ARTURO

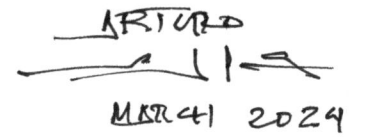

MARCH 2024

Organic Cinema

Organic Cinema

*Film, Architecture,
and the Work of Béla Tarr*

Thorsten Botz-Bornstein

berghahn
NEW YORK · OXFORD
www.berghahnbooks.com

Published in 2017 by

Berghahn Books

www.berghahnbooks.com

© 2017 Thorsten Botz-Bornstein

All rights reserved. Except for the quotation of short passages for the purposes of criticism and review, no part of this book may be reproduced in any form or by any means, electronic or mechanical, including photocopying, recording, or any information storage and retrieval system now known or to be invented, without written permission of the publisher.

Library of Congress Cataloging-in-Publication Data
Names: Botz-Bornstein, Thorsten author.
Title: Organic cinema : film, architecture, and the work of Bela Tarr / Thorsten Botz-Bornstein.
Description: New York : Berghahn Books, 2017. | Includes bibliographical references and index.
Identifiers: LCCN 2017008686 (print) | LCCN 2017022140 (ebook) | ISBN 9781785335679 (eBook) | ISBN 9781785335662 (hardback : alk. paper)
Subjects: LCSH: Tarr, Bela, 1955---Criticism and interpretation.
Classification: LCC PN1998.3.T363 (ebook) | LCC PN1998.3.T363 B68 2017 (print) | DDC 791.4302/33092--dc23
LC record available at https://lccn.loc.gov/2017008686

British Library Cataloguing in Publication Data
A catalogue record for this book is available from the British Library

ISBN 9781785335662 hardback
ISBN 9781785335679 ebook

Contents

List of Illustrations — vi

Introduction — 1

1 Cinema, Architecture, Literature — 23

2 Central Europe — 39

3 What Is "Organic?" — 48

4 The Melancholy of Evolution — 57

5 Where Is the Center? — 65

6 Modernism and Postmodernism — 76

7 Organic Harmonies — 89

8 Back to Humanism? — 116

9 Politics of Harmony — 136

10 The Spiritual — 153

11 Organic Places — 162

12 The Organic Camera Shot — 179

Conclusion — 198

Bibliography — 201

Index — 217

List of Illustrations

1.1	Interior of Mortuary Chapel in Farkasrét, Budapest, by Imre Makovecz.	28
5.1	Janos Valuska in *Werckmeister Harmonies* (2000).	60
5.2	Church in Gazdagrét, Budapest, by Imre Makovecz.	71
5.3	Greek Catholic Church in Csenger by Imre Makovecz.	72
6.1	Cultural Center in Szigetvár by Imre Makovecz.	82
11.1	Interior of Holy Spirit Church in Paks by Imre Makovecz.	165
11.2	Holy Spirit Church in Paks by Imre Makovecz.	167
11.3	Still from *The Man from London* (2007).	169
11.4	Still from *Werckmeister Harmonies* (2000).	173
11.5	Church in Siófok by Imre Makovecz.	175
12.1	Estike in *Satantango* (1994).	187

Introduction

This book is about the philosophy of the organic and how it interacts with the aesthetics of cinema. Organic is anything relating to a living entity. Organic matter can evolve, but it can also decay. In philosophy, the living aspect of the organic structure has prompted several generations of thinkers to develop approaches able to see various cultural and natural phenomena as dynamic: the organic has often been described as the interplay of evolution and decomposition.

The main purpose here is to develop the idea of "organic cinema." The essence of the organic will derive from not only cinema theory but also the theory of architecture, where the organic has reached a high level of sophistication. Many organic philosophies of the nineteenth and twentieth centuries explored in this book have had an immediate impact on architectural theory. Surprisingly, film theorists have generally been unaware of this body of thought revolving around organic architectural theory or have only tentatively shown interest in it, usually by approaching segments of this tradition via the work of Henri Bergson. Both organic cinema and organic architecture base their activities on the idea that the image character of their medium needs to be overcome and that creativity in their respective arts should be seen as a sculpting of space or time. As a result, techniques, as well as theoretical aspirations, move to the background, while practical aspects of the arts are emphasized.

Slow Cinema, Contemplative Cinema

Organic cinema is related to "slow cinema" and "contemplative cinema." However, while the latter two remain, in my opinion, relatively vague terms,[1] organic cinema is supposed to be more precise as a theoretical notion. Unlike slow and contemplative, "organic" is not merely atmospheric. One reason the terms "slow cinema" and "contemplative cinema" have remained relatively vague until recently is because they tend to be used as "foggy, dark, monotonous, and nostalgic" in order to cover the styles of many film directors. I extract the definition of organic cinema from an analysis of three Béla Tarr films, more precisely, his trilogy of *Damnation* (1988), *Satantango* (1994), and *Werckmeister Harmonies* (2000). However, Tarr is not the only organic film director. Andrei Tarkovsky, Aki Kaurismäki, Theo Angelopoulos, and Reha Erdem, to name but a few, are similarly organic because they attempt to capture life in a wandering fashion by following its haphazard rhythm and paying as much attention to details as to "cosmic" questions.[2]

However, for some reason, Tarr must receive privileged treatment. First, in terms of slowness, Tarr is arguably more emphatic than anybody else. Second, Tarr says the "rhythm [of his films] is provided not by the story but by the actors, by the play of the actors" (Breteau-Skira 2010: 18). He also says his films "are not action/cut, action/cut" but that he is trying to "understand the temporality without forgetting that this is a life and that it is happening" (22). I find that these claims correspond best to a cinema based on the principles of organic development. The fluid, long takes follow a rhythm inspired by the inherent qualities of the shot footage, not of the editing. This rhythm is precisely how one of the pioneers of organic architecture, the German organicist architect Hugo Häring, defined his architectural method: "Search for shapes rather than impose them, discover forms rather than construct them" (1925: 4).[3] As will be shown, contemplative cinema can learn a lot from the theory and practice of organic architecture, particularly from Gestalt theory, which sees single architectural components as parts of a system of dynamic relationships. The Gestalt evolves as a hybrid of form and being and has self-organizing tendencies.

Hungary

Generally speaking, our present age is not organic but rather marked by the brutal competition of different universalisms—clashes that seem to be programmed in the near future. According to Islamic extremists, a universal moral order should be obtained by imposing the rules established by God on an Islamic state. This God-based universalism clashes with another universalism: the rationality with which "Western" thought is often identified, whose most famous derivatives are democracy and egalitarianism. Quasi-religious environmentalism represents another universalism. In this world of competing universalisms, organic thought formulates an alternative.

Ambitions to develop an organic vision of the world have become a serious undertaking in a place perhaps few people would expect to find it: Hungary. Film director Béla Tarr, architect Imre Makovecz, and writer László Krasznahorkai have been obsessed with organic forms of expression for decades. Their organic ambitions become manifest in various ways and cover a spectrum reaching from the politically conservative to the progressive and from the religious to the atheist. But all three share a rootedness in Central and Eastern European culture.[4] Equally important is a strong connection with rural culture and tradition, as well as questions about their possible decline/resurrection in a modern and globalized world. Hungary thus becomes a showcase for a certain form of organicism able to define the universal beyond individual/universal paradigms. In organic philosophies, the universal is not spelled out in the form of abstract rules, nor does one cling to individual, communal, national, or private expressions. The search present in the work of these three Hungarians goes for the universal in the sense of "cosmic."

Béla Tarr

The three films chosen for demonstrating organic cinema are distinct from Tarr's earlier ones—with the exception of *Almanac of Fall* (1985)—because they show the director's pronounced interest in formal experiment. All three films also present elaborately designed, bleak, run-down, and desolate settings that many foreign spectators might spontaneously associate with rural parts of Central and Eastern Europe. Similar Hungarian films existed before, for example, Zoltán Fabri's *Hungarians* (1978) or *Bálint Fábián Meets God* (1980), in which an emphasis on poverty, drunkenness, and ignorance portray rural life.

Krasznahorkai's novel *Satantango* was published in 1985, and Tarr's eponymous film is from 1994. Thus, the film has roots in the communist world but also stretches into the capitalist era. *Satantango* tells the story of a ruined collective farm whose inhabitants are having affairs with each other, conspiring against each other, and constantly being observed by a drunken doctor (Peter Berling). The charismatic trickster Irimiás (Mihály Vig) manages to cheat most of the villagers out of the little savings they have, though he himself is manipulated by the local government. In the film, he and his companion, Petrina (Putyi Horváth), represent both the former totalitarian state and the new economy.

The elliptical narrative of *Werckmeister Harmonies*[5] revolves around a traveling exhibition featuring a dead whale accompanied by a mysterious, crippled guru called "the Prince," who is trying to bring social unrest and violence to the village. The Prince's political strategies are absurd and megalomaniac, and they culminate in random ransacking. The reclusive, elderly musicologist György Eszter (Peter Fitz) and the young mail carrier Janos Valuska (Lars Rudolph) oppose the Prince's undoing. Eszter's estranged wife *Tünde (Hanna Schygulla)*, who is allied with the local police chief, also opposes the Prince, though her purpose is to take command of the village. At the end of the film, troops are stationed on the streets, and the mysterious whale is destroyed. Valuska falls into a vegetative state and is interned in a mental asylum.

In *Damnation*, a provincial cabaret singer (Vali Kerekes), her husband Sebestyén (György Cserhalmi), her former lover Karrer (Miklós B. Székely), and the bartender Willarsky (Gyula Pauer) betray each other in all possible ways. The plot ends with the former lover's denunciation of the other three characters. The film was released in 1988—one year before the downfall of the Iron Curtain—but it already plays, like *Satantango*, on the dual ground of communism and capitalism, one being as decadent as the other. Sebestyén has debts and, according to Karrer, he faces "irrevocable disintegration." Similar to what Irimiás does in *Satantango*, Karrer cunningly suggests "there might be a way to stop the ruin."

Organic Cinema?

Roughly speaking, organic architecture has existed since Frank Lloyd Wright, but the concept of the organic can be traced to philosophical sources from romantic thinkers like Samuel Taylor Coleridge, August Wilhelm Schlegel, and Johann Wolfgang Goethe. Despite its historical and contemporary importance in the humanities, the idea of the organic in film theory remains highly underdeveloped. Tarkovsky provided potentially one of the first metaphors destined to define cinema as an organism when writing, "the time that pulsates through the blood vessels of the film, making it alive" (1986: 114). He expresses a similar pattern through his organic intention to create "an entire world reflected as in a drop of water" (110). More recently, Daniel Frampton's ambition to grasp a cinematic thinking process he calls "film-mind" (filmind), which he believes to be capable of conceptualizing "*all* film as an organic intelligence" (2006: 7), accounts for another attempt of employing the organic in the service of cinematic aesthetics. Among the more concrete associations of the organic with cinematic structures is James Goodwin's proposal (made in his book on Sergei Eisenstein) to contrast an organic cinema with an intellectual cinema: "Where form in intellectual cinema establishes ideological perspective and critical distance, in organic cinema form fuses author, content, and individual spectator" (1993: 176).

A few other attempts at seeing film as an organic phenomenon without naming it as such do exist. In the 1960s, film critic and director Paul Mayersberg claimed: "[Michelangelo] Antonioni and [Jean-Luc] Godard conceive their films in shots. They don't write a scenario and then think how to do it. A distinction between the event and the treatment is meaningless for *The Eclipse* because the shots are events in themselves" (Perkins et al. 1963: 32). Steven Marchand has picked up Mayersberg's thread of thoughts in order to sketch the rules of an "event-based" cinema in which "nothing happens apart from the shot itself" (2009: 139). From Antonioni's "pure events," which are produced by autonomous camera movements and describe "nothing," Marchand draws a line to Tarr's "emphasis on the concrete physicality of the event" (143). Tarr systematically develops the "event cinema," especially in *Werckmeister Harmonies,* by favoring the sequence shot. Marchand concludes that this way of filming is organic because "what is captured whole is the event in the fullness of its occurrence" and the shot as a whole "is undivided from what happens in it" (147). These ideas overlap more or less with how organic architecture approaches the "materiality" of its elements.

Gilles Deleuze frequently mentions the word organic—it appears 114 times in *Cinema 1* (1986) and 34 times in *Cinema 2* (1989)—without exploring its intrinsic character determined by a specific philosophical tradition. This lack of investigation is surprising given that Deleuze's own distinction between the movement-image characterized by action, the time-image emerging with neorealism, and the French New Wave characterized by stillness prefigures some points that appear in contemporary discussions of slow cinema. Nevertheless, the organic for Deleuze is simply a sort of unity he deals with in a chapter on montage (1986, chap. 3). The organic input will be relevant mainly for matters of image composition. In "The Laws of Organic Composition," a section in chapter 9 ("The Action-Image"), Deleuze introduces the action-image as an "organic representation in its entirety" (1986: 151). The meaning of the word organic here is likened to that of "concrete," especially since Deleuze decides to contrast the organic image with the "crystal-image," which is more abstract, virtual, and self-contained. However, Deleuze never uses the organic as a critical tool to evaluate the potential formalism of action-images. For him, the organic action-image is simply "structural because the places and the moments are well defined in their oppositions and their complementarities" (1986: 151). In *Cinema 2*, Deleuze calls montage the "organic composition of movement-images" (1989: 28), which is the source of classical narration. In this sense, Eisenstein is "organic" for Deleuze because his representation "includes spatial and temporal caesuras" (1986: 152).

Organic Cinema and Organic Architecture

Space and Time

This book's parallel treatment of film and architecture is justified for several reasons. In general, themes concerning the production and perception of space, surfaces, and light are essential to understanding both film and architecture. Films offer spatial experiences just like buildings do. Furthermore, buildings can be cinematic because people interact in dramatic or nondramatic ways in built spaces. Theoretical terms like aura, representation, narrativity, montage, place, rhythm, and typology concern both film and architecture. Architect Jean Nouvel has said: "architecture exists, like cinema, in the dimension of time and movement. One conceives and reads a building in terms of sequences. To erect a building is to predict and seek effects of contrast and linkage through which one passes" (Rattenbury 1994: 35). Some contemporary architects have even decided to replace the word "site" with "plot" in order to do justice to the particularity of local sites, which is fading more and more. According to the British architects collective Urbanomic, the change from site to plot was necessary because sites "become increasingly assimilated into the capitalist logic of regeneration and value creation" (from the blurb of *When Site Lost the Plot*, Mackay 2015). For the Urbanomic team, a "plot" in the sense of a story line is supposed to make the place more authentic.

Another way of making architecture organic is to integrate time into the design. Again, by doing so, architecture comes closer to film. The organic Japanese architect Tadao Ando once forced himself to see a building as a garden and to observe "subtle changes taking place from moment to moment, from season to season, and from year to year.... There is life in the parts, and these parts together breathe new life in the whole. When I look at a garden that, like an organism, is never complete but, instead, exists in time, I wonder if I cannot create buildings that live, that is, buildings that are adrift in time" (1991b: 19). Here, architecture becomes a "cinematic" event determined by time and organic development.

Materiality

Another key topic of organic cinema and architecture is "materiality." Both organic cinema and organic architecture value a contemplative exploration of spatial and temporal experience through a rediscovery of the material. Once again, Tarkovsky is the forerunner, as his long and fluid takes are based, according to Vlada Petric, "on the director's belief that the camera is capable of unearthing the hidden significance of the material world" (1989: 29).

Organic versus Constructivist in Architecture and Film

The "nonorganic" approach has often been called the "constructing" approach and remains a pertinent expression in not only architecture but also cinema. Dudley Andrew uses an architectural metaphor, suggesting that, in what I call nonorganic cinema, the shots are simply bricks: "In its realist genres, Hollywood cinema molds and bevels every shot into a brick that can be smoothly attached to neighboring bricks in forming the bridge of the story" (2005: xiv). Organic cinema does not construct with bricks but tries to formulate different relationships between particular expressions, as well as the time/space they are in.

Social Critique

Organic cinema and architecture have yet another point in common. Both run counter to the perspective of mainstream cinema and architecture, which either seek comfort in familiarity and predictability or work with spectacular image-driven effects aimed at impressing the masses. This means organic architects and film directors are distinguished by an anti-capitalist critical potential willing to critique consumerist "fast architecture" and action cinema. In Hungary, the organic has traditionally been used in this political sense, because, according to Judit Frigyesi, the "emphasis on organicism was itself a political statement. It was the declaration of the liberation of art from political propaganda and a clear stance against both artistic conservatism and the emptiness of mass culture" (2000: 92).

Contemplative cinema and slow cinema have been related to "poetic cinema," with which Tarkovsky is often associated. This is an interesting fact in its own right that deserves further exploration in a separate study. Obviously, thoughts and feelings are more efficiently transmitted in poetry when the performance is slow, allowing contemplation. Poetic elements often enter Tarkovsky's films via the metonymy, a figure of speech in which one term is substituted for another. The metonymy does not necessarily help engender an understanding of the item but refers us to something else. Tarkovsky's use of metonymies makes his cinema slow because metonymies make the viewer stand and contemplate. They are not like metaphors, which can be understood and integrated in the overall flow of the narrative. Metonymies interrupt the time flow or make it tenacious and sticky, creating a certain mood or atmosphere. In poetics, metonymies are said to provide profundity.

In contemplative cinema, slowness becomes a virtue, just like the waste of time and space can become virtues in architectural designs that do not follow the rationality or functionality of the grid. Song Hwee Lim points to the explicit link between slow cinema and the Slow Food movement, which attempts to rediscover the flavors and savors of regional cooking: "The Slow movement advocates downsizing to the level of the local and places emphases on organic origins, artisanal processes, and ethical products. These values are anathema to speed" (2014: 3). Both slow cinema and organic architecture represent lifestyle revolutions and are likely to have a liberating function. Forty years ago, Paul Virilio (1977), architect by profession, singled out speed as the primary force shaping civilization. Finally, speed will lead us to "war at the speed of light" (Virilio 2002). If this is true, then slow cinema and organic architecture formulate alternative directions of the development of human civilization.

The idea of "resistance" is very important in many of the works discussed here. The title of Krasznahorkai's book *The Melancholy of Resistance* (1998)—which Tarr adapted into *Werckmeister Harmonies*—suggests a curious fusional concept composed of melancholy and resistance. I will show that the film can also be seen as the key notion for any "revolution through slowness." The theme is indeed proper to Krasznahorkai. In many of his works from the 1980s and 1990s, Krasznahorkai depicts vanity, perfidy, treason, and paranoia by showing how characters act slowly within an absurd universe. Those people are not passively and naïvely submitted to the absurd world they live in but are constantly trying to move forward. Of course, in the end, they do not get anywhere, which makes them melancholic. However, the melancholy has been part and parcel of the special form of resistance from the beginning. A resistance working through melancholy (by thus being a "resistance of melancholy," for that matter) tends to employ slowness in order to create a complex critique of social conditions. For Krasznahorkai, this seems to be a matter of lifestyle, as he affirms to having staggered all his life "between the deadly sweetness of sadness and the irresistible desire to revolt" (2001: 86). His characters seem to do the same.

Silence and Melancholy

A supplementary dimension concerning the intrinsic link between slowness and the organic is produced by the particular status of sound. Again, this concerns both cinema and architecture. Lim suggests that slow films privilege "silence and abstinence of sonic elements usually heard on film" (2014: 10). Ira Jaffe also refers to silence as an essential component of slow cinema, especially for Antonioni (2014: 69). In film, silence can represent a form of essential purity, which is why film directors often use it to produce dreamlike impressions (cf. Botz-Bornstein 2007a: 40–43). The same is true for architecture, as Ando highlights: "I prefer for the space to speak and for the walls to produce no sense of their own identities" (1991: 1). For Ando, the silence is inspired by the Buddhist concept of emptiness (see Botz-Bornstein 2015, chap. 6). According to the Hungarian architect Botond Bognar, organic architecture considers that "silent spaces cannot be seen with the eyes; they are felt with the heart" (1982: 19). The silent spaces are here "felt" in a way similar to how time is felt in slow cinema.

A clear link appears between silence and melancholy: silence has something melancholic about it. Silence is not the mere absence of sound, but it can be experienced as a "soundless bass," to borrow the beautiful words of the Hungarian philosopher Béla Hamvas, whose thoughts on melancholy will be of interest later. Hamvas believed he heard in the melancholic works of older artists the "low, monotonous and almost soundless bass [which is] the only place of Being that is not more intensive than the paradise of logos" (2008: 17). At the beginning of his book on the Taiwanese director Tsai Ming-Liang, Lim reproduces a sentence from Mary Ann Doane about the emergence of time feeling in modernity: "Time was indeed felt—as a weight, as a source of anxiety, and as an acutely pressing problem of representation" (Doane 2002: 4; Lim 2014: 11). Doane still perceives the reverberations of this break today in the instantaneity of modern electronic media. Lim, on the other hand, draws from here a link toward slow cinema because he believes "time itself" is represented in these films, which can best be felt within the periods of slow cinema silence.

When Bognar says "silent spaces are felt with the heart" (1982: 19), he means there is no speech in those spaces except the speech uttered by the empty space or by the walls. Through silence, organic architecture—and organic film—can produce a certain style or atmosphere that will not be expressed by means of rules and principles. The "style" of this architecture simply appears—silently. Ando holds that in his buildings, it is the space that speaks, not the (noisy) concrete elements surrounding or occurring in the space. In other words, the silence creates this architectural form or style. Ludwig Wittgenstein, whose philosophy relates to the mathematical and scientific problems central to *Werckmeister Harmonies* and whose ideas will be discussed accordingly (chapter 7), would say such a style is a quality that "shows itself" in the form of a silent expression. This silence of the space expresses everything that one cannot speak about: "Whereof one cannot speak, thereof one must be silent" is the last line of Wittgenstein's *Tractatus Logico-Philosophicus* ([1921] 1990: 111). In the present discussion on aesthetics, silence turns those architectural and cinematic expressions into self-sufficient entities. Some might find this input "transcendental," and much of this book discusses whether this word can grasp the essence of both organic cinema and organic architecture.

The Silence of Evolution

This study on the organic is very much concerned with philosophical questions of nature and evolution. Here, "silence" remains a relevant theme. In the context of organic philosophy of nature, silence represents a moment of standstill in which evolution stops and invites us to a brief instance of contemplation. There are several such moments in Krasznahorkai's writings:

> There was a moment when the world stood still, and during this moment the leaves stopped vibrating, the elastic swinging of the branches stopped, but also the flow inside the veins of the trees and stems and roots, an ant population that had so far been carrying its possessions diagonally across a path, stumbled, a pebble that had just started rolling did not roll further, and the wood worms in the pillars and consoles stopped ... in a word, everything, animal and plant and stone and all secret interior processes, everything was, for one moment, canceled in its existence—for the only purpose that the next moment could come and everything would continue where it had stopped. (2005: 13)

Contemplation and the Art of Being Disinterested

The main topic of *Werckmeister Harmonies* is the confrontation of science with art or of mathematics/analysis with contemplation. The opposition of analysis and contemplation represents a classic philosophical theme prominent in the history of science since antiquity. One point at issue is that the "perfect" image of a mathematized reality does not necessarily correspond to the reality "out there." Rather, this reality can be grasped through a contemplative approach. For "the preeminent ancient theorists of the cosmos, Plato and Aristotle, physics was not fully mathematizable because only whatever was perfect could be perfectly mathematical" (Wallace 1987: xxix). These philosophical ideas are at the root of musicologist Eszter's obsession with music as a phenomenon "being close to an approximation to perfection" (Krasznahorkai 1998: 112–13).

Based on these observations, one can conclude that contemplation and analysis are two different attitudes: psychologically, culturally, and scientifically. It is necessary to examine contemplation as a philosophical concept more closely. Contemplating is different from looking and seeing, as well as from scientific observation. Contemplation provides a cognitive surplus because the contemplation of the present often goes together with reflections about not only what is seen in the present but also what has been in the past and what will be the future. Thus, contemplation often has a stumbling and hesitating quality. While we contemplate, we constantly guess proximate meanings we derive from neighboring sources. This is also why "slowness" becomes such an important feature in contemplation. Obviously, the contemplative approach is different from analysis because the latter should be effectuated in an increasingly "time-efficient" fashion in the modern world.

However, the meaning of the word "contemplation" must be further fine-tuned if it is to function within the present theoretical discussion of the organic. Attention has been drawn to the critical potential that both slow cinema and organic architecture can hold their own against consumerist "fast architecture" and action cinema. In philosophical terms, the word "contemplative" can appear slightly misleading because it does not necessarily make this critical potential obvious. "Contemplative" could mistakenly be related to the idealist tradition attempting to see the world in purely theoretical terms. However, in the type of cinema in question here, contemplation has more concrete and more existential connotations, because by contemplating the world, the contemplator also contemplates the meaning and—possibly—the organic finiteness of her own existence. In this sense, and despite its faltering and meditating qualities, contemplation is not merely idealist and otherworldly but also (self-)critical. Moreover, the contemplating mind can declare solid and everlasting structures supported by official regimes to be fragile and "merely" organic.

In any case, contemplation is only possible when the contemplated element appears in a detached form, independent of all contingencies and random circumstances to which it was submitted within its original environment. Only then can the contemplated object be understood "as something," that is, its essence can appear. Hermeneutic philosophy holds that contemplation can provide new insights into an already-known element. I derive those thoughts from the theory of understanding involving anamnesis (recollection) as developed by Plato in the dialogues *Meno* and *Phaedo*.[6] Most important for the present discussion is that contemplation is submitted to a paradox: its critical input is due to not only a potential engagement but also its intrinsic disinterestedness. Paradoxically, just because contemplation is to a considerable extent disinterested, it has often been frowned upon in revolutionary places such as Stalinist Russia. In ethico-aesthetic terms, contemplation describes the approach of the autonomous artist and consumer eager to observe and record reality independently. And they do so by maintaining a critical distance from the world they contemplate. Today, "contemplation" is frowned upon in certain Islamic countries where existentialism or other philosophical exercises advertising themselves more or less explicitly as contemplative are often undesired. To my knowledge, a film program on "Existential Cinema" at the American University of Sharjah was canceled in 2014 because the administration found that such efforts "to contemplate one's existential conditions" contradict religious belief. The ambition to maintain a critical distance from reality in order to obtain a fresh relationship through contemplation can appear subversive in any system eager to establish the existence of "reality" in an authoritarian fashion (this process probably became clearest in socialist realism), no matter if the regime is communist, capitalist, or religiously oriented.

All of this means that melancholic contemplation leads to resistance, and the "melancholy of resistance" must be understood in this sense. The fusional concept of melancholy and resistance is provocative because it implies a resistance of melancholy implemented by a contemplative approach toward reality. As will be shown, this melancholy is not so much "disinterested" in the sense of a negation of reality. The latter would indeed be pathological along the lines laid down by Sigmund Freud in his *Mourning and Melancholia*. For Freud, melancholy is characterized by the "cessation [*Aufhebung*] of any interest in the outside world" and the "inhibition of all activity" ([1917] 1957: 244). However, the disinterested contemplation sparked by melancholy and its silence—topics of Tarr's and Krasznahorkai's works—is not pathologically passive but active: it can lead to resistance.

Contemplating the Stars

The astronomical theme so heavily exploited in *Werckmeister Harmonies* also bears a close relationship with the idea of contemplation. Tarkovsky once said one should watch his films "as one watches the stars" (1986: 9), and the observation of the nightly sky is perhaps the most original contemplative activity humanity has ever engaged in. Hans Blumenberg writes in *The Genesis of the Copernican World* that the cosmos was seen in antiquity as something whose "contemplation" could be man's highest fulfillment (1987, sections 5 and 6), and Thomas S. Kuhn begins *The Copernican Revolution* by explaining the contemplation of the sky as, in the first place, a poetic activity:

> Seen on a clear night, the sky speaks first to the poetic, not to the scientific, imagination. No one who views the night sky can challenge Shakespeare's vision of the stars as "night candles" or Milton's image of the Milky Way as a "broad and ample road, whose dust is gold, and pavement stars." (1957: 7)

I will show (most lengthily in chapter 7) that *Werckmeister Harmonies* is linked to the discipline of "musical theology" practiced in the seventeenth century, at which the theoretician Andreas Werckmeister was adept. The harmony of the stars was supposed to reflect the harmony of music because God created both the stars and music. In European culture, the idea of the perfect overlap of nature, math, and God has always had a strong tie to astronomy. The search for harmony, especially in the Werckmeisterian musical context, has always had cosmological aspirations.

Contemplating Reality

How should we see reality? Is the world measurable and fully mathematizable, or does contemplation provide a surplus of information about reality in the same way anamnesis, according to Plato, provides new insights about elements that are already known? The contemplative approach bears a strong link with philosophical questions concerning the reality character of its medium. What is "reality" for (or in) organic cinema? Once again, the answer can derive from comparisons with organic architecture, which does not imitate nature but rather is meant to *be* nature; similarly, organic cinema does not imitate reality but is an existential reality that organically develops out of certain elements. Accordingly, Marchand describes the "event-based" cinema of Tarr in such existential terms: "Eszter's house is indivisible from the event it depicts. It *is* that event" (2009: 147).

Tarr's and Krasznahorkai's treatments of the "Werckmeister harmonies" musicological problem reflect the principles of the organic particularly well. In this book, I demonstrate that "natural harmony" in musical theory is called the "organically created space" in architectural theory. Drawing lines in architecture or editing a film in the Eisensteinian manner, on the other hand, represent a sort of Werckmeisterian tuning. Overall, this study shows that contemplation, as opposed to mathematical analysis, locates an organic web in the form of an immanent, self-sufficient, hermeneutically determined, "natural logic" present in the form of neither empirical facts nor of abstract rules. The Hungarian philosopher Georg Lukács once brought this constellation to a point when writing in *The Theory of Literature*: "When life quae life finds an immanent meaning in itself, the categories of the organic determine everything: an individual structure and physiognomy is simply the product of a balance between the part and the whole, mutually determining one another" ([1920] 1971: 65). This idea is important in musical theory and architectural theory and should also be discussed in the context of film theory.

Organic Practice

The imaginary musicologist György Eszter's obsession with "natural harmony" directly follows from the above considerations of organic philosophy. Moreover, theories of organic architecture offer close examinations of the "natural" and the "calculated," as well as of potential conflicts arising between them. However, the discrepancy between the natural and the calculated are also manifest in how organic architecture and cinema proceed in practical terms. Organic architecture often works without a preconceived plan because its forms are supposed to develop on the site. Makovecz, for example, did not "trust architects who claim the program must be learned as a function," but instead the design "reveals itself during the planning process" (Gerle 2010: 33). Newly created spaces must be contemplated first; only then can the next step be undertaken (to describe the process as the concept of "contemplative architecture" here would be not at all misleading). Sometimes the drawings are made only to obtain building regulations permissions—and only after the building is accomplished. Likewise, Tarr (2001) affirms to "never use the script. We just write it for the foundations and the producers and we use it when looking for the money.... We have a story but I think the story is only a little part of the whole movie." Through this in situ process of detail development, the aesthetics of the organic aims to fully exploit the location.

Construction, Deconstruction, and the Organic

The junction where the organic model of evolution-decomposition meets postmodern philosophies of "deconstruction" will receive special attention in this book. In Tarr's films, forms are not merely deconstructed; rather, a sense of (an often uncanny) totality subsists. The Hungarian-American film scholar Yvette Bíró sees in Tarr's long takes the "imperative to follow through" (2008: 169) because the long takes often convey a feeling of inevitability or even of the power of destiny. The length of the shots is not due to the director's aesthetic decision in the first place, but instead the shots are experienced as self-determined or perhaps even determined "from above." This artistic ability to install a totality clearly opposes postmodern ideologies of deconstructive fragmentation. Instead, this artistic ability denotes a modern approach that must be called organic. In this sense, the organic offers an interesting alternative to both modern constructivism and postmodern deconstructionism.

In architecture, the term "organic" in connection with a particular way of using form, space, and material has prospered for more than a century. Organic architecture goes back to Frank Lloyd Wright and Louis Sullivan but is also linked to other famous architects such as Hugo Häring, Bruce Goff, Antoni Gaudí, and Ödön Lechner (nicknamed "the Hungarian Gaudí"). In this book, I concentrate on Imre Makovecz, the initiator of Hungarian organic architecture (*organikus építészet* or *szerves építészet*) or living architecture (*élőépítészet*). The book might sometimes read like a sociocultural history of Hungary and Central and Eastern Europe, which is not entirely unintended.

László Krasznahorkai

László Krasznahorkai, whose demanding novels *Satantango* (1985) and (the central part of) *The Melancholy of Resistance* (1989) served as the blueprint for Tarr's films *Satantango* and *Werckmeister Harmonies*,[7] manifests a similar obsession with the organic. The analysis of Krasznahorkai's writings will provide valuable input for "organic philosophy" from the field of literature. First, Krasznahorkai's novels are very much about decay, which provides a clearly organic aspect. In *Kegyelmi viszonyok* (Under the conditions of grace) (1986), Krasznahorkai explores death, or, more precisely, absurd and arbitrary death. At the same time, he presents decay as something aesthetically and even spiritually elevating. In the story "Milyen gyönyörű" (How beautiful), Krasznahorkai explains, "We can perceive in a landscape in the profoundest beauty and in the profoundest decay something—something that refers to us" (contained in 2015b: 25). Throughout his work, Krasznahorkai describes in vivid and lengthily detailed language how organic matter is given to decomposition. The "Werckmeister Harmonies" part of *The Melancholy of Resistance* ends with a two-page description of a decaying corpse, rendering technical details from chemistry and concluding that "from the moment of birth every living organism carries within it the seeds of its own destruction" (Krasznahorkai 1998: 314). Similar—often-excessive—descriptions of organic processes appear in the novel *Seiobo There Below* (2013c) (see chapter 2). Krasznahorkai's world is organic up to the point that even nonorganic matter is bound to decay and rot, as described in *Satantango*: "So that, in the unremittingly brief time allowed for the purpose, the walls might crack, the windows shift and the doors be forced from their frames; so that the chimney might lean and collapse, the nails might fall from the crumbling walls, and the mirrors hanging from them might darken" (2012a: 115). This is more or less what really happens in Tarr's last film, *The Turin Horse* (2011).

Passages containing an "organic message" are even more frequent in Krasznahorkai's novel *Északról hegy, Délről tó, Nyugatról utak, Keletről folyó* (From the north by hill, from the south by lake, from the west by roads, from the east by river), where a cypress is presented as an envoy transmitting "a message about its history and its existence that nobody will ever understand because this understanding is not the matter of humans" (2005: 88). The natural tree is meant to contain bits of philosophical information, which is a pantheistic idea sometimes used in organic philosophy. Furthermore, the jet stream—with its billions of particles, including viruses, bacteria, vegetal parts, pollen, and algae colonies—circulating around the earth is described in great scientific detail. The division of cells is described in a similar fashion, which the author believes to be an "unbelievably long and strange story." An insistence on the literary depiction of cyclical structures also "bring us back to the point where the whole cycle had started, that is, the genesis of spore capsules" (90).

Of course, the description of the world as an organic phenomenon also has metaphorical dimensions, as people and the existing society have been slowly but notably disappearing from rural communities during the slow breakdown of the communist system. The breakdown itself had been a long process of decomposition announced by Emmanuel Todd as early as 1976. In *The Final Fall: Essay on the Decomposition of the Soviet Sphere,* he examines suicide rates, infant mortality, and alcoholism but also absurdities like the delivery of truckloads of shoes for only the right foot. In agreement with the principle of "melancholic resistance," Krasznahorkai's agenda is one of decomposition and resisted decomposition. Accordingly, the protagonist of the story "Rozi a trükkös" (Rozi the tricky one), in *Kegyelmi viszonyok,* writes that he attempts "to master the process of deterioration and decomposition in order to obtain a state of total solitude and independence" (2015c: 87).

The Whole and the Part: Hermeneutics

The organic in Krasznahorkai's work (as well as in Tarr's) is also presented as an aesthetic device closely related to hermeneutic discourses on the relationship between the part and the whole. Krasznahorkai in particular is very much aware of this philosophical theme's importance. He notes, for example, about the photos of cameraman and photographer Gábor Medvigy, that "the whole we are seeking is not simply an accumulation of individual elements" and that "those to whom it is obvious that it is impossible to make a whole out of all these billions of available images ... instinctively look away from the billions of fragments" (2013a: 12).

In *Seiobo* and *Északról hegy,* such organic statements often relate to explorations into Eastern philosophy, affirming that "everything is though nothing is" (Krasznahorkai 2005: 21) and that an ancient thought beyond definition becomes alive when we gain the sudden insight that "there is only the whole and no parts" (22). In *Északról hegy,* the hermeneutic whole/part relation is even expressed through detained descriptions of organic architecture. The protagonist first finds the extraordinary complexity of the monastery "inaccessibly monumental" because the "arrangement of the main buildings, the condo and the lecture hall, the dorms, the office, the cells, the dining hall, the reception rooms and the abbot's residence as well as the sophisticated placement of the kitchen, of the guest rooms, the bath and the laundry" (27–28) follow a system normal eyes cannot grasp. Only much later the protagonist realizes that this complexity enables the relationship between the whole and the parts. Still, the feeling he will never be able to produce a mental image of the entire map persists. The spatial organic metaphor in this passage is valid for human life in general. The particularly human individual and the godly universal can never match, though all human culture and civilization strives toward the unification of both dimensions. Accordingly, Krasznahorkai writes in A Théseus-általános (The universal theseus) that the human spirit is detached from this world "in order to turn toward a mysterious, splendor, toward an inscrutable undecipherable greatness that he names universe or god of the universe. Of course he cannot succeed (which is sad but I have to say it) because the object of his quest does not exceed his own small person" (2001: 61).

The Cultural Context

A large part of this study compares the aesthetic principles of Imre Makovecz (the most famous Hungarian organic architect) and the films of Béla Tarr. Naturally, a question that must be seriously addressed is whether Tarr and Makovecz can be compared at all, particularly in a Hungarian context. My Hungarian friends were often bewildered when hearing of my project. They hastened to explain to me that Tarr and Makovecz represent "two different worlds" and that the conservative and the progressive, the religious and the atheist, the symbolic and the unsymbolic can simply not be dealt with in the same study. How can a highly ideological and deeply mythological architectural style be compared to a fundamentally nonmythological, unsymbolic cinematic form with entirely different ideological convictions behind it? There are three answers to this question. First, Makovecz is not conservative and religious in the same sense understood in postcommunist Central and Eastern Europe today, a region that has most recently witnessed the surge of right-wing nationalist politics and religious revival. Makovecz's religiosity is not sectarian but rather spiritual and generally pantheist and therefore opposed to all dogmatism. Nor is his interest in local culture determined by traditional humanism or by nationalism. Makovecz is similar to Béla Bartók, who incorporated folk music into his compositions but whose compositional achievement, according to Theodor Adorno, depended "on its power to suppress his nationalist instinct" ([1925] 1981: 128). Second, and more importantly, Makovecz's and Tarr's styles have a common source: the modern cult of natural organicity. It is often forgotten that a part of modernism is deeply rooted in the idea of essential naturalness, which founded the ornamental branch of modern styles. This development can encompass very different aesthetic approaches, as the comparison of Makovecz and Tarr demonstrates. Third, the common "modernism" theme is, in both cases, based on a rejection of postmodernism. True, the cult of naturalness, most manifest in Art Nouveau, did also engender a postmodern, eclectic, ornamental branch, but Makovecz, Tarr, and Krasznahorkai do not follow this path. Instead, all three twist modernity in a very personal way by staying away from (at least most of the time) postmodern approaches that favor the ironical play with extant forms of historical or commercial culture or their mere quotation. It is on this deeper level (not on the level of politics) that I see similarities between Makovecz, Tarr, and Krasznahorkai.

A problem is, of course, that all the above patterns cannot be revealed by means of purely empirical studies, that is, by merely looking at shapes and images or at political convictions. The challenge of this study is therefore to reveal parallels through an ethico-aesthetic "conceptual" analysis to show that Makovecz and Tarr/Krasznahorkai do not opposed each other along the lines of a traditionalist versus modern dichotomy. Organic architecture (including Makovecz) *is* modern and even has futurist tendencies. References to the past and to tradition are no indicators of premodern, antimodern, or postmodern approaches: what matters is *how* images and symbols of the past are used.

The worst option would be to describe the differences between Tarr and Makovecz along historically established political lines, perhaps even by attributing the positions to Budapest's divided geography. In that case, Makovecz would be located in Buda and Tarr in Pest, separated by the Danube.[8] The division corresponds to old geographical and cultural distinctions. Traditionally, "populist" politics celebrating folk virtues and *Kultur* were settled in the hills of Buda, while cosmopolitan urbanist (often Jewish) intellectuals looking for *Zivilisation* lived in Pest. Timothy Garton Ash has described these conflicting worldviews that have continued to make sense for centuries: the Pest people "have looked outward to Vienna and the West rather than inward to the Transylvanian strongholds of agrarian Hungarianness. They have been drawn to sociology rather than to ethnography, and to socialism rather than to nationalism" (1985: 6). Even postcommunist politics maintained those fault lines (though not necessarily geographically) in the form of the opposition of the center right-wing Fidesz—Hungarian Civic Alliance and the Socialist Party. If we follow this pattern, Makovecz's fascination with myths can indeed make him look more "right wing," the more so because, as Boris Groys argues, "myth is the opposite of revolution" (1992: 116). Groys understands revolution as an activity able to "make the world," while myths are seen as static and authoritarian patterns coming from the past and contradicting dynamism. To support his claim, Groys (1992: 166) quotes Roland Barthes (1987: 147) from his *Mythologies*: "Wherever man speaks in order to transform reality and no longer to preserve it as an image ... myth is impossible." However, Makovecz's peculiar approach shows that myth *is* possible, even in situations where we aim at a transformation of reality. The conclusion: myth is not necessarily conservative. The present comparison of Tarr/Krasznahorkai and Makovecz aims to overcome Barthes's conceptual distinctions by describing the organism—as well as the myth—as not a static but rather a dynamic phenomenon. Two centuries of organic philosophy support this view. Thus, instead of contrasting rightist and leftist intellectual attitudes by referring to right-wing populism and socialism, respectively, I prefer to trace the differences between Tarr/Krasznahorkai and Makovecz to another opposition that has left its mark in Central and Eastern European intellectual history: the confrontation of Russian left-wing intellectuals with the more right-wing Eurasianist philosophies of the 1920s, the former supporting the revolution and the latter working on "Turanic" elements evaluating the importance of a spontaneous folk principle and the Orthodox Church. Here, both the left and the right were modern (as opposed to antimodern), and neither side was ready to foster traditional humanism. The suggested change of perspective will eventually lead to a reevaluation of the entire body of "leftist" poststructuralist thought and of the allegedly more "rightist" organic thought in an international context. In the end, the organic model of evolution-decomposition does not necessarily overlap with postmodern philosophies of deconstruction.

Another echo from the past is audible in the opposition of the revolutionary/leftist/deconstructionist versus the conservative/organic/religious. I am referring to the case of nobody other than André Bazin, whose work is very important here. Bazin developed his highly personal philosophy in a Catholic intellectual environment. He would quickly be denounced by his "progressive" contemporaries as a bourgeois idealist steeped in Christian theology and possibly an opiate addict (see Gray 2005: 10). The revolutionary spirit eager to deconstruct existing structures and Bazin's more conservative organic spirit searching for dynamic, holistic perspectives were bound to clash. Hugh Gray's defense of Bazin in his introduction to *What Is Cinema?* is highly relevant in this context because it points to the origins of the most organic thought Western philosophy has to offer. And those are also, at least indirectly, the sources this book draws on:

> Have they never heard of the philosopher Xenophanes who, gazing up at the heavens, proclaimed "the all is one"? Or of Parmenides who saw this whole as a continuum? Indeed if there had been cinema in those days one could imagine a similar argument to the present one going on between the schools of Parmenides and Heraclitus. It was these philosophers who first saw the cosmos or "reality" as a whole. (2005: 12)

Hungary has produced a cosmic director, a cosmic writer, and a cosmic architect. The precise meaning of "cosmic" will be explained by drawing on several philosophical sources, but a preliminary understanding can be provided by looking at its contrary: the "acosmy" (*acosmie*), a neologism invented by the French geographer Augustin Berque (2015). Acosmy designates a worldview engendered by the nonorganic abstraction of the modern cogito: when the vision and experience of the world is based on an "I think" instead of an "I dwell within a cosmos," either individual or universal perspectives are the only options. However, both the individual and the universal are abstractions. Therefore, in the history of philosophy, a whole string of organic thinkers has elaborated on the meaning of the more concrete, cosmic perspective.

Notes

1. Two recent books, Song Hwee Lim's *Tsai Ming-Liang and a Cinema of Slowness* (2014) and Ira Jaffe's *Slow Movies: Countering a Cinema of Action* (2014), have helped clarify the subject. However, given the large number of "slow films" that have recently appeared, as well as the large interest this phenomenon has received online, it is surprising that more books have not been published on this topic. While Lim's book has very much contributed to a general clarification of slow cinema, Jaffe's *Slow Movies* does not entirely eliminate the vagueness of the terms. I deal with both books here and in the first chapter. On contemplative cinema, see also a forthcoming book on Plotinus and film studies (Botz-Bornstein and Stamatellos 2017).
2. Lim has made a list of twenty directors he considers representative of slow cinema, but only contemporary directors are included (Tarkovsky and Yasujirō Ozu thus do not appear). The top five are Tsai Ming-liang, Béla Tarr, Alexander Sokurov, Lisandro Alonso, and Theo Angelopoulos (Lim 2014: 14).

3. All translations are my own unless otherwise indicated.
4. The legitimacy of the terms "Eastern Europe" or "Central Europe" is a controversial subject. Geographically, Hungary fits into both areas. For many people, "Eastern Europe" has negative connotations of backwardness. For some, it simply "stretches too far to the East" because it can also include Ukraine and Georgia, whereas "Central Europe" can also include major European cultures/countries such as Austria and Germany. In order to avoid all controversies, I use here most of the time the term "Central and Eastern Europe," which designates the region between the German-speaking countries and Russia.
5. The film *Werckmeister Harmonies* is based on the 220-page central section of Krasznahorkai's novel *The Melancholy of Resistance* entitled "The Werckmeister Harmonies: Negotiations."
6. See Gadamer 1989 (esp. p. 11) for more details.
7. Krasznahorkai also cowrote the script for *Damnation* with Tarr, though *Damnation* is not his novel.
8. "Budapest" is the combination of the city names Buda and Pest, which were united into a single city in 1873.

CHAPTER 1
Cinema, Architecture, Literature

Imre Makovecz

Imre Makovecz (1935–2011) was an architect internationally recognized as a foremost representative of the organic style. One of the most obvious organic features of his work is a preference of wood over manufactured materials like concrete, bricks, or iron. Wood is "organic" in the sense that it is bound to rot and decay. However, using organic material is not enough to make architecture organic, just like the decision to film ruins or forests does not turn the film into organic cinema. Makovecz shapes his timber architecture in an expressionist fashion, taking care to integrate both the surrounding nature and some—not necessarily Hungarian—folk traditions into his architectural creations. Makovecz describes his buildings like this:

> Our buildings evoke an ancient, often dark atmosphere.... We are involved in the revival of ruined and deserted villages and towns, and the story—recognition, discovering one another, conflicts, struggle for a national future—must be concentrated in the villages, roofs, halls and rooms, in the fabric of the houses, plots and streets. (Heathcote 1997: 7)

Béla Tarr

Béla Tarr's films are known for the rather abstract aesthetics of their black-and-white images and camera shots that can be as long as eleven minutes (the complete length of a 35mm film roll) but also for the bleak environment they expose. In fact, the environment looks very much like the one Makovecz described in the above passage. Several observers have noticed Tarr's organic input. Rose McLaren (2012) speaks of Tarr's coordination of "gritty detail and a sense of the universal in a way that some see as visionary and others find tedious." Universal themes are combined with individual human tragedies, big themes with trivial issues, the "cosmic" with the mundane, and fullness with emptiness. Yvette Bíró finds that Tarr "gives shape to the variability inherent in pulsation and the incomplete (uncompletable) nature of the flow of time" (2008: 160).

However, the link between Tarr and Makovecz is not only guaranteed by a similar formal interest in organic compositions but also concerns a similar conception of "organic space" present in Makovecz's buildings and Tarr's films. First, the "organic space" connects to Tarr's cinematic treatment of architecture. A lot of architecture appears in Tarr's films, though it has nothing to do with the architectural beauty current in the films of Federico Fellini or Michelangelo Antonioni, nor does it relate to the spirit of urban exploration by which French New Wave cinema is fueled. In film, Tarr's preference for ruins brings him close to Andrei Tarkovsky, and in architecture to the organic style developed by Makovecz and his followers. The Makovecz–Tarr link this book elaborates on is thus based on three criteria: (1) there are similarities with regard to the form of the compositions; (2) Tarr's films use architecture in a special way; (3) Makovecz and Tarr produce organic space in a similar fashion. The last point will receive much attention in chapter 12, where I establish the long camera take as a strategy dependent on the aesthetics of the organic.

Architecture in Tarr and Krasznahorkai

Architecture is a protagonist in many of Tarr's films. *Journey on the Plain* (1995) is not only a journey into a lost world but also a film about architecture mixed with poetry from the Hungarian national poet Sándor Petőfi. The film takes us to the postfeudal and postindustrial ruins of postcommunist Hungary. Architectural themes appear very early in Tarr's oeuvre, at least indirectly, with the film *The Prefab People* (1982). The title alludes to prefabricated mass housing in Hungary called *panelkapcsolat*, which was mostly made of Soviet-style precast concrete panels. The Hungarian title of the film is indeed *Panelkapcsolat*. The film *Family Nest* (1997) also addresses architectural conditions, presenting life in Hungarian prefab houses where large families must share small spaces. Architecture again becomes a striking feature in *The Man from London* (2007). Maloin's (Miroslav Krobot) illuminated and temple-like tower was built for the film and hovers like a UFO over the small city. Being both transparent and unreachable, the tower seems to contain a holy grail. From there Maloin governs the world by pulling his levers. Disproportionate though simultaneously integrated into the environment, the tower parallels some of Makovecz's structures.

Many ruins and decrepit buildings appear in later Tarr films. David Bordwell (2007) notes that the display of architecture makes Tarr's later films more "tectonic" and also that Tarr "shifts our attention from human action toward the touch and smells of the physical world." Walls receive attention in their own right through long, almost obsessive camera shots of their decrepit textures and plasters. In *Damnation*, a long sequence is composed of the slow alternation of walls and persons. The same principle is used in a sequence of *Satantango* where walls and people alternate. Also in *Satantango*, the doctor screens the walls vertically with his binoculars, as if attempting to read an encrypted story. In *Damnation*, there is a long, apparently insignificant, shot of the toilet ceiling while people are conversing. In this film, the process of rainwater slowly covering the walls is shown twice.

Walls receive a similar kind of attention in László Krasznahorkai's novels. The protagonist of "Once on the 381"—in *Megy a világ* (Going to the world)—finds deep in the thicket of the Serra de Ossa a hidden convent, which is a ruined palace whose decomposed walls Krasznahorkai describes in detail: "A large number of the many tiles had fallen from the wall and broken. The walls and ceilings that had once been carefully painted were eaten by mold" (2015b: 165). Why are those walls so important? In *Satantango*, Krasznahorkai describes walls as canvases on which reality is projected: "Even if it was plain to him that the sense of vacancy and tedium radiated by the very walls was only an appearance, and even if this spot was to the site of as yet invisible but therefore all the more feverish forces in the coming hours would soon engulf them" (2012a: 87). The walls do not have an identity spelled out in terms of ornaments, functions, or anything *on* them. Rather, they speak the silent language of emptiness precisely in the way required by Tadao Ando, who wanted "the space to speak" and "the walls to produce no sense of their own identities" (1991: 1).

Architecture in Tarr's films has yet another function, concerning the production of cinematic time-space. The camera's slow, horizontal movements alongside walls can also be seen as cinematic exemplifications of what Frank Lloyd Wright called the "principle of plasticity working as continuity" (1941: 183). Those slow shots along the ruined walls in *Damnation* and *Satantango* present people not directly but through wall openings. In *Damnation*, the conversation in the police office is filmed through the window from the outside, after which the camera moves along the wall onto the street level, where we see Karrer leaving through the main entrance. Here, as well as elsewhere, the long camera shots along walls make the space fluent as the walls create an organic unity of time and space. The walls are not merely physical borders but also function as temporal intervals leading from one object (one person) to another.

The Whale

A prefab house appears again in *Werckmeister Harmonies,* this time in the form of the "package" the huge stuffed whale has been put in, which is dragged into town on a circus wagon. On the outside it looks like an ordinary container, but on the inside, the *panelkapcsolat* is structured like a house with different rooms. In his "universal theseus" lectures from 1993, Krasznahorkai added further details explaining that the truck is "out of all proportions" and about thirty meters long (2011: 10). Strangely, as is written in *The Melancholy of Resistance,* the "monstrous truck" is hermetically closed because "the whale's domicile could apparently be opened only from the inside" (Krasznahorkai 1998: 87).[1] Soon the curious observers notice:

> there was neither handle nor grip nor any kind of chink in that riveted tin box, nothing at all that might suggest a door, and therefore it seemed (however impossible it might be to apprehend) that here, before the eyes of several hundred spectators, stood a contraption without any opening whatsoever at front, rear or side, and that the strong confronting it was in effect attempting to pry it open through sheer dumb obstinacy. (85)

At the end of *Werckmeister Harmonies,* the walls have been torn off the package, and the metaphysical object it contains (the whale) is visible. The whale as such has metaphysical connotations for several reasons. First, it signifies destruction because it belongs to the violent preacher, the Prince. Many commentators have seen this whale as the sea monster from the Old Testament, the leviathan. In the film, this provides an important input. Though the whale has no direct satanic powers, the townspeople will be spontaneously link it to the Prince's "vast murderous fury." However, the Old Testament also offers another, very different, whale story, the one of Jonah, who is miraculously saved when thrown overboard a ship by being swallowed by a whale. While in the whale, Jonah prays to God and God commands the whale to spew Jonah out.

In Krasznahorkai's original story, contrary to what we see in the film, the townspeople flock to see not only the whale but also what is hidden inside the whale, which means it is possible to enter the animal. This fact brings the symbol closer to the Jonah story while reinforcing the architectural metaphor. However, the whale still symbolizes something else. John Hodgkins sees the whale as "a symbol for Hungary's repressed modernist events [and] traumatic historical moments that are now breaching the surface after a long psychic submersion." Through the whale, the "townspeople find themselves forced from their cocoon of temporal nebulosity and thrust back into the processes of history" (2009: 52). This interpretation is indeed plausible. Krasznahorkai himself describes the whale as "the past ... crawling remorselessly ahead below the windows of unsuspecting people" (1998: 24).

A comparison of the whale with Makovecz's architecture is not far-fetched. Makovecz's buildings are often round and bodylike (most famously the church in Paks and the cultural center in Bak), which justifies further reflections on the whale in the present context. In fact, organic architecture often evokes the image of a living body's inviolate interior (see Toy 1993: 7), and a recurrent metaphor in descriptions of organic architecture is the expression "like a stranded whale." There are two reasons for the preference of whales in discourses on organic architecture. First, many organic architects find the round and bulging shapes appropriate. Second, the whale's physiognomy and cultural connotations (especially in light of its resemblance with Noah's ark) allows it to appear as an organic, living creature simultaneously able to function as a houselike shelter for humans. In other words, nature becomes culture through the whale because the animal is "stranded" and no longer functional. Third, Goethe saw fish (though not necessarily whales) as an example of a system representing the perfect reciprocity of organism and environment for which nothing can exist in isolation because "the fish is not fashioned for water nor does it adapt itself to water; rather the fish exists in and through water" (1833: 536).

Another association the shape of an inhabitable body produces is, of course, the return to the protective environment of the maternal womb. Makovecz himself has reproduced, in a very literal fashion, the interior of a whale in the form of the Mortuary Chapel in Farkasrét, Budapest (1975). In this mysterious space, wooden undulating ribs are held together by the "backbone" of the ceiling.[2] Makovecz relied here (like in the Seville Pavilion, the Paks Church, the Siófok Church, and the Csenger Sports Hall) on shipbuilding techniques. The ark shape (sometimes confusingly similar to that of a whale) is also metaphorically significant

Figure 1.1. Interior of Mortuary Chapel in Farkasrét, Budapest, by Imre Makovecz.

because European sacral buildings are formally related to ships, as indicated by the word "nave" to describe a part of a church. Therefore, a metaphysical allusion to the ship as a connecting device between this world and the afterlife might also be important when it comes to the metaphorical use of a whale.

Organic Architecture

Frank Lloyd Wright used the term "organic architecture" for the first time in 1914 in an article called "In the Cause of Architecture" for the journal *Architectural Record* explaining that the organic must be a fit between form and spirit (Wright 1975: 45) and an expression that avoids symmetry and literal repetition. Since Wright's times, theories of "organic architecture" have spread in many directions. Sometimes the imitation of curvy lines is seen as enough to make a building organic; sometimes the use of local materials and traditions is pointed out as essential; finally, many contemporary organic architects also refer to ecology and a New Age–style pantheistic kind of spirituality as the most important characteristic of the organic. I do not intend to cover the phenomenon of organic architecture as a whole here but am mostly interested in certain principles established by Makovecz, Wright, and the German organic architect Hugo Häring, whose theories are reflected in the Hungarian organic tradition. Hungarian organic architecture connects to Wright's aesthetics (as well as that of other organicists like Alvar Aalto), though its appearance is generally more rustic, less elegant, and less sophisticated. Organicism has been particularly important in the aesthetics of both Hungarian and Viennese modernism. Here, more than anywhere else, organicism helped to undertake the shift from romanticism to modernism, which becomes most obvious in the musical works of Arnold Schoenberg, Anton Webern, and Béla Bartók, whose input will be discussed in the context of Andreas Werckmeister's musicological problems.

Circularity

Aesthetic devices and conventions concern the form of a work of art. From a formal point of view, Krasznahorkai's texts are organic in many respects. *Satantango* has a circular structure, which represents the organic circle of disintegration and restoration. The book begins and ends with the depressing description of a gloomy day in the Hungarian countryside. In terms of style, the author reproduces a logic of the organic by pushing long sentences to such extremes that their only apparent purpose is to "be there." Inside those sentences individual elements remain significant, but the logic holding the individual and the general together is not static. Those patterns are organic and the long take, as Tarr practices it, exemplifies this organic philosophy.

In "El último Lobo," Krasznahorkai (2009) uses a spatial metaphor to explain his own approach: a "depressing logic in claustrophobic prose." The eminent literary critic James Wood has described Krasznahorkai's prose as a "dynamic paralysis in which the mind turns over and over to no obvious effect" (2012: 282). Obviously, it is not without reason that Krasznahorkai fans have thought of starting a "Slow Reading movement" (see Roy 2015). Here, "dynamic paralysis" will serve as a keyword for analyzing several elements in Hungarian film, literature, and culture. Elements in Krasznahorkai's texts are often repeated, and the language adopts coil-like structures. The sentences are similar to the looping melodies played by a wheezing accordion in *Satantango*'s dance scenes or to the "organic" music Mihály Vig composed for Tarr's films. The circularity is also very well exemplified by the cable car buckets in *Damnation*, which turn around in a circle and which Karrer counts all over again. Any central point able to establish a Cartesian order in terms of mathematics is avoided with the result that movement becomes non-movement. Like in organic architectural shapes, Vig's transitions are processlike and elements will not appear suddenly. This is paralleled by Tarr's films, where cuts are rare and where the camera seems to "drift" from frame to frame. The impression is that no authoritarian, central narrative (or a melody in music) exists but rather that one narrative element emerges from another narrative element. Tarr alludes to precisely this pattern when saying there are no events in real life but only series of conditions: "I despise stories, as they mislead people into believing that something has happened. In fact, nothing really happens as we flee from one condition to another" (Ebert 2009: 847). The result is the emergence of organic time, which means more precisely that narrative time is suspended. Finally, as the camera movement is stripped of its narrative function, we experience a feeling of slowness.

Slow Cinema, "Cinema Povero," Cool Cinema

Real slowness is organic, and the organic is always slow. Goethe held that Gothic architecture is not an imitation of nature. Instead, such architectural forms emerge slowly and transform. In art, this idea of slowness is more closely linked to poetry than to music. As the introduction pointed out, concerning Tarkovsky's "poetic cinema," thoughts are more efficiently transmitted in poetry when the performance is slow because intentions need to be grasped and meanings "lived." In organic thought, the emphasis on slowness is important, and for this reason alone, the slow movements in Tarr's films can appear organic.

In recent discussions of contemporary film, "slow cinema" or "contemplative cinema" have emerged as catchwords. However, they have mainly been employed by theoretically minded film enthusiasts writing on blogs and cannot be considered well-founded theoretical notions. Besides Song Hwee Lim (2014), Ira Jaffe (2014) has made a serious attempt, in his *Slow Movies: Countering the Cinema of Action*, to establish "slow cinema" as a coherent notion. However, is it really possible to find a common denominator of so many film directors' styles simply by concentrating on slowness? In Jaffe's book, slow cinema appears neither as a genre nor as a well-defined style but rather like a "family resemblance."

First, slowness is a matter of time. Jaffe writes, "retarded motion and prolonged moments of stillness and emptiness distinguish contemporary slow movies" (2014: 3). Here, stillness and emptiness are equated. However, stillness concerns time, while emptiness concerns visual and narrative components. Therefore, Jaffe adds two more items—the "austere mise-en-scène" and "lack of expressiveness":

> Editing or cutting in slow movies tends to be infrequent, which inhibits spatiotemporal leaps and disruptions. Not only do long takes predominate, but long shots frequently prevail over close-ups. Consistent with these stylistic elements, which may distance and irritate the viewer, is the austere mise-en-scène: slow movies shun elaborate and dynamic decor, lighting and color. Moreover, the main characters in these movies usually lack emotional, or at least expressive, range and mobility. Indeed, the characters' "flat," affect-less manner.

Jaffe thus concludes that slow movies "gravitate toward stillness and death, and tend, in any case, to be minimal, indeterminate and unresolved" (2014: 3). The lack of cutting produces long scenes, which obviously concerns time. The austere mise-en-scène, on the other hand, concerns not time but visual design. The last point, the actors' blankness and lack of expressiveness, is a matter of acting style, which is central in Jaffe's analysis of Jim Jarmusch's *Stranger Than Paradise* (1984), where the lack of expressiveness appears in the form of a pervasive "deadpan manner." One might wonder whether "slow cinema" is really the right term to hold all of these elements together because, obviously, only the first point deals with time.

In a broader context, the slow movement is, of course, related to "antiliterary" (in both senses of the term) movements of late modernity represented by absurd theater, the Nouveau Roman, and the French New Wave, to name but a few. In order to establish pertinent parallels between slow cinema and preexisting movements, I believe choosing the expression "cinema povero," derived from the Italian *arte povera* movement of the 1960s, would be very suitable because *arte povera* also attacked the corporate mentality prevalent in culture by returning to simple objects and messages. Of course, it is also possible to link, in a transversal fashion, the stylistic device of minimalism to the concept of time by saying long takes are minimalist because they tend to provide less information per second. In that case, the more suitable term would be "minimalist cinema."

Matters become more complex if one considers that "being minimalist" is not the only function of long takes; it might even be merely a side effect. True, when takes are long, there is often less to be filmed, but this is not necessarily the main purpose of taking long camera shots. Jaffe mentions critical reflections on recent Romanian cinema—particularly on Cristian Mungiu's *4 Months, 3 Weeks and 2 Days* (2007)—in which the long-take camera "maintains a distance" and "an impassivity" resembling "the stare of a peculiarly empathetic surveillance camera" (2014: 99). Thus, not only the long take itself but also the intentions behind the long take matter for its aesthetics. In this sense, the long take becomes emblematic for a paradox of modern experimental aesthetics because it can be long for two different reasons: first, because elements have been added and second, because some elements are missing. The problem is not limited to film and is even more current in modern literature. James Wood (2011) has pointed this out in his essay on Krasznahorkai, noting that, in general, "postwar avant-garde fiction has moved between augmentation and subtracting." Samuel Beckett, for example, started out as an augmenter and ended his life as a subtracter. Slow cinema is also moving back and forth between augmenting and subtracting.

Another concept that comes to mind in the context of slow cinema is the idea of "cool cinema" derived from Marshall McLuhan's principle of "cool media," which the Canadian philosopher understands as a model of communication leaving information partly unexplained and open to interpretation. To "cool media," McLuhan opposes "hot media" destined to provide high-definition information (1964: 37). Hot media favor analytical precision while cool media's lack of emotion is likely to challenge the viewer's own production of emotion. According to McLuhan, hot media "leave not much to be filled in" and thus allow less participation, but in incomplete cool media, the consumer must reenact emotions. Jaffe also uses the metaphor of coolness when writing about *4 Months, 3 Weeks and 2 Days*: in a "horrific long take" here, the camera "continues calmly and coolly" (2014: 101). Similarly, in Gus van Sant's *Elephant* (2003), long takes "keep the audience distant and the film's emotional temperature low" (57).

That all of this relates to the organic might not be immediately obvious. However, contrary to what most people might think, the concept of coolness is generally highly compatible with organicism. In music, at the time of Bartók, Schoenberg, and Webern, more structural, intellectually controlled approaches were to function as antidotes to the "lukewarm" sentimentality of romanticism. This shift toward a generalized aesthetics of restraint is most visible in the works of those composers who have been considered organic (see Frigyesi 2000: 25). In film, minimalism can be effective in the décor, place, and action but also in the narrative when information that *could* provide coherence and narrative soundness is suppressed. Jaffe concentrates on this last point in his chapter on Béla Tarr. The characters in *The Turin Horse* are unable to abandon their home after their well dries up, and nothing indicates "what causes the expanding darkness that signals their deepening paralysis and the end of the world" (2014: 14). Furthermore, in *Elephant,* "the absence of explanation is matched by the lack of emotional expression [when] the suddenly slow, soft, gliding motion seems to occur without cause or explanation" (50). Those intellectual patterns are in agreement with McLuhan, who attends to the narrative aspect by declaring nonlinearity an attribute of coolness and by dismissing melody as a continuous, connected, repetitive structure (1964: vii–viii). Linear and sequential ordering is hot, while fractured and discontinuous structures are cool. Of course, matters are a little more complex than this scheme indicates. The suppression of coherence is not always in agreement with the logic of the organic and can also lead to a postmodern aesthetics of fragmentation. The subtle line separating the organic from postmodern playfulness will be discussed at length in chapter 6.

The idea of "holding back" is a recurring theme in Jaffe's *Slow Cinema,* though it is never highlighted as a particular part of a theoretical system. We have to ask, what is held back? First, in slow cinema the director tends to hold back the protagonist's point of view. Jaffe analyzes Lisandro Alonso's *Liverpool* (2008) and Pedro Costa's *Ossos* (1997). In those films, the "'withholding' pattern entails a refusal to track either promptly or closely the actions of characters as well as their shifts of attention or points of view" (2014: 114). More generally, "strong political and social views are withheld" in slow movies. Open rebellion is also limited because of "the extreme indeterminacy of these films" (151). Despite this "holding back," long takes have been seen as participatory because they create the feeling of being present and of moving around in the space.

Importantly, the aesthetics of the long take as a "cool device" works only in combination with this strategy of withholding. In strictly temporal terms, the long take is continuous, as Tarr affirms when saying he prefers the long take because he likes the continuity. Furthermore, this continuity "matches that of real life, and it's very important to make the film a real psychological process" (Tarr 2000). Tarr's desire for continuity, should any "withholding" effect be absent, would clash with McLuhan's "discontinuity" as a main feature of cool media. Vice versa, the "spatiotemporal leaps" that slow cinema avoids can also work in the service of discontinuity, while continuous and connected long takes leave little to be filled in. First, this means that cool or minimalist cinema does not depend on long takes. Second, long takes are minimalist only as long as certain elements within the shot are withheld.

Jaffe presents many cases. He also extends the scope of the long take toward the metaphysical, saying there is not only a lack of expression but also the attempt to express something inexpressible. Jaffe finds this in Jia Zhangke's *Still Life* (2006), where both Sanming and Shen Hong seem locked "in inexpressible sadness" (2014: 143). Tarr's slow pace also points to "the existence of human beings deprived of action and events in their allotted time" (Bíró 2008: 169) The minimalism of the narrative structure thus needs to be distinguished from a minimalism of content. Jaffe refers to this when quoting Jonas Mekas's attempt to distinguish "silence" from "emptiness" in Antonioni's films: "They say Antonioni rediscovered silent cinema, he is going back to the true principles of cinema. They look at it formalistically. But ... Antonioni's silence comes from his content" (2014: 69).

Slow Motion

Another important aspect of slow movies must still be addressed. In general, slow movies are unrelated to slow motion as used in scenes of violence and martial arts films, where the slowness actually *adds* information because details (often of horror) are blown up in time. This slow motion does not create the detached mood slow movies are famous for. A "slowness of fullness," not a "slowness of emptiness," creates anxiety. Slow motion in slow cinema—rare as it is—will always have another function. An example is Tarkovsky's selective use of slow motion, which contributes to the aesthetics of the oneiric and which Vlada Petric has called an instrumentation of Vsevolod Pudovkin's "close-up of time" (1989: 30). This kind of slow motion reflects the characters' psychological or emotional fixations manifest in body movements and objects that the director wishes to observe more closely over time. As a result, slow motion creates a whole range of unnatural sensations clearly transcending the augmentation of horror and brutality to which slow motion is almost limited in action cinema.

What about the stroboscopic undercrank or "step printing" effect (also called "stop printing"), which Wong Kar-wai and others use to obtain a particularly haunting sense of simultaneous animation and retardation? This stylistic device clearly slows down the film's pace and creates a contemplative mood in the spirit of slow movies.

Bazin and the Organic

The general idea of slow movies is that less is more. But what is the "more" supposed to be? Is it aesthetic beauty, reality, unreality (dream), a meditative mood, or "the metaphysical"? Do long takes capture the reality of everyday life in a more efficient manner? Without doubt, slow cinema or contemplative cinema "lays bare" (to use the words of André Bazin) the world and reality before us as it takes "a close look at the world," including all its cruelty and ugliness. Bazin puts forward silent era director Erich von Stroheim, who rejected "photographic expressionism and the tricks of montage [aux artifices du montage]." Stroheim's aesthetics can here easily be extended toward that of slow cinema because "one could easily imagine as a matter of fact [à la limite] a film by Stroheim composed of a single shot as long-lasting and as close up [aussi gros] as you like" (2005 1: 27; Bazin 1961 1: 135). Most important for Bazin is the decision to preserve the natural continuity of the time and space of everyday life in film. Thus, the ideas present in volume 1 of *What Is Cinema?* represent a prototypical version of organic film theories, often reinforced by the use of metaphors derived from organic life.

Bazin's organic tendency becomes particularly clear when he plays out René Descartes's constructivism against the theories of the naturalist and cosmologist Georges-Louis Leclerc (also going by the name of Comte de Buffon), who influenced the evolutionary theorist Jean-Baptiste Lamarck. Bazin writes: "In any event, the margin of error is greater on the side of Descartes and his animal-machine than of Buffon and his half-human animals" (2005 1: 43; 1961 1: 51). Slow cinema should have an evolutionary structure that Bazin decides to oppose to the narrative structure of the melodrama. The melodrama is not spontaneously evolving but calculated. As a result, its movements are often too predictable:

> Unfortunately the demon of melodrama that Italian film makers seem incapable of exorcising takes over every so often, thus imposing a dramatic necessity on strictly foreseeable events. But that is another story. What matters is the creative surge, the special way in which the situations are brought to life. The necessity inherent in the narrative is biological rather than dramatic. It burgeons and grows with all the verisimilitude of life. (2005 2: 31)

Jaffe confirms the importance of Bazin's determination to "preserve the natural continuity of the time and space of everyday life" (2014: 54). For postsurrealists like Bazin and Siegfried Kracauer, cinema looks for its most genuine form of expression within a paradoxical kind of realist expression "in which the imaginary is permitted to simultaneously include reality and replace reality" or "in which our imagination is fed by a reality that it will soon replace" (Bazin 2005 1: 47). Kracauer even insists that "reality" should enter film immediately in the form of "camera reality" (*Kamerarealität*) and that we should be moved by the "raw and unpainted presence of objects" while the "umbilical cord between image and reality remains uncut" (1973: 224). This corresponds precisely to Bazin's promotion of documentary immediacy over the mediations of script.

However, when emphasizing the necessarily paradoxical character of this approach, Bazin goes one step further: if our imagination is fed by a reality that will soon be replaced by this same imagination, "the fable is born of the experience that it is supposed to transcend" (2005 1: 47). Here, Bazin anticipates Tarkovsky—though the latter never mentions Bazin in his *Sculpting in Time* (1986)—by declaring montage "anticinematic." What is so wrong with montage? The problem is that it does not respect the organic character of cinematic space and time, which is the only "reality" that remains once "the fable is born of the experience that it is supposed to transcend." Montage can only create narratives when it follows, in Bazin's terminology, a "literary" approach ultimately bound to disrespect the "unity of space" whose production is nevertheless the task of cinema (46). This means Bazin calls for the "respect of spatial unity" because realism "resides in the homogeneity of space" (50).

The fact that resides in the homogeneity of space, even more than the promotion of documentary immediacy over the mediations of script, represents an outline of an organic philosophy of film. The "ontology of the cinematographic tale" (48) depends on the realism of cinematographic space, while montage creates an unwanted shift from the real to the imaginary (50), that is, a shift from the cinematic to the narrative-literary. Whether this happens depends on the film's "spatial density" (48). Only when the space is "dense" will the imaginary have a chance to shift backward toward realism. Montage, on the other hand, destroys this density. Finally, to the density of space must be added the density of time in the sense of concrete time. Dense time must oppose abstract time. This is how Bazin's "reborn realism" becomes capable "of bringing together real time, in which things exist, along with the duration of the action, for which classical editing had insidiously substituted mental and abstract time" (39).

Once again we must ask what kind of surplus is produced by slow movies or contemplative movies. It is a "density of space" for Bazin, but Tarr suggests something else: since nothing happens in his movies, "all that remains is time. This is probably the only thing that's still genuine" (quoted in Jaffe 2014: 161). Tarr's view is radical and more reminiscent of Tarkovsky than of Bazin. And, certainly, not all "slow" directors would agree on those points. Thus, different devices can be used to slow cinema down, but the purposes for which they are chosen differ from director to director.

Notes

1. Krasznahorkai's story can be traced to a real event. In 1961, 1962, and 1963, a stuffed whale, captured in 1954 off the Norwegian coast and named Goliath, was touring in Hungary. It weighed 68,200 kilos and was transported, exactly like in the film, on a heavy-duty truck. Apparently, it was possible to enter the whale itself. On posters the whale was presented to the public in a truly "organic" way: organ by organ, that is, indicating that the heart weighs 450 kilos, the kidneys 560 kilos, the liver 600 kilos, and the tongue 2,200 kilos. This is strongly reminiscent of Makovecz's attempts to attribute the names of body parts to parts of buildings like eye and mouth but also column, bottom, elbow, forehead, hair, and so on (Beke 1987: 26). Tickets for the whale circus were sold by the thousands, and people were brought from neighboring villages to places where Goliath was on show. In his "universal theseus" lectures, Krasznahorkai (2001) describes the whale story from his own point of view as if he himself went in the 1960s to see the whale exposition. The problem was that Goliath came from the other side of the Iron Curtain. Rumors that the CIA had sent the truck in order to spy on the Hungarian people spread quickly (*Dunaújvárosi Hírlap* 1962; Funzine Media 2012). The event also inspired Lajos Parti Nagy's (2006) short story "Giuseppe undo Pusztay" in which the sharklike circus director gets rid of the decomposing whale by throwing it into the swamp of the Danube Delta. Romanian forced laborers building a canal discover the remains decades later. Historians conclude they are the bones of a mammoth and put them into the Museum of Natural History.
2. Another whalelike appearance can be seen in the 268-meter-long Hungarian Parliament Building. Completed in 1904, it is superlative in many respects in order to symbolize the political function of the second capital of the Austro-Hungarian monarchy. Its size (it contains almost seven hundred rooms) was already found uncanny when it was built. The bicameral system for which it was conceived switched to a unicameral system in 1920 because the unicameral legislation was found more suitable for the small,

homogeneous unitary state Hungary had by then become. The change has deprived the entire northern half of the building of its function (it can now be rented for conferences). Moreover, Viktor Orbán's controversial new legislation has recently almost halved the 386-member parliament. As a result, the parliament lies like a stranded, half-empty whale on the claimed land of the former Tömö Square. Endre Dányi has called the parliament an "inhabited ruin" (2013: 58).

CHAPTER 2
Central Europe

As mentioned in the introduction, there is something "Central or Eastern European" in the work of Imre Makovecz, Béla Tarr, and László Krasznahorkai. In Krasznahorkai's writings, the cultural exceptionalism is sometimes caricatural. The bureaucratic archivist hero from *War and War* (2006), György Korin, is depicted as a crazy, unintelligible foreigner from Central Europe who must be judged by special standards. András Bálint Kovács (2008) holds that Tarr's films "offer the most powerful and complex vision of the historical situation in the Eastern European region over the last decade." Again, I believe this perspective pertains to the organic. To understand the organic works of Tarr and Krasznahorkai outside the particular cultural context in which they are placed is indeed impossible. They share this trait with artists of earlier generations. The organic compositions of Anton Webern, Arnold Schoenberg, and Béla Bartók were already a response to the social anxiety in Central Europe at the time: they connected to a desperate fight against a disintegrating society in which the organic was supposed to provide coherence. The Hungarian situation from the 1980s onward is characterized by similar concerns.

Dynamic Paralysis

Some might find the concept of "dynamic paralysis" (Wood 2012) a perfect illustration of the Central European way of dealing with the political and cultural events affecting the region over centuries. The organic can serve as a conceptualization of the paradoxical pattern called dynamic paralysis, as well as an illustration of a typical Central and Eastern European attribute. The idea of dynamic paralysis as a simultaneous expression of resignation and nonresignation is a pertinent cultural concept summarizing the spirit of Central and Eastern Europe. The concept clearly underlies Krasznahorkai's personal life philosophy when he describes the psychological dimensions of his creative production: "After every book a disappointment, and after that, let me try again ... a Beckettian cage in which I live ... 'Try again. Fail again. Fail better'" (Beplate 2013: 163). "Fail better" succinctly summarizes the complex process of dynamic resignation.

Formally speaking, the organic evolves circularly, as it submits to a life cycle endlessly moving from life to death and back again to life. Robert Boyers has called this quality a "stoic doctrine" (2005: 170), which he sees particularly well exemplified in Krasznahorkai's works. Dynamic paralysis is generally typical for Krasznahorkai's thinking, as he seems to revel in the formulation of logical paradoxes. For example, in *Seiobo There Below*, he speaks of the "logical irrationality" of Indian myths (2013c: 37). He has repeatedly described this state of natural circularity literally: "[The Japanese crane] comes from a world where eternal hunger is the ruler, so that to state that it hunts means that it takes part in the general hunt, for all around it every living being falls upon its prescribed prey in the eternal hunt: falls upon it, strikes down upon it, it approaches and seizes it, grabs it ..." (5). Organisms are entities that constantly struggle for survival, and Krasznahorkai's passage represents nothing other than a literary description of organic development in nature. The insistence on eternity and repetition can also let this entire organic process appear as one "long take" on nature.

The organic life-death-life cycle is more embedded in the consciousness of Central and Eastern Europeans than of Western Europeans, which is why the former have also been more prone to an understanding of organic cultural expressions. The organic evolves and declines and evolves again, which is a perfect description of the Central and Eastern European cultural situation that has unfolded over many centuries. Rarely can we observe a linear model of evolving colonial or progressive enthusiasm; rather, the most typical fare has been a paradoxical combination of dynamis and stagnation. *The Essential Guide to Being Hungarian,* in a chapter suitably called "Fate," states: "Generally speaking, to be Hungarian is to be dealt a real blow by life. It is misfortune itself; it is to be an outcast, persecuted, beaten, forced into migration, live in penury or backwardness; it is to be orphaned, to be misunderstood in life" (Ráz 2012: 16). Other Central and Eastern Europeans will recognize those feelings, as well as the ironical connotations attached to them. Hungarian philosopher Gáspár Miklós Tamás has summarized Hungarianness as "the feeling that we are finished, but that at the same time the whole thing is a joke" (2013: 23). The cycle of oppression, frustration, resistance, and defeat has created a cultural consciousness of "dynamic resignation" similar—though not necessarily identical—to the state of consciousness dominant in the appreciation of absurd art, which, according to Lilla Töke, grew out of a historical necessity in Central and Eastern Europe. Absurd art "exists owing to a particular historical continuity evolving from the traumatic turmoils of two world wars, from political extremism, authoritarian repression, the failures of (fascist, socialist, and capitalist) economic experimentation, and from the ongoing bureaucratic chaos and despotism" (2011: 102–3). Hungarian absurd literature thus belongs to a realist aesthetic tradition, which is highly unusual. (That the absurd appears here as not an estranged reality but a depiction of normal reality will interest us in chapter 7, where Krasznahorkai's particular understanding of realism will be examined).

Disappearance and disintegration have occurred everywhere in the world, but Western Europeans at least have had at times a chance to see the evolution of time in a more linear fashion. Hungary lost two-thirds of its territory after World War I. The territorial loss is still considered a national tragedy and creates—if not nationalism and chauvinism—a curious, disciplined form of melancholy that can be named "melancholic resistance." Budapest has been declared the "indestructible city" not because it has never been destroyed but because it constantly re-emerges "despite great waves of emigration, of invasions, of wars of independence by Tartars and Turks, of robberies and explosion" (Peter Hanák, quoted in Gyáni [1998] 2002: xi). Gábor Gyáni concludes that "discontinuity has always been a feature of [Hungary's] long history" (xi), and Jean-Marie Samocki even holds that in the East "disintegration appears less as a consequence of historical time but as an origin, it is the matter of a spooky and eternal Mitteleuropa" (2011: 118–19). Thus, disintegration is not what history produces but rather the origin of historical creation itself, which is indeed a strange model of history. If we had to label it, we would call it organic.

Central and Eastern Europe is also a candidate for applications of organic thinking because the entire political culture here was once expressed in the form of "the System." Hungarian writer György Konrád explains the difference between socialist and capitalist countries, stating of the former, "I used to criticize the system, now I criticize particular things" (1995: 41). In communism, people were forced to think organically because details were linked through not only fluid cultural traditions (like in the West) but also a rigid overarching structure represented by "the System." Consequently, the tiniest mistake would be seen as the system's fault. During the last decades of the communist regime, "the System" had been paralyzed and ceased to function. The result of this rigid organic constellation is dynamic paralysis, producing a feeling of absurdity and unreality. Correspondingly, Georg Lukács explained in one of his last interviews, "the bureaucracy generated by Stalinism is a tremendous evil. Society is suffocated by it.... Everything becomes unreal, nominalistic. People see no design, no strategic aim, and do not move" (Marcus and Tarr 1989: 215–16). Furthermore, Central and Eastern Europeans will probably always understand the organic defined as the contrary of "constructed" in subtler political terms than most other people in the world. The recent historical experiences brought about by the shift from communism to capitalism have made Central and Eastern Europeans aware of the socially constructed nature of any political system.

Yet another way to grasp the concept of dynamic resignation can be described as a kind of Central and Eastern European "fragility." Costica Bradatan writes about this cultural particularity in the preface to a special issue of *Angelaki* entitled "The Unbearable Charm of Fragility":

> The Eastern European modality of insertion in the world is a paradoxical one: it always presupposes the expectation that the world can collapse at any time. In Eastern Europe everything barely exists. If tomorrow the universe were to fall back into nothingness, this would hardly surprise anyone here: the dividing line between existence and nonexistence is always blurred, and that is exactly what makes everything (institutions, people, ideas, projects) so fragile. (2010: 4)

It is precisely this kind of fragility that is evoked in *Werckmeister Harmonies*'s hospital scene (see chapter 5). In art, this fragility can create an experience of (spatial and emotional) emptiness that remains unique to Central and Eastern Europe. We find it, for example, in Milan Kundera's description of a walk he takes through Prague in the 1970s with a philosopher friend whose thousand-page manuscript was confiscated by the police a few hours earlier. Kundera describes the situation with empathy: "We walked toward the square in the old city near which I was then living, and we felt an immense loneliness, a void, the void in the European space from which culture was slowly withdrawing" (1984: 36).

Organic Architecture and the Search for Harmony

Central and Eastern European fragility as a theme inspiring the aesthetics of the organic connects to a typically Hungarian cultural discourse desperately attempting to dichotomously define the organic and the rational. In Hungarian architecture, this cultural and political paradigm has been discussed for more than a century and has helped to make Hungarian architecture a subject of international interest. In Hungary, architecture is not merely a matter of aesthetics or technology but a site where social ideals and national identities are fabricated. Historically speaking, the Hungarian definition of the organic has its roots in the particular position that Hungarian culture holds within the Austro-Hungarian Empire. Edwin Heathcote explains:

> Just as Expressionism and the Bauhaus share roots in the Romantic Medievalism of postwar Germany, both Hungarian Rationalism and Organicism can be traced back to the specific cultural condition that existed in the late nineteenth century, an era in which Budapest began to compete for dominance with its twin capital in the Austro-Hungarian Empire, Vienna. (2006: 35)

Within this political context, the opposition of the rational-international to the national-individual has managed to become part and parcel of the philosophy of the organic. Early Hungarian organicist architects like Ödön Lechner (1845–1914)—sometimes called the Hungarian Antoni Gaudí—experimented with national symbolisms, which developed into a distinctive wave of national architecture. While Lechner thought a Hungarian style needed to be invented from scratch (by referring to a general idea of "the East" as the cradle of Hungarian culture), the younger Károly Kós (1883–1977) found that a Hungarian style did indeed exist and engaged in serious research into Transylvanian folk culture. Hungarian identity should be sought not in Asia but in the Middle Ages. Kós's conservative architectural group, the "Youth" (Fiatalok), synthesized modern technology with folk themes. In the 1970s and 1980s, a group of younger architects, the Pécs Group, practiced an adventurous organic style (sometimes under the leadership of György Csete) in the relatively liberal environment of the city of Pécs in southern Hungary. Such autonomous initiatives were extremely rare in any socialist-realist environment. The search for harmony, which is one of Krasznahorkai's main themes, was already important here. The Pécs Group manifesto from 1973, entitled "Only from Pure Sources," promised to create "harmony in new works, with the old, with the region, with nature, with man, and with human settlement" (Cook 1997: 7).

National culture bloomed in Hungary because the country had had such a long history of oppression from the outside, which made the development of a distinct national culture essential for the creation of a national identity. Of course, Hungary is not unique in this respect but is paralleled by other European countries. In the nineteenth century, especially in Central Europe, the hunt for origins was rather obsessive. At earlier stages, Hungarian romantic nationalist sentiment had not been much different from Pan-Slavism (see Kohn 1953). Later, in the 1920s, national revival styles were dominant in many European countries. However, the development that this identity search took in Hungary is unique, which relates to the political constellations Heathcote describes above. The Art Nouveau movement in Hungary was often secessionist and adopted a special aesthetics for this purpose. In order to be distinct from the Austrians, exotic influences needed to be emphasized. A certain contradictoriness became part of the cultural consciousness: on one hand, Hungarians poured "resources into chartering their grand ancestry to somewhere out in the Asian steppe" (Winder 2013: 6); on the other, they required being coequal with the Austrians within the large European empire of the Habsburg. On one hand, they defined their "Hungarianness" (*magyarság*) via links with non-European minority cultures and eagerly attempted to express Hungarian identity in "exotic" terms; on the other, they wanted to be recognized as a "rational" European leading power. Contradictions concerning Hungary's relationship with Europe still regularly surface. Members of the far right, anti-European party participate in steppe rallies in Kazakhstan together with other Siberian peoples and reproduce romantic clichés of the wild, nomadic Hungarian; at the same time, a not-much-less right-wing governing Fidesz party receives European subventions for renovating the Budapest Parliament Building. All this is bound to produce a twist in the country's cultural consciousness. Delusions of grandeur and self-pity are often fused into one political package, of which the strong desire for a harmony to reconcile those contradictions comes as a part.

Later, the Hungarian architectural style had to adapt to the modern age, and, consequently, the "rational" component had to be emphasized. After Lechner, Béla Lajta (1873–1920) managed to bring together the modern (rational) and the organic (national) within one architectural expression. In principle, Lajta overtook Lechner's universal ideas but not his details. István Medgyaszay—who would later find "proof" that Hungarians are related to Huns, Persians, and even Chinese and Japanese (see Gerle 1998: 251)—undertook the same task at the same time. On one hand, Lajta's fusion of the modern and the national paved the way for the more "cosmic" organicism of Makovecz and his followers. On the other—and this makes the Hungarian situation so different—the story is not as straightforward as it appears. The socialist interlude brought about a polarization, putting progressive rationalist and conservative organicists into opposing camps without leaving much possibility for communication between them. During socialism, the dichotomy Lajta had attempted to dissolve was spelled out in terms that were even more radical.

However, overall, nationalist and identitarian ambitions in architecture rarely produced nationalist results. Lechner indulged in exotic Far or Middle Eastern themes when designing the Museum of Applied Arts in Budapest, but the result was not a redefinition of Hungarianness in terms of Eastern culture. Rather, a completely new language that is interesting in its own right emerged, even in an international context. Contemporary reactions illustrate this contradiction: while, in the eyes of some, Lechner had succeeded in wrenching Hungarian cultural identity from the Austrian aesthetic realm, Hungarian nationalists simultaneously thought this style did not express "Hungary's national essence" (Brandow-Faller 2011: 182). The important point is that Lechner's formal compositions are based on neither ethnographic studies of village life nor imported Asian shapes but were simply imagined archetypes. Accordingly, Lajos Fülep wrote at the time, "looking for national he found international, searching for Asian he found the modern and topical" (Gerle 1998: 226). In this context, the individual does not remain individual but rather acquires a general meaning. This contradiction can make Lechner the forerunner of the organic, just like the Austrian architect Otto Wagner is the forerunner of functionalism. The situation is very similar to that of Béla Bartók, whose art is not merely folkloristic. He also reinterpreted folk sources for a completely new purpose, often ensuring that "his folklorism could not be used to support the nationalism of the political establishment; on the contrary, it undermined the basic tenets of contemporary nationalist ideology [as] he used Romanism, Slovakian, and Arabian music in pieces that he thought of as examples of Hungarian art music" (Frigyesi 2000: 21).

In subsequent phases of Hungarian history, labels would change several times: socialist modernism could identify with conservative positions, while the organicist approach could appear as a radical oppositional stance ready to provoke the authoritarian regime. Whatever happened, the logic would remain the same: the system opposing the organic to the rational would remain intact. After socialism, the organic school adopted an antiglobalization position.

Does all of this really concern Hungary alone? Despite the undeniable fact that similar movements did exist in other European countries, I believe the search for musical harmony—the topic of Tarr's film and

Krasznahorkai's section of the novel that bears the word harmony in its title—is very Hungarian. Around 1900, a Hungarian national identity would be created through an impressive amount of productions in many fields of the arts, though Hungarian music is best recognized on an international level. How did this new style come about? In fact, the entire process appears like research into the particularities of musical harmonies. In principle, the emergence of a distinctly Hungarian musical style in the late eighteenth century depended on the mixing of certain elements of Hungarian folk harmonies with the harmony of classical music. The anthropological and musicological research of Bartók and Zoltán Kodály consisted very much in the analysis of older harmonies that needed to be identified in terms of origin in order to be converted into new harmonies.

Similar "harmonizations" took place in architecture. In general, organic Hungarian artists attempted to reestablish a lost harmony between local (rural) and international culture avoiding the fragmentations characteristic of urban culture. Moreover, organic harmonization was on many Hungarian social scientists' agenda at the turn of the century. The historian Gyula Szekfű (1883–1955) produced an—arguably flawed—cultural geography of the nation by practicing geopsychology, whose purpose was to establish connections between the land and its people. The nationalist geographer Ferenc Fodor (1887–1962) attempted to shape Hungary's geographical, historical, and psychological elements into a total unity (see Jobbit 2011). And the historian Sandor Pethő (1885–1940) strove to integrate modern science and national traditions. Building on German *Geistesgeschichte* and other "spiritually informed" historiographical and methodological approaches developed half a century earlier by Leopold Ranke and Wilhelm Dilthey, these modern scholars attempted to fuse "subjective elements such as memory, feeling, and tradition" with modern science (Jobbit 2011: 64). Being remarkably similar to later ethnophilosphy or "ethno-scientific" approaches (with all their essentialist shortcomings), conservative nationalist scholars desperately sought to render cultural and scientific fragments into meaningful organic totalities. The result was supposed to be a harmonious science of national meaning.

This chapter has shown that the aesthetics of the organic in Central and Eastern Europe relates to a typically Hungarian cultural discourse attempting to dichotomously define the organic and the rational. In the specific cultural context of Hungary, *Werckmeister Harmonies* has both a metaphorical and literal meaning. James Goodwin also put forward the opposition of the organic and the rational, which remains important in Hungarian architecture today, in one of the first statements on organic cinema: "Where form in intellectual cinema establishes ideological perspective and critical distance, in organic cinema form fuses author, content and individual spectator" (1993: 176). Goodwin's statement, though related to film, echoes a classical statement by the architectural historian Bruno Zevi (1950: 65), who, in his treatise *Toward an Organic Architecture* (1946) opposes the organic to the theoretic. For Goodwin, together with the "intellectual" comes the "ideological." Therefore, since ideologies are generally assumed to have been done away with in the postcommunist world, "organic cinema" should logically be seen as the next step in the realm of cinema. In Hungarian organic architecture, this step was taken a long time ago. In cinema, a similar step must be expected.

CHAPTER 3

What Is "Organic?"

The Individual, the Universal, and the Anti-Universal

Historically, the scope of philosophical reflections on the organic has been broad because the organic addresses universal and individual ways of interpreting the world order and of how people should live within that world order. The organic concerns ethics, aesthetics, and religion. In the history of philosophy, the organic has very often represented a paradoxical fusion of the particular and the universal, of the concrete and the abstract. The "dynamics" of the organic, addressed in chapter 2 in the form of a "dynamic paralysis," represents a similar paradox, as it insists on the interplay of evolution and decomposition: though all living structures are held together by a coherent and evolving "organic" model, the organic element can at the same time "decompose" all static structures. Even while the organic evolves, it will still be the product of decay. In an organic context, nothing can be static, not even evolution.

In the nineteenth century, the idea of the organic served as an intellectual model in many cultural areas, but in the latter half of the twenty-first century, organic thinking was pushed into a peripheral niche. Prominent today are discourses on "universal" values on one hand and various forms of individualism on the other. Postmodern philosophies attempting to deconstruct universalisms do exist, but they typically do not engage in organic thinking or deconstruct universalisms in view of alternative, coherent "organic" models (see chapter 8). Examples of nonorganic ways of thinking, however, are abundant. First, there are the "universalists." Attempts to force general rules on individual expressions are probably as old as human civilization. Those who find a truth to express "all and everything" often become intolerant. Instead of seeing the general truth as a tool to use within sophisticated dialectical, cosmological, or monadological systems, these people tend to see "the universal" as an end in itself.

The opposite approach also exists: ethnic pride and nationalism are often expressions of individualisms unwilling or unable to join more universal values and structures. Here, the individual clashes in the most dramatic way with the universal. Most nonorganic tendencies remain inscribed in a system where the individual and the universal are perceived as clear oppositions. A certain form of economic globalization that some like to call McDonaldization (see Ritzer 2001) follows the scheme of straightforward universalization. Benjamin Barber's (1995) "Jihad vs. McWorld" scenario, on the other hand, expresses conflict: a regionalistically oriented "jihad" clashes with the busily expanding and universalizing world of McWorld capitalism. Barber understands jihad as a generic concept comprising all individual countercultural movements. However, this "individualism" will not necessarily remain purely individual either; it can become very pervasive once it decides to universalize its individual values.

A typically "Western" anti-universalism also exists and heads toward the other extreme. Being against all universal truths, it formulates a relativist position declaring that all things cultural, political, or religious have equal value. This "vertigo of relativity" (Berger and Luckmann 1966: 17) was partly sparked in the early twentieth century by new discoveries in science, philosophy, and anthropology, and it culminated in Albert Einstein's replacement of the absolute with the relative. Believing history has proved all values and cultures to be individual and self-contained, this anti-universalism interprets the relativity of truth as a moral postulate. General truths do not exist: the moral world is nothing more than a random accumulation of single elements. Allan Bloom (1987) has criticized this kind of fundamentalist relativism in *The Closing of the American Mind*. He finds this exaggerated relativism typical for North American students of the humanities, as well as for their teachers. In this book, the three models sketched above—the individual, the universal, and the relativist anti-universal—will be located in concrete situations regarding the characters in *Werckmeister Harmonies* and other films. This analysis will enable us to define the particular position of the organic.

In a world of competing universalisms, of equally absolute individualisms, and of anti-universalisms, negotiating compromises is becoming increasingly difficult. Fortunately, not all philosophies are "totalitarian." Poststructural philosophies have long been attacking totalitarian structures and universal values and essentializing dichotomies by developing theories meant to deconstruct the rigid Western metaphysical heritage. The result is not really a compromise between the individual and the universal but rather an approach to transcend their dichotomy. However, "deconstructionists" are not the only ones working toward this end. Other philosophers have been working on the same project but in different ways sharing. All those philosophers share the ambition to define the relationship between the universal and the individual not in terms of oppositions but of fruitful paradoxes. Some such philosophies come from the Muslim hemisphere: Jamal ad-Din al-Afghani (1838–1897) and Muhammad Abduh (1849–1905) attempted to accommodate universal modernity and local culture within one philosophical discourse. More recently, transculturalism, intercultural thinking, and hermeneutics must be listed among these efforts. All of these philosophies reflect on an ontological or existential self-contradictoriness able to simultaneously affirm the existence of both single elements and their unity. Any form of organic thinking is part of this project.

Hermeneutics

Philosophical hermeneutics plays a prominent role in the contemporary organic landscape. Here, the notion of play is meant to transcend the dichotomy of the individual and the universal. For Hans-Georg Gadamer, the most important hermeneutic philosopher of the twentieth century, the organic metaphor of play or game serves as a model for social interaction and aesthetic expressions. All Dasein ("being there"), according to Gadamer, is implicated in the organic structures of language and culture, which means the subject has no absolute control over those structures. Even art is always organic, communal, and collective. Gadamer draws an explicit analogy between biological and social organisms, highlighting the importance of the equilibrium within organic constellations (1976: 32). Social life is never a matter of social engineering, because the latter runs the risk of upsetting the delicate balance of stratified social forces (1971: 314–17). Finally, Gadamer suggests an organic model of time, which will be important in chapter 12 when analyzing the temporal logic of long camera shots. From Gadamer's hermeneutic perspective, time "develops in its very nature out of the suffering of flesh of human experience" (1970: 348). He suggests, for example, that "old age" has its own time. In this sense, the time of any epoch represents an autonomous mode of "Being."

Defining the Organic

Organic architecture goes back to Frank Lloyd Wright and Louis Sullivan, but in intellectual history, reflections on the organic are, of course, much older. They have existed at least since Aristotle's extensive elaborations on the spatial paradox of the *chôra,* and they stretch into contemporary physics through the big bang theory or chaos theory. Some roots of organic thinking can even be traced to pre-Socratic and Indian philosophy. The simultaneous philosophical affirmation of single elements and their unity (an idea most widely reflected by idealism) has developed at different ages. All philosophies experiencing, in this paradoxical way, the tension between the individual and the general are "organic" in the broadest sense of the term. The philosophies of Plotinus, Spinoza, Bruno, Eckhart, and Hegel are examples. Spinoza held that even though there is only one substance, this substance has infinite attributes. Hegel saw wholes and parts as united in their oppositional contrast, which means that even opposing elements could rely on an underlying complicity. A large part of Western philosophy is fueled by a stimulating tension between descriptions of the world composed of clearly definable singularities on the one hand and a unifying generality on the other.

The dangers of organicism can also be found in this tension. In Western philosophy, the organic has always had an ambiguous status, mainly because individual elements must be reflected against a "totality," which can have both positive and negative connotations. No matter how "total" the totality is, the singularities should always remain clearly definable: in an all-encompassing "dark" totality, we will simply be lost. In other words, the rooting of the empirical world in the world of the absolute should never bring about the total disappearance of the border between the natural and the supernatural order. If philosophy simply negates any differences within an abstractly established totality, it abandons ratio altogether and turns into mysticism.

A large part of organic thought connects to evolutionary theory. In the eighteenth and nineteenth centuries, cultural theories were increasingly influenced by Jean-Baptiste Lamarck's and Charles Darwin's studies of evolutionary history. Consequently, biological analogies attempting to retrieve an organic, functional unity in Aristotle's sense became popular. The German romantic philosopher August Wilhelm Schlegel used the term organic in 1809 in lectures on architectural theory describing how the mind can translate an indefinite plurality of distinguishable parts "into an entire and perfect unity."[1] In the Germanic region, Schlegel is the most important organic philosopher of his time, paralleled by Samuel Taylor Coleridge in England. Schlegel opposes the organic process to the mechanic process, criticizing that the latter imposes rules on material despite the quality of this material. In his lectures on architecture, Schlegel lays down an understanding of the organic relevant for many later generations:

> Form is mechanical when, through external force, it is imparted to any material merely as an accidental addition without reference to its quality; as, for example, when we give a particular shape to a soft mass that it may retain the same after its induration. Organic form, again, is innate; it unfolds itself from within, and acquires its determination contemporaneously with the perfect development of the germ. ([1845] 1933: 335)[2]

In light of its history, it is certainly not surprising that until the beginning of the twentieth century, discussions of the organic focused mainly on architecture—leading to the creation of the term "organic architecture"—and were less often evoked in other contexts. In architecture, parallels between the organism and the building go back to the High Renaissance and had already been noted by the Vitruvian architect Andrea Palladio, who referred to the villa plan as a digestive system (Gans 2003: vi). Apart from architecture, music is the only other art for which the term "organic" has had some importance. Modern musical theory (up to more recent deconstructive tendencies) has even been said to take "for granted the idea of 'organic form' as an absolute aesthetic value, that is to say, the premise that all great works—those that truly merit the analyst's attention—should manifest a deep-laid unity of style and idea, whatever their apparent (surface) lack of any such unifying features" (Kerman 1983, quoted in Norris 2005: 38). Furthermore, in cinema theory, consistent allusions to organic philosophy are almost nonexistent.

Almost a hundred years after Schlegel, William Morris and John Ruskin were interested in the organic, this time in the context of Gothic architecture. Of course, the "Gothic versus the Classic" theme is not entirely new either but goes back to a much older debate on architectural theory sparked by Goethe's 1772 essay "Von deutscher Baukunst" (Of German architecture). Around 1800, both Schlegel and Goethe adhered to the romantic view that Gothic architecture is close to nature, first because it had developed from the morphology of plants, and second because it seemed to represent a forest. Goethe had first celebrated the

Gothic cathedral because here, "just like in nature," all elements contribute purposefully to the establishment of a magnificent whole. In this context, Goethe addressed some of those dichotomies that became important much later in modernity, such as the themes of "measuring versus feeling" and "geometry versus organic." The topic's indirect connection with Goethe's biological metamorphosis doctrine (published in 1817), which explains that forms slowly emerge and then transform, already projects certain concepts of natural organization and evolution, making those ideas on architecture even more relevant for any discussion of the organic. Rudolf Steiner would call Goethe "the Galileo of the organic" (Pearson 2001: 40).

In the last two decades of the nineteenth century and in the first three decades of the twentieth century, organicism transgressed the limits of architectural theory, and even the limits of aesthetics, in order to become a full-fledged philosophy. This happened in various regions of the world. At the time when Frank Lloyd Wright and Béla Lajta most actively developed their particular architecture, the organic became a prominent theme for several new philosophies. In all of those philosophies, the idea of the organic as a coherent whole in which single elements are interrelated in a nonmechanic fashion remains the most important guideline. The organic unity is seen as the result of a natural growth emerging from within and thus is not totally controllable from without. Among the most famous organic terms emerging within the first two decades of the twentieth century are Henri Bergson's notion of *durée pure* in which past, present, and future form an organic whole, Nishida Kitaro's notion of *basho* ("place") signifying an existentially defined locality, and Wilhelm Worringer's influential concept of *Einfühlung* (empathy), which has clearly organic undertones.

When it comes to the organic, there is a lot more to report about Russia. In Russia, philosophers living around 1900 were more active than anybody else in establishing a unique philosophy around the idea of "all-unity" (*vseyedinstvo*), which represents an organic "unity in multiplicity" of all beings. The so-called Russian Silver Age overlaps with the decades in which organic philosophies were booming worldwide, and the Russian productions are impressive in terms of both quantity and quality. All-unity as an organic totality fascinated prerevolutionary organicist thinkers like Vladimir Soloviov (1853–1900) and Lev Lopatin (1855–1922), as well as more modern philosophers like Semën L. Frank (1877–1950) and Nicolai Berdyaev (1874–1948). In politics, the organic concept of *sobornost,* (spiritual community) first launched by the Russian Slavophiles, is partly inspired by the organic romantic conception of nationhood as developed by F.W.J. Schelling, who criticized Immanuel Kant's view that a priori elements do not exist in the real world but are simply "put into it" by the human mind. As a result, Schelling reestablished nature as an organic quality in possession of its particular reason (*Naturvernunft*) and able to organize itself (cf. Schelling [1798] 1967: 336ff). Schelling also uses the terms *Allheit* and *Einheit*.

The Russian line continued into later decades of the twentieth century, mainly represented by Nicolas Lossky's (1928) idea of the "world as an organic whole," as well as by Mikhail Bakhtin's philosophy of the polyphonic and harmonized totality and his idea of the chronotope as an "idyllic relationship of time and space" (1981: 229). Finally, even a subgroup of the Russian formalists (led by Victor Zhirmunsky and Vladimir Propp) reverted to the less mechanic forms of what it decided to call "organic formalism" and which was inspired by biology (see P. Steiner 1979: 19). That organic philosophies developed much more in Eastern than Western Europe might be important for the present considerations of Hungarian culture, though direct connections between those philosophies and the work of Makovecz, Tarr, and Krasznahorkai do not seem to exist.

Nature versus Math

The nature versus math dichotomy is the main topic of *Werckmeister Harmonies*. Most of the organic concepts produced by philosophers over a span of 150 years attempt to draw both time and space away from Newtonian geometrical or mathematical definitions. The organic represents a fundamental and coherent order underlying the incoherent patchwork of elements by which our reality is constituted. However, contrary to the structuralist anthropologist or the Newtonian physicist, the organicist looks for an order that is not merely rational or scientific. She looks for the organic as a quality that remains distinct from the "universal." More precisely, she looks for an order that is more fundamental than merely mathematically established universal structures. This order will most typically be likened to a certain idea of nature. This problem, which focuses on the dichotomy of the mathematical-calculated versus the natural-organic, is also a prominent topic of *Werckmeister Harmonies*, which is why I expand those explanations in this chapter. Both the film and the book revolve around the findings of musicologists from various époques, who indicate that harmonious ratios existing in nature do not necessarily overlap with mathematical order. Suggestions are made that a harmonic system can be "naturally" sound but appear, at the same time, irrational when seen from a mathematical point of view.

The Organic Today

The organic as a subject of intellectual interest has had its ups and downs, and specific reasons explain these fluctuations. After a post-Renaissance decline and a peripheral existence during the Enlightenment, Lamarck's and Darwin's studies of evolution led to a fresh interest in organic unities in the late eighteenth century and throughout the nineteenth century. Theoretically, the latest discoveries in biology today should be able to turn organic systems once again into a subject interest. The mapping of the human genome (the Human Genome Project) should inspire new reflections on the meaning of organic unities in society as well as in art. Furthermore, this interest in the organic should concern not only the scientific but also the social, political, and aesthetic. The challenge is bigger than ever because the Internet, as it seems to work toward a nonorganic world of fragmentation, sets here an interesting counterpoint. The renewed engagement in organic ways of artistic expression by the Hungarian artists of this book needs to be read in this context.

In the introduction, I referred to the necessity of overcoming the dichotomy of the progressive versus the conservative and showed that André Bazin's theories immediately connect to those problems. His organic and holistic philosophy that was trying to see—like Parmenides and Heraclitus—the cosmos or reality as a whole (Gray 2005: 12) could be denounced as reactionary by his "progressive" contemporaries. Today, the fake dichotomy that opposes organic thought to deconstructive thought seems to repeat those patterns. The conflict between the revolutionary/leftist/deconstructionist and the conservative/organic/religious perpetuates itself. I want to show that a work like *Werckmeister Harmonies* cannot be approached with ideologically hardened tools exemplified by many poststructuralist philosophies. Organic cinema continues the tradition of Bazin's liberal analyses whose spirit has been characterized by his collaborator Emmanuel Mounier in 1932, when summing up the position of their journal *Esprit*. Mounier writes that he and his colleagues "are looking for a camping ground somewhere between Bergson and Peguy, Maritain and Berdyaev" (Gray 2005: 4). Eighty years later, it is possible to add a few more poststructuralist authors to Mounier's list, but, the organic approach Bazin and Mounier suggested appears to have remained as unusual and revolutionary as ever.

Notes

1. The lectures were published only after his death.
2. Schlegel's influence on English romanticism is so important that Coleridge is said to have plagiarized this passage from Schlegel in his *Lectures* (1987). Coleridge is often quoted as a precursor of organic theory because he was arguably the first who contrasted an innate development made from within with a mechanic effectuated from without (see Bloom and Trilling 1973: 66). However, Coleridge's version of this passage is interesting in its own right because he incorporates a "clay metaphor" into the text that does not occur in Schlegel: "The form is mechanic when on any given material we impress a pre-determined form, not necessarily arising out of the properties of the material—as when to a mass of wet clay we give whatever shape we wish it to retain when hardened. The organic form on the other hand is innate, it shapes, as it develops itself from within, and the fullness of its development is one and the same with the perfection of its outward form. Such is the life, such is the form" (1987: 362). On the plagiarism reproach, see Wellek 1982: 151–57.

CHAPTER 4

The Melancholy of Evolution

In organic philosophies, "nature" is often, though not always, understood as an unknown, "metaphysical" element whose organic rules do not necessarily overlap with the rules expressed by mathematics, logic, and science. In principle, the organic order of nature is hidden for science but can be made visible—at least temporarily—by philosophers and artists. András Bálint Kovács describes Béla Tarr's and László Krasznahorkai's expressions exactly in this sense by, right at the beginning of his important article from 2008, pointing to the "holistic vision and worldview of great artists." Organic art or, according to Kovács, all great art, "sees the world in its entirety." On the other hand, Kovács also acknowledges that such arts striving toward an expression of the universal "rob things of their colorful, ambiguous, and accidental nature," that is, of their individuality. He says, "Minor artists, who say but little of the world, think small and are therefore truer to the ultimate diversity inherent in everything," while "great artists force their will and vision on the entire world." Kovács believes "it is just this arrogance that helps the recipient to discover in everything what a viewer—stuck in diversity and everydayness—cannot see." Organic art creates neither uniform systems nor visions of events only of individual interest. Instead, it creates cosmic visions of individual incidents.

Kovács's reflections on art echo those of the Hungarian philosopher Béla Hamvas, who shares certain traits with Krasznahorkai and Makovecz. This thinker, author of *The Melancholy of Late Works*, believed, exactly like Krasznahorkai and Makovecz, that essential elements of human culture have been lost in modern civilization. In his essay on Beethoven, entitled "The Seventh Symphony and the Metaphysics of Music" (2007), Hamvas describes the "minor artist" precisely in Kovács's terms:

> Here we recognize the difference between the novice and the master. The novice paints, writes or sings for his own enjoyment and this

enjoyment in painting or writing or singing is important to him. She becomes her own audience, is both the composer and listener in one, at once within the work and observing from the outside. The resulting mess is characterless, dilettante art, like autoeroticism, giving joy to no none but its creator.

As an alternative, Hamvas sketches an aesthetics of resistance or of self-resistance, in which the free evolution of the ego striving for the universal power must be restrained by the anti-egoistic powers of humility:

> He fails because of this power. He keeps winning and winning and winning, mere victory and triumph. Meanwhile, he doesn't realize that part of him is empty, exposed, weak, fragile and incomplete. He lacks the power to stand up and drop to his knees. He lacks restraint, morality, religion, weakness; he lacks the strength to be weak, and the capacity for gratitude. Thus in this emptiness he must vanish, and from this inadequacy, become nothing.

Hamvas sees "the strength to be weak" as an indispensable part of the creative production of mature works, and he links it to melancholy. In *The Melancholy of Late Works,* Hamvas defines this restraint as the main characteristic of melancholy, particularly the melancholy of old age. Artists who reach an old age tend to abandon all showy magic with which they tried to impress the world when they were younger; now they return to silence and slowness (Hamvas 2008: 19). This does not mean the art of melancholy is simple: it is complex and multilayered (27–28).

Curiously, Hamvas's ideas about the importance of melancholy are almost literally found in the writings of his archenemy Georg Lukács, who also formulates the "strength to be weak" through the mechanics of melancholy by writing, "the need for reflection is the deepest melancholy of every great and genuine novel" ([1920] 1971: 84). The two men were enemies because Hamvas opposed any realist concept of art, which led to serious quarrels with the Hungarian communist regime, and Lukács in particular because he was a fervent communist.[1] Both Hamvas's and Lukács's accounts of mature artistic styles use themes that also appear in Edward Said's *On Late Style* (2006) in which the mature style is established as a reflection of a life of learning, as well as of sadness coming from wisdom. Like Hamvas, Lukács emphasizes the link between melancholy and matured creativity:

> The melancholy of the adult state arises from our dual, conflicting experience that, on the one hand, our absolute, youthful confidence in

an inner voice has diminished or died, and, on the other hand, that the outside world to which we now devote ourselves in our desire to learn its ways and dominate it, will never speak to us in a voice that will clearly tell us our way and determine our goal. (85)

Both Hamvas and Lukács divert from Freud. For Hamvas, melancholy makes suffering "sweet as never before. So tempting and full of hope" (2008: 24). Melancholy is typically double-faced, "which has nothing to do with schizophrenia because it is not pathological. Melancholy is the last benediction in the life of humans" (30). Lukács also sees the voluntarily chosen fragility of the mature artist as a virtue. Freud, however, in his *Mourning and Melancholia*, declares melancholy pathological because, unlike mourning, it grieves for a loss the subject is unable to identify. Melancholy represents for Freud "an extraordinary diminution in [the subject's] self-regard, an impoverishment of his ego (*Ichgefühl*) on a grand scale" ([1917] 1957: 244). While Freud characterizes this situation—where "for the melancholic subject the attachment to the lost object supersedes the desire to recover from the loss"—as pathological, for Hamvas and Lukács just this diminution of the ego is so important for the creation of mature works. The contrast is even more pronounced. For Freud, melancholy is always one of evolution, because this strange disease signifies "an overcoming of the instinct which compels every living thing to cling to life" (246). Freud's idea of evolution is not organic but linear. However, the organic position, which sees evolution as a purposeless and circular process of decomposition, will also depict melancholy as an ironic combination of disintegration and evolution. Freud's evolution is functional and hierarchic, whereas organic evolution is playful.

Lukács seems to have in mind the Kierkegaardian concept of melancholy as an ironic approach producing "irony as a mastered moment" that can exercise a "chastening effect on the personal life." The latter formulation comes from Abrahim Khan's article "Melancholy, Irony, and Kierkegaard," in which the author demonstrates that Søren Kierkegaard saw melancholy "not as a problem to be resolved, but as a means and motive for becoming a genuine or complete person" (1985: 68). Detachment and indifference are the qualities able to connect melancholy and irony. Freud, however, would have never drawn this link from melancholy to irony because he treats melancholy as parallel to the very "serious" mourning. At the same time, even Freud admits that resistance is not excluded but rather enclosed within melancholy by definition. Freud cites the example of "a woman who loudly pities her husband for being tied to such an incapable wife as herself is really accusing her *husband* of being incapable" ([1917] 1957: 248). Even for Freud, melancholy and resistance are connected.

Krasznahorkai's elaborations on melancholy reinforce this connection. In his "universal theseus" lectures, Krasznahorkai maintains that "this sadness ... has overshadowed my whole life and overshadows it still today; there is in me an insatiable desire to observe the axis of the world, but this desire is entirely obscured by the devouring haze of this sadness" (2011: 22). However, instead of striving toward an elimination of this sadness, Krasznahorkai describes how this melancholy connects to the world of musical harmonies and the existence of beauty:

> The second source of sadness emanates from the passage in music from major to minor mode, everywhere and at all times, whenever I witnessed this moment: when in a musical composition, no matter what kind, there suddenly appeared a major note after a minor one, for example after C-major appeared A-minor, and as a result the music tore my heart, I had the impression that this passage in minor was addressed to me personally, my face tensed ... I listened and said to myself, ah, this beauty, while what I had was sadness. (24)

The organically produced beauty leaves us sad because, though our spirit is detached from this world "in order to turn toward a mysterious splendor, toward an inscrutable undecipherable greatness that he names universe or god of the universe we do not succeed because the object of our quest does not exceed his own small person" (61).

The Logic of Nature

The logic of organicism tries to draw the entire world (art, politics, religion, and science) into a coherent, harmonious structural network by following a model that is not formal but imitates the immanent, self-sufficient logic of nature. Like math and logic, the organic structure evolves by following a general ideal, but it moves toward this ideal by following individual steps that do not necessarily fit into the overall plan of the general structure at every moment. In other words, contrary to abstract structures issued by mathematics, the organic structure does not follow a predetermined and static order invented by the human ratio. The organic structure is rational (it makes sense) as a whole, but it can also accommodate single elements that can look irrational to the mathematical mind at certain moments. The organic constellation sometimes looks senseless in terms of logic not because it contains no logical order but because humans cannot grasp this logic.

Organic structures are not supposed to follow a final design issued by a human mind beforehand because the model of the organic is not math or logic but nature. This is precisely the topic of *Werckmeister Harmonies*. What this "reason of nature" actually is can be spelled out in different ways, all of which will never be merely scientific but strive to embrace the unknown dimension of a total structure. In purely scientific explanations, contingency has no place, but it does in organicism. While pure science establishes abstract structures in which the general necessity and the individual event perfectly overlap, organicism refuses to reduce nature to such a known structure. As a result, the organic evolves within a tension unfolding between the general and the individual, the abstract and the concrete, the logical and the illogical. This tension is not mechanic or dialectical, but it represents the essence of the organic itself, which cannot be canceled because that would make the organic aspect of the structure disappear.

The Organic and God

In many discourses on the organic, spiritual connections and links with God are striking, though not always expressed in the form of theism. True, romanticism with its nostalgia for the unity of God, nature, and man has left its own imprint on organic philosophy. However, the God of the organic—if there is one—is generally more likely to be the pantheist God contained in nature. András Ferkai says the buildings of Hungarian organic architects tend to be "pagan cult sites" (1998: 290), and even Frank Lloyd Wright made no attempts to discard pantheist evocations: "God is the great mysterious motivator of what we call nature, and it has been said often by philosophers, that nature is the will of God. And, I prefer to say that nature is the only body of God that we shall ever see. If we wish to know the truth concerning anything, we'll find it the nature of that thing" (1987: 21). Hugo Häring also held that the secret of Gestalt is always a "divine plan," and his use of the word God always remained tied to the idea of creation and to the order of things, constantly pursuing how human beings come to terms with the ordered world in which they find themselves. Of course, mysticism is knocking at the door here, as is always the case when pantheism has been invited. Still, this spiritual tendency has nothing to do with the God-based universalism of religious extremists; it is not universalist but organic.

Putting Order into Chaos

Wright expressed a "desire for simplicity that would yield a broader, deeper comfort ... a growing idea of simplicity as organic ruthless but harmonious order called nature" (1941: 178). Organic architecture is simple because its scheme and design are clear. However, the "simplicity" of this organic structure is diametrically opposed to that of the mathematical structure. It is not the universal simplicity of modern architects pursued, for example, by Ludwig Mies van der Rohe, who has rightfully been called a "universalist" (see Blundell Jones 1996: 7). The organic looks simple from afar, but a closer view suggests it is determined by infinite complexities. The simplicity of the mathematical structure, however, looks confusingly complex from afar, and its "simplicity" can only be discovered through close examination. This is why Wright says "simplicity in art is a synthetic positive quality in which we may see evidence of mind, breadth of scheme, wealth of detail and a sense of completeness found in a tree or flower" (Wright 2003: 60).

Organicism today represents an increasingly tempting option in a world that has been made overly complex through the abundance of scientific research spreading in all directions. The scientific world is fragmented and lacks coordination. Despite its mystical temptations that always remain present, the philosophy of the organic seems willing to retrieve a "common sense" perspective in a world that is basically unstructured. In contemporary science, even nature itself no longer appears coherent and organic. Nuclear physics and gene technology have atomized and split up nature into its tiniest components and never attempted to "put it back together" again. We learn, for example, that the yeast genome has 6,200 genes, perhaps even more if regulator and structural genes are included. There are an infinite number of details, but what do those details tell us about the reality of yeast? The world as a lived, coherent place that simply "makes sense" is getting lost. Things have no essence; they appear to be in science, not what they are in reality. In 1992, Eric Drexler showed that molecular nanotechnology enables us to transform coal into diamonds and sand into supercomputers, as well as to remove pollution from the air and tumors from healthy tissue. What is, in this context, the logic of nature, and what is the meaning of organic? Applying rules and structures cannot make the world a coherent place, because they would merely establish abstract links between elements (atoms, genes) that would still not appear "real" in the way reality is understood in everyday life. What is lacking is the structure of the world as it *really* exists, not as it exists in the view of a science that becomes increasingly specialized, abstract, mathematical, and computer-dependent.

Zygmunt Bauman sees the state of disorientation produced by these scientific paradigms as a typical manifestation of social experiences during the postmodern age. He attempts to grasp this disorientation by describing it as the "liquid" state of modernity characterized by social, economic, political, and cultural fragmentation: "we are becoming more and more flexible and ready to abandon commitments and loyalties without regret" (2007: 4). The liquid element is simply too slippery for our hands to grasp. In other words, the liquid has no organic structure, as it is too similar to the abstract: it is mathematically measurable but still strangely absent in terms of meaningful, "palpable" relationships between elements because those relationships need to be shaped with regard to both the individual and the universal components of social life. Only then can we have meaningful ("organic") totalities and not just networks. According to Bauman, such meaningful totalities are missing in contemporary industrialized societies.

This state of affairs is precisely what Krasznahorkai's novels express. Korin in Krasznahorkai's only urban novel, *War and War*, is falling into the trap of the liquid as he is attracted by the totality of the Internet, which he decides to interpret in quasi-religious terms. He discovers a text he believes to have "foundation-shaking, cosmic" (2006: 83) dimensions and attempts to make it immortal by uploading it to the Internet. However, by enmeshing his own life with such universal questions of immortality, Korin makes the biggest mistake of his life: he leaves behind the concrete world of the organic and enters the liquid, amorphous universe of the virtual, which leads to his tragic end. Bauman shows that liquid societies have difficulties determining overarching solid—or at least half-solid—totalities. All we have is a liquid universe without organic structures: "Forms, whether already present or only adumbrated, are unlikely to be given enough time to solidify, and cannot serve as frames of reference for human actions and long-term life strategies because of their short life expectation" (2007: 1). Here, the organic becomes attractive as a model able to provide a graspable sense of "totality."

What about philosophy of science and critical theory, both of which so actively deconstruct universal structures? They do not strive to retrieve an organic unity but instead work in the opposite direction by defining scientific truth through cultural rhetoric and power relations. This is even generally true for critical approaches toward science. What the *Werckmeister Harmonies* protagonist Eszter would call the "natural" foundations of truth are erased and replaced with socially coded, politically enforced patterns that can (and certainly often need to) be deconstructed. The well-meant discursive unification of science, ethics, and culture provided by critical philosophy, which aims to deconstruct universal truths, is certainly justified. At the same time, the unification leaves a lot of doubt about not only ethical values but also scientific validity. Individuality, self-determination, diversity, difference, and *différance* are the headwords often so strongly pronounced that they can appear dogmatic. In this context, organic philosophers suggest an alternative that most poststructuralist philosophers are unwilling to accept. To the latter, the unification of thought organicists seek can only appear suspect and possibly related to paternalistic Socratic (or perhaps even Christian) dialectical scientism. Michel Foucault, for example, rarely misses an opportunity to point out all unifying structures as repressive.[2]

Organic philosophy also rejects the Socratic, dialectical scheme of thought, so organic thinking very often finds itself on common ground with postmodern philosophies. The difference is that organic philosophy constantly attempts to reflect otherness against some kind of unity that it attempts to keep in sight. Of course, the "paternalistic" dangers that postmodern thought and critical philosophy see in organic philosophies are not entirely unfounded. Therefore, it is necessary to constantly specify which kind of organicism is acceptable and which is not. This book shows that Krasznahorkai's, Tarr's, and Makovecz's organic expressions are acceptable examples.

Notes

1. Lukács has been charged of actively participating in the elimination of noncommunist intellectuals, such as Hamvas, István Bibó, and Karl Kerényi, who were either confined or forced to do unskilled labor. See the "Georg Lukacs" entry in the *New World Encyclopedia*, http://www.newworldencyclopedia.org/entry/Georg_ Lukacs (accessed 3 December 2016).
2. Chapter 8 will show that Derrida represents an exception and that his idea of "play" can very well be understood as an organic notion.

CHAPTER 5

Where Is the Center?

Centered Organicism and Fundamentalism

Talking about the "center" in Central and Eastern Europe is a tricky project. During Austro-Hungarian and Soviet rule, politics was very much "centralized." This does not mean localities did not exist; rather, those localities were regional cultural centers without much political power. In the 1990s, the center disappeared, and for some time, ethnic strives replaced politics, especially in former Yugoslavia. The position of a potential center within organic models in Eastern Europe is thus a very important topic.

As noted, the model of the organic contains some eminent dangers that concern possible centralizations of organic configuration. Because of its "fundamental" nature, organicism can easily be used by fundamentalist rhetoric. Strictly speaking, this is a strange state of affairs, to say the least, since organic models practiced in Gadamerian hermeneutics, for example, are explicitly designed to *avoid* extremism. Most often, the organicist is simply what Richard Rorty has called a "liberal metaphysician" who wants "a final vocabulary with an internal organic structure" (1989: 92) and simply cannot bear the existence of a patchwork of contradicting meanings and situational truths. In general, the most important component of this kind of organicism is not the center but the equilibrium. Extremes are never beneficial for organic constellations, as they tend to be conceived on the basis of abstract and transcendental criteria external to organic-hermeneutic reasoning. Utopian or puritan extremism, for example, normally arises in the realm of the nonorganic abstract.

However, in some cases, even the organic metaphysician will become a fundamentalist, mainly when she is no longer looking for an equilibrium establishing an "absent" center but desires to spell out a central notion, location, or concept in concrete terms. This organicist search for a unifying structure can easily become the basis of religious or nationalist fanaticism, primarily because the existence of the organic will be seen no longer as a continuous development (in the spirit of a Bergsonian creative evolution) but as a deterministic and progressive pattern meant to develop toward a predetermined central idea. Against this background, it is certainly no coincidence that, eleven years after the fall of communism, the whalelike Hungarian parliament was equipped with a new center. In 2000, the royal crown was transferred from the National Museum to the Parliament Building, where it resides right under the central dome.

Contrary to what many people might believe, having a center is not a necessary condition for the organic structure. The organic constellation can also simply be declared extant without attempting to specify its center. The problem is that organic constellations often tend to be conceptualized in order to extract central terms like "God," "essence," or "national style" from elements that do not necessarily contain such central notions. Organic structures defined by following the latter scheme are "universal" simply because they are based on central ideas. Approaches adhering to this tendency can also be called "compulsive organicisms." Along such lines, Philippe Lacoue-Labarthe (1987) has traced the "national aestheticism" of the Nazis, who saw the state as an organic machine, to this compulsive interlinking of national identity and an organic concept of culture.

There is another problem with the organic. The fusion or union of opposites, as well as the contradictory overlapping of the part and the whole, are bound to leave a certain number of things unexplained. This gives the organic a quasi-constant mystical ring. Paradoxically, the organic model, which merely affirms that some things cannot be explained, can then be used as an "explanation of everything." This is how the lack of a center can so easily become a positive "central" notion in fundamentalist thought. The circular avoidance of meaning and foundation can become a meaningful foundation in its own right. In critiques of religion, this fallacy is known as the "appeal to ignorance." Since no one can "rationally" prove why the world exists, we *must* conclude that God has created it. God will be used as a rational foundation of those things that lack a foundation. Fundamentalist, centralized, or universalizing organic discourses follow this scheme: since all we have in this world is an organic order that transcends reason, this order must be accepted as a new form of reason equipped with its own center.

Uncentered Organicism

László Krasznahorkai's, Béla Tarr's, and Imre Makovecz's organicisms evolve along paths very different from those just described because their organicisms are uncentered. An alternative organic approach emphasizes the existence of a freely evolving organic structure that does not universalize ideas about which it believes to have individual knowledge. This "uncentered" approach can be called cosmic and must oppose the universal approach. The difference between centered and uncentered organicisms can be rendered by drawing on the difference between Goethe's *Urpflanze* (the "archetypal plant") and modern gene technology. Both the *Urpflanze* and the gene grasp something "original" from which larger organisms could develop. However, Goethe's morphology is not meant to "explain everything." Goethe did not believe essential secrets are hidden inside the shapes of certain natural phenomena; he did not believe the correct detection of these shapes explain the generation of other shapes. Goethe never spoke as a physicist pretending to have found concrete causal links. Instead, he described shapes forming an organic whole, and he presented insights about similarities. In the end, the *Urpflanze* (the "original plant") does not exist in reality but can only be imagined (see Goethe 1817), whereas the gene claims to be a central notion having the status of a fact. Here, Goethe acts very much like an organic philosopher analyzing nature.

The arts of Krasznahorkai, Tarr, and Makovecz are not universal but cosmic. The noncenteredness plays an important role here. Many people actually think organic architecture depends on it being "somewhat off center" on principle (Robinson 1993: 9), which places it in the right relationship with the above political claims about the position if Hungary in within Europe. In Hungary, a certain noncenteredness might even come in naturally: in terms of geography, the Hungarian center, the Puszta, is rather an empty noncenter. The desolate, wide-open expanses of this plain in the middle of the country with not a single human being on it, which became a semidesert after Turkish invaders destroyed the irrigation systems and everything else (Winder 2013: 120), are what Paris is for the French and the forest for the Germans. The doctor in *Satantango* even reads out a text confirming this plain had once been a huge lake. A priori, these are bad conditions for the development of a centered organism able to spark nationalism or positive feelings about the beauty of Hungarian nature.

Second, Krasznahorkai's, Tarr's, and Makovecz's organicisms do not follow the Socratic-Platonic, rational approach steadily advancing, through systematic dialectical reasoning, toward a unique and supreme truth. Krasznahorkai is even against such dialogue and propagates the organic as a single voice constantly bifurcating and spreading out in order to create polyphonic patterns. In Krasznahorkai's view, the organic voice avoids all dialogically engineered compromises, as he explains in an interview with Mauro Javier Cardenas (2013):

> I don't believe in dialogue. I believe only in monologues. And I believe only in the man who listens to the monologue, and I believe I can be the man who listens to your monologue the next time around. I believe only in monologues in the human world. The dialogues, in American prose, after the Second World War, to be honest, the best dialogue writers, are here in the USA, but dialogue doesn't work for me because I don't believe in dialogues.

Of course, those reflections are reminiscent of Goethe's suggestions to use the dialectical in a different, more dynamic way. The actions in Krasznahorkai's novels follow a similar pattern of the "uncentered organic." Korin, the hero of *War and War*, goes to New York and believes he is at "the very center of the world, the place where matters were actually decided, where things happened" (2006: 19). However, the "center" remains a mythical, religious, and visionary center unable to establish a geographical order. It is rather a place like the Garden of Eden or ancient Rome. The same is true for "the manuscript" that will provide, so Korin hopes, an answer to the puzzle of his life. The puzzle will not be solved but will be seen as the answer to the question of—the puzzle of the world. Without center there is no measurable progress, only circularity. András Bálint Kovács points out, with regard to Tarr, that the "circularity of dramatic form characterizes stories in which characters go through events but these events do not get them closer to the solution to their initial problem" (2013: 118). This is precisely the logic of the uncentered organic. If the organic were centered, it would form a "perfect" circle, which would, strictly speaking, be the end of the organic configuration. As a result, things would neither develop nor die. The medical scientist of pre-Socratic times, Alcmaeon of Croton, pointed this out when writing about the organic condition: "Human beings perish because they are not able to join their beginning to their end" (1952: Fragment 2). The conclusion is that the circle should never close.

In other respects, *Werckmeister Harmonies* is also a prime example of an uncentered narrative. János Valuska, the film's central figure we follow from station to station, is no classical central figure, because he is undecided by definition. His position remains undefined as he floats

Figure 5.1. Janos Valuska in *Werckmeister Harmonies* (2000).

between Eszter; Eszter's ex-wife, Tünde and the Prince. Still, he is the most important ("central") character. The only thing he clings to is some vague pantheistic belief. The spider web of polyphonic messages created during his long trajectories in the film is imposed on the viewers as they perceive the film's space usually through Valuska's eyes, making the film a radiant example of uncentered organicism. How are the lines of the web held together? Is there a narrative in the sense of an authoritarian logic? No, there is only the organic logic actively sustaining evolution and evolving out of itself.

Satantango also has a fake center. At first sight, the doctor can look like a plausible, well-established central point because he is a center of gravity in both the metaphorical and literal sense of the term. Heavy and immobile, he is the contrary of Valuska in *Werckmeister Harmonies*. The doctor is also the only "authority" in the sense of an author. It is indeed possible to interpret the principle story of *Satantango* as written by the doctor. However, in reality, he has no authority at all but is losing more and more of it, as the cooperative system of which he was once part has been dismantled. Now he is weak and decadent, and he does not even have a name: what kind of "author" is this? While he is waiting to slip back into the system, "retrospectively" by receding into the past on a tango-like pattern (six steps forward, six steps backward), he imagines conspiracy theories consisting of spider webs drawn by foreign agents.

In the last scene of *Werckmeister Harmonies*, Eszter visits the town square to look at what he had believed to be "the center," which is the whale or, more precisely, the whale's eye. However, though the mysterious prefab house into which the Melvillian creature was put is now dismantled, there is absolutely nothing to discover. The metaphysical center is there for all to see, but it is meaningless. The "symbol of God's organic creation," as Valuska called the whale, is simply decaying like any organic matter. The whale's eye is no metaphysical window to unsolved questions, and the center is a blatant noncenter. Valuska suspected this from the beginning, believing it highly possible that "the ramshackle truck belonging to 'this bunch of con-men' contained either nothing at all, or, if anything, then a stinking corpse whose plain lack of interest they disguised by a factitious, if effective, piece of market publicity about some so-called 'secret'" (Krasznahorkai 1998: 86).

Organicism and Kitsch

We find the same pattern in Makovecz's architecture. Makovecz looks for a universal order but always takes care that this order remains without a center. Of Transylvanian traditional art he say, "their content does not contain any hint of a nationalistic or tribal message, but is far deeper, more universal, and significantly easier to comprehend than any manifestation of nationalism could ever be" (Gerle 2010: 7). This strong statement is difficult for new Hungarian nationalists to swallow. Because "noncentral" paradigms dominate this organic philosophy, Makovecz's reevaluation of folk motives does not lead to nationalist kitsch, which is notable because, as Edwin Heathcote also affirms, "much of the organic output can be easily dismissed as kitsch" (2006: 39). Makovecz even openly praises kitsch, which is amazing for an artist who has lived in—and been opposed to—a socialist (and even Stalinist) world whose aesthetic environment was once strongly determined by propaganda kitsch. But Makovecz can clearly praise kitsch only because he operates in a realm where mere kitsch fundamentalism is impossible: "Many like to sneer at kitsch but I happen to like it. Kitsch analyzes everything that is missing from the confused, barely understandable art of the twentieth century. Since more and more is missing in art, the world of kitsch is becoming more and more interesting and rich in variety" (Gerle 2010: 50).

Purism, minimalism, the suppression of information—these are all modern diseases. Why not be simply straightforward? Makovecz goes even further by propagating symmetry, which in aesthetic contexts can

Figure 5.2. Church in Gazdagrét, Budapest, by Imre Makovecz.

very easily appear simplistic, naïve, or kitsch: "All human movement, at least when expressing the entire human structure and not performing some kind of utilitarian purpose, is instinctively symmetrical. When either blessing or cursing, I lift both arms and hands" (Gerle 2010: 33). Still this is not *real* kitsch because it does not claim to have a metaphysically defined center. Real kitsch is always an organic expression with a center, or, more precisely, it is an expression reduced to its center. Kitsch is straightforward and has only one particular message (for example, in propaganda art). However, without this ideologically defined center, kitsch is not really kitsch. Heathcote aptly notes that Makovecz's aesthetics could "probably never be hijacked by corporate big business as an architectural style, a system or a language with which to decorate otherwise faceless and inhuman buildings. It therefore cannot be tamed" (1997: 9). The untamable force of this architecture also connects to the ecological material. We simply cannot imagine Makovecz in Las Vegas, and his architecture could probably not be used for a "Makovecz theme park" in the way Friedrich Hundertwasser's aesthetics has been used in Vienna, because Makovecz's work (with some exceptions) is not image-driven enough (see Blundell Jones 1996). Sometimes it might *look* like kitsch but, unlike kitsch, its expressiveness remains too uncentered. Unlike Hundertwasser's, Makovecz's architecture remains based on the premises of critical regionalism (see Botz-Bornstein 2015), whose critical component distorts the straightforward messages the tourist industry normally looks for.

Tarr also has been confronted with the kitsch problem, which sticks out as a surprising occurrence for a typical representative of so-called

Figure 5.3. Greek Catholic Church in Csenger by Imre Makovecz.

art cinema. Within the "trash versus taste" controversy, art cinema is usually identified with the latter. Less surprising is that the kitsch reproach would occur in the melancholic, sensitive, and often eerie music produced by Mihály Vig, Tarr's longtime collaborator. Vig's organ music is organic by definition, not only because it imitates nonelectronic instruments like traditional organs and accordions but also because it attempts to gradually "evolve" chords, which are consistently held for a long time while a few new notes emerge. New notes come into being only while others still persist, which means nothing comes out of nothing: every new note must be engendered by other notes. Vig's music thus appears like an audible version of a Deleuzian rhizome: it evolves through coherent schemes of repetition and circularity without ever culminating in one central point, which is actually why it remains distinct from kitsch. The folkloric accordion tunes played during dance scenes in Tarr's films follow patterns similar to Vig's. There are no refrains, no codas, and no dramatic ends; all we have is the constant and purposeless process of "evolution." Or, according to Janice Lee (2014), writing about Tarr, "we are going nowhere." Vig is a sort of musical Krasznahorkai, and watching a Tarr scene with a Vig soundtrack is like watching an overlong music video. The actions are self-contained, and so is the music.

When deciding to have the torch singer (Vali Kerekes) in *Damnation* sing Vig's song "Kész az Egész" ("Everything is over") in a cool Nico style while heavy rain pours outside the Titanik bar, it was Vig who was worried that kitsch would finally take over. He feared that the song's initially ironical message would not be palpable in the newly established context of the film and that the parodic character of the song would not be understood. There was a real risk that verbal clichés could be taken for granted (see Kovács 2013: 121). Vig asked Tarr to choose another song. The fear turned out to be unfounded, as the overall impression of the scene is not that of kitsch. Critics have found more instances of near kitsch in Tarr's later films, for example, in the hospital scene in which the hooligans abruptly abandon their destruction spree at the very moment they see the old man in the bath. Again, Vig's organ music kicks in. A Hungarian reviewer has judged that this scene "does not make sense psychologically" and should therefore be classified as "metaphysical kitsch" (see Kovács 2013: 152). The constellation is highly unusual: the scene meant to lead to the cancellation of what could otherwise have been the kitsch-like narrative climax of the entire film can be identified as kitsch in return. But is it really kitsch? True, this scene does not make sense within the (psychological) logic of real space (where it would indeed be kitsch), but it does work within the logic of the organic space the film creates. Therefore, the scene is not kitsch because, once again, no dramatic center leads us to a narrative climax.

More can be said about this scene regarding its representative status as a dreamlike reality. The hospital scene does not appear in Krasznahorkai's book, and one can speculate about Tarr's reasons to add it. In many respects, the scene is extremely stylized and "unrealistic." For example, no nurses and doctors are in this hospital. On the other hand, in historical terms, the scene is strongly reminiscent of the ransacking of the Communist Party's municipal branch headquarters in Budapest on Republic Square during the "Hungarian Revolution." On 30 October 1956, insurgents sieged the building, and occupants who tried to surrender were shot, beat to death, or hanged on the spot. Tarr's submission of factual brutality to such an extreme stylization lets the scene appear like a dream. Again, this "holding back" of reality contradicts common kitsch strategies. Furthermore, the hospital scene can be read as an illustration of the particular form of Central and Eastern European fragility. It shows how institutions and systems can collapse at any moment for no particular reason. The scene can be watched like a fragment of an absurd theater play, which would be a truly "Eastern European" reading (see Töke 2011).

Tarr himself has explained how he manages to deprive kitsch of its center: by creating an organic system employing opposing powers. For Tarr, neither love nor dark hopelessness should exist alone: "both have to be present, because if only the first one is present, it will generate kitsch, if only the second is there, it is just purely frightening" (Kovács 2013: 169). On the other hand, an intrinsic link exists between organism and kitsch: organic expressions are simply more "primitive" and spontaneous than "edited" and mathematically calculated forms, especially more so than those most typically represented by modern aesthetics. This paradox of kitsch as non-kitsch is what makes those organic expressions so interesting. Makovecz's tendency to linger on kitsch is part of the same system. Robert Venturi, with whom Makovecz admits to have affinities, found that kitsch opposes the simplistic progressivism of modern capitalist society. If we really oppose this system, we should be "positive" toward kitsch, as Venturi points out in this famous passage on the high street aesthetics of Las Vegas:

> The commercial strip, the Las Vegas Strip in particular, the example par excellence, challenges the architect to take a positive, non-chip-on-the-shoulder view. Architects are out of the habit of looking nonjudg-

mentally at the environment, because orthodox Modern architecture is progressive. (Venturi et. al. 1972: 3)

Kitsch is definitely organic, but not everything organic is kitsch. Kitsch is not controlled by intellectual structures, nor does it work with calculated devices like *Verfremdung* ("alienation"). In this sense, kitsch is purely spontaneous. However, kitsch becomes unbearable should its message be formulated in terms of commercial, political, or religious ideologies. This would be "centralized" kitsch, most often manifested as blandly consumer oriented or simply as propaganda. Neither Makovecz nor Venturi sees kitsch in this way, as a centered phenomenon. Their "kitsch" has no central message that can be taken home and consumed. As noted, Las Vegas or corporate businesses can probably never hijack Makovecz's style—if it is a style at all—because its message is not "centralized" enough and cannot be packaged in terms of "a style." If it were, it would indeed become kitsch. If style turns out to be no more than a random aesthetic expression ignoring its particular ethical and existential context, then this style will not be organic or exemplify aesthetic ambitions resulting from organic life constellations. Thus, the aesthetics of the organic always keeps a critical distance toward the notion of style. Wright held that organic architecture "never can become a mere style" or "stultify itself as a mere style" (1941: 181, 189). It always grows from within a cultural situation by following the imperatives of a relatively complex environment and does not simply adhere to the rules of a certain style. Makovecz repeats those words almost literally in his foreword to the 1991 *Biennale Catalog*: "It would be a mistake to think that this mission is only a stylistic inquiry. I do not believe in the concept of 'style' as it has been used recently in architecture and other realms. ... I believe in ancient dramaturgic rules and in Fate" (Cook 1997: 180). In other words, the "organic style" should have no image quality. These ideas concerning style correspond perfectly with the principles of the "organic" composer Arnold Schoenberg, whose structural and intellectually controlled approaches were to function as an antidote to sentimentality and kitsch. For Schoenberg, "style is the quality of a work and is based in natural conditions, expressing him who produced it. ... But he will never start from a preconceived image of style; he will be ceaselessly occupied with doing justice to the idea" ([1946] 1975: 121).

CHAPTER 6
Modernism and Postmodernism

Organic architecture rebels against the doctrines of modernism and can thus be understood as a postmodern critique of society and of political systems. Nevertheless, as shown in the preceding three chapters, important differences between the organic and the typically postmodern persist. Therefore, the discourses of the organic and the postmodern must be disentangled. This task is not easy because in many respects, organic and postmodern discourses do overlap. Even in Imre Makovecz's works, the distinction between the postmodern and the organic is not always obvious. For example, his attraction to Robert Venturi's proverbial postmodern style accounts for some superficial similarities, which became even more pronounced in his later projects such as the Seville Pavilion (1992) or drafts of a hotel in Berlin (1997). The same is true for Makovecz's often seemingly naïve use of literal elements like the wings attached to the steeple of the Pázmány Péter Catholic University's church or artificial trees inside buildings. His last works might indeed be postmodern in appearance.

Central and Eastern Europe and the Postmodern

In order to draw a separating line between Makovecz and postmodernism, it is necessary to consider the historical and political constellations described in chapter 2, which have initiated in Hungarian culture (especially in architecture) a peculiar perception of (Western) modernity. Only this Hungarian view of Western modernity can account for the fact that after socialism, a critique of modernism, to such a large extent, joined the style of an organic architecture that had already been defined in previous decades. This critique joined postmodern trends much less frequently. Of course, postmodern architecture does exist in Hungary, but it could never attract the same amount of national—and therefore international—interest as organic architecture, let alone be seen as representative of a national style. Today, in the worst case, postmodern architecture can be found in the villas of the newly rich middle class in the form of incoherently employed iconic and historic elements.

A common denominator underlying the organic aesthetics of Makovecz, as well as that of Béla Tarr and László Krasznahorkai, is indeed that they remain "modern" in the sense of not giving in to "postmodern" impulses. International postmodernism arose simultaneously with the fall of communism and was enthusiastically applied in many other Central and Eastern European countries in the 1980s. In the anti-utopian atmosphere of disillusionment toward totalities and systems of this decade, the aesthetics of postmodernism could appear as the most consistent method to dismantle totalitarian cultures. Totalities needed to be fragmented and deconstructed. Furthermore, everything that was once forbidden (like formal experiments and free-form associations) could now be tried. Thus, despite unbridgeable differences, postmodernism and organicism share a common starting point: both thankfully embraced the new freedom that had become available in the postindustrial (postcommunist) era. This is also the perception of Charles Jencks when he—rather boldly—classifies both the Pécs Group and Makovecz as protagonists of the postmodern movement (2002: 84).

Hungary is organic, which makes it unique. In the 1980s, most other Central and Eastern European countries went for postmodernism.[1] In Estonia, for example, the young architects of the so-called Tallinn School framed a critique of Soviet modern architecture by developing a rather Americo-centric postmodern style inspired by Venturi and Peter Eisenman.[2] In Poland, postmodernism was understood as an appropriate form of pluralism (see Górski 2002; Janaszek-Ivaničková 1997). Things were very different in Hungary. Imitating Western architecture had been a taboo for years in alternative architectural circles, and a value-based search for new forms of expression was, by preference, led independently. Instead of imitating American postmodernism, the continuation of a Hungarian organic tradition appeared more attractive. The organic line of American architecture established by Frank Lloyd Wright and Bruce Goff provided inspirations, though it was not merely imitated. In general, Hungarian organic architecture is a homemade phenomenon and not so much a product of international influences.[3]

The organic style had already announced itself seventy years earlier at a similar moment of disillusionment: at the end of World War I, when the trust in liberal capitalism and individualism had been dramatically shattered. Paradoxically, and similar to what would happen decades later in the postcommunist situation, the value crisis sparked by World War I also brought new liberties: old empires (Czarist Russia and Austria-Hungary) had been swept away, and small nations could now experiment with new ways of self-determination. Moreover, even socialism could be prematurely experienced in Hungary at about the same time. It came with Béla Kun's so-called Soviet Democracy (Council Democracy) experiment, which later developed into a dictatorship.

The paradoxical combination of disillusionment and enthusiasm experienced in the 1920s could be restaged in the 1980s. Now the styles were either postmodernism or organic. Krasznahorkai taps into precisely this environment when he describes, in a metaphorical fashion, the state of disillusionment that determines *The Melancholy of Resistance*. Eszter discovers that what he had for years believed were "the most wonderful harmonies and most sublime mutual vibrations, a position in which every note of every masterpiece had, over several centuries, contrived to suggest some great platonic realm," were in reality no more than a "cheat," a "fraud," and an "infuriating and shameful position" (Krasznahorkai 1998: 115). For Eszter, so the parable continues, the musicological ideologist Andreas Werckmeister invented this "cheat."

One cannot insist enough that compared to Western Europe and North America, the "modern style" in Central and Eastern Europe remained linked to entirely different cultural experiences. Around 1900, Central and Eastern European modernity would still develop in parallel with Western movements. However, in the nationalist and conservative atmosphere of the interwar period, the region became more peripheral. Things became even worse after World War II when modernism had to face oppression, distrust, and harassment from the Stalinist regime—particularly in Hungary, where we do not even find something like the Prague Linguistic Circle of structuralism, the Tartu-Moscow Semiotic School, or the Polish school of phenomenology. Roman Ingarden had already initiated the latter before World War II. In Hungary, until the 1950s, the official cultural politics rejected modernism as being formalist and cosmopolitan. Even Georg Lukács drafted an—admittedly sophisticated—critique of literary modernism.

After Joseph Stalin's death, modernism emerged mainly in the form of functionalism. In Eastern Europe, modernism was not only experienced through a time gap; it was loaded, as a social phenomenon, with completely different ideological connotations. For those reasons, in many Eastern European countries, postmodernism could be experienced as a liberation. Curiously, the attraction even worked the other way round. Some Western postmodernists—for example, representatives of postmodern classicism like Aldo Rossi, Philip Johnson, and Ricardo Bofill—showed an outspoken interest in the—now historical—expressions of socialist realism (see Jencks 2002: 128). Another important question is whether Central and Eastern Europe really wanted to obtain this Western type of modernity. Western modernity, which is very much based on the experiences of the French and American revolutions, as well as on liberalism, was certainly perceived differently in a region that had earlier been submitted to a socialist type of modernity. The idea of a third way to modernity or of an "alternate modernity" (Arnason 2005) to integrate typically modern achievements like technology and a market economy with traditions and culture certainly had further effects on the choices made by some Hungarian architects.

Organic versus Postmodern

The next chapter will analyze the potential antagonism of the organic and the postmodern, but a few points can be mentioned here. While the postmodern deconstructs totalities, the organic constantly searches for new totalities it wants to be not static (universal) but dynamic. Strictly speaking, the decision to let totalities subsist inscribes the organic into the realm of the modern and makes the organic incompatible with postmodern and deconstructive approaches. Peter Blundell Jones thus aptly calls organic architecture the "alternative tradition of the modern movement" (1996: 7). Yet another reason organic architecture cannot be postmodern is that, historically and by definition, the organic relates to the idea of modernity, however differently this modernity might have been interpreted. Hugo Häring took care, during his attempts to distinguish his own works from the archaic tendencies of Nazi-promoted architecture, to insist on the modern character of his organic architecture that he found incompatible with Nazi-style historicism. Frank Lloyd Wright is generally also seen as modern, just like the Hungarian and Viennese composers at the turn of the century. Those artists are modernists, though they also constantly insist on the importance of the "organic whole." In fact, the entire movement of Hungarian modernism is intimately connected with organic philosophy (see Frigyesi 2000, chap. 4). Overall, aesthetically, the organic vocabulary tends toward a modern universe up to a point where, in more recent writings, the organic has often been presented as futuristic (see Pearson 2001: 24).

The association of the organic with the futurist might appear surprising in light of Makovecz's (and others') tendencies to present "living architecture" (a distinctively Hungarian appellation) in opposition to international modernism. Seeing the organic as modern can also look counterintuitive if one considers that the typically natural materials used by organic architecture differ radically from modern glass, steel, and concrete. The assumption looks even stranger considering the link organic architecture has maintained with romantic ways of thinking, including the anti-Enlightenment heritage sticking to many of those philosophies, as well as with certain spiritual and quasi-religious traditions. However, while organic architecture is critical of a certain kind of technological and mechanical culture, its aesthetic expressions are always future-oriented. Organic architecture is different from merely conservative or traditionalist architecture attempting to reconcile tradition with modernity (represented in Hungary in the 1930s by Iván Kotsis and Pál Viragh).

Organicism wants a different kind of modernity, and Hungary has turned out to be a suitable ground for staging this experiment. Makovecz and his followers are not folkloristic, nor do they engage in a romanticization of the past. Organic architecture is even outspokenly progressive the moment it criticizes modern Western architecture for its "reactionary" consumerism (see Magyar 1991: 19). Here, organic architecture follows the principles of critical regionalism, which is also a modern movement. Like organicism, critical regionalism has a utopian potential because it overcomes the naïve realism of regional architecture. While the organic can connect to the futurist, the outspokenly backward-reaching aesthetic gestures of the postmodern are incompatible with the spirit of futurism. The postmodern mainly extracts the geometrical form from modernism, as well as the emphasis on the image, which is precisely what organicism avoids. In cinema, this turn toward the image happened by the end of the 1930s with the introduction of a standardized aesthetic system assimilating cut, fade, dissolve, and image in movement. According to Graham Cairns, film was downgraded to "a site for spectacular sets" and ceased being "a radical melting pot for spatial theories" (2014: 3).

Organic architecture concentrates on the building's functions by developing its works from the inside out. Organicism will never put the "outside" aspect (that is, the building's image) to the center of its aesthetic approach. "Ornament should be the thing and not on it," said Wright (1941: 74). Makovecz, Tarr, and Krasznahorkai do not indulge in exuberant imagery, futile grand gestures, or willful belatedness, nor do they recede to the premodern vernacular. Contrary to what superficial impressions can yield, Makovecz is not recalling the vernacular but is rather inspired by myths that confer a more cosmic dimension to the buildings. This interest in myths especially makes his creations different from "realist" regional architecture. Makovecz's aesthetics emphasizing round shapes might be reminiscent of traditional peasant houses, but in reality there is no link with vernacular architecture. The symbols are not local, and old shapes receive new interpretations. At the same time, the effect of strangeness is not postmodern, because its aim is not to destabilize the ontological value of the space but to frame and solidify it. When Makovecz integrates a building into the cosmos by placing astrological signs on walls and pillars (as he did in the cultural center in Szigetvár), and when he occasionally arranges the placement according to astrological constellations, this is the contrary of playful deconstruction (even though some irony might be involved). At the same time, Makovecz's "mythological mix" is not an impenetrable whole presented as an impersonal, superindividual unity. Instead, the mythological network is laid bare and made visible, which is why some people mistakenly find Makovecz postmodern.

For the same reason, Tarr (2004) confirms that the human condition for him is not absurd: "No, it's not absurd. The world is moving and turning and people are seeing films." Makovecz's ambition to confer a more cosmic dimension to his buildings also parallels Krasznahorkai's interest in myths. The techniques of dislocation or the creation of uncertainty proper to postmodernism produce a kind of play that can easily be experienced as empty because the holistic character of the whole experience is missing. True, similar to postmodernism, the organic expressions are equivocal, and an ultimate meaning is often unavailable within the circular flow of the organic discourse. These two features are also among the most striking ones of Krasznahorkai's writings. However, the organic is more than an open-ended system of signs endlessly referring to other signs. This kind of system is rather the result of postmodern approaches aiming to make meaning unavailable on principle. Organicism, on the other hand, has never made the "linguistic turn": the world is not just language, and cinema is not just images. Rather, in organic expressions subsists a sense of cultural reality able to exist independently of mere language games.

The organic becomes postmodern only when it imitates the image of nature. Häring already recognized this approach as a major mistake and insisted the "principle rather than the form of nature ... should be followed" (Blundell Jones 1996: 186). Art Nouveau architects were typical

Figure 6.1. Cultural Center in Szigetvár by Imre Makovecz.

imitators of nature, as they eagerly reproduced natural beauty, the most obvious example being the imitation of the natural shapes presented by biologist Ernst Haeckel in his biological atlas, *Art Forms in Nature* (*Kunstformen der Natur*, 1899–1904). The problem is that the organic is not a manifestation of "anthropomorphy or biomorphic shapes but of open-endedness" (Blundell Jones 1996: 85). What matters is the development of open-ended shapes within certain circumstances. A typical example of fake organicism is Japanese Metabolism, which adopted organic forms without ever joining the philosophical agenda of organic architecture (see Kuma 2009: 56). Into the same category fall Hungarian experimentations with tulip-shaped facades applied to *panelkapcsolat* buildings with which the Pécs Group in Hungary experimented in the 1970s. Communists and organicists alike criticized those attempts because they concerned only exterior modifications and decorations (see Molnár 2005). It is not enough for a building to look like a tulip to be considered organic.[4]

Most recently, "curvy" architecture has become increasingly popular because computers make the design of complex shapes easy. However, to be curvy does not mean to be organic. In popular understanding, organic architecture is any architecture avoiding straight lines. The problem here is that nature is merely imitated, which again means it is presented as an image. The "imagification" is in line with postmodern strategies in general, but it opposes the spirit of the organic. The contemporary organic architect Bart Prince says he "would never start with the idea that the building was going to look like anything else, because this is applying a form from the outside rather than arriving at it from the inside." If people tell him, for example, his buildings look like whales, they wrongly "assume that I must have been trying to make it look like what they think they saw" (2001: 92). Nothing can be more opposed to Venturi's (postmodern) theory of the duck and decorated shed.

In film culture, the digital—the central driving force of postmodern image culture—has brought about a parallel turn toward imitation. Reproducing reality by using a cold and perfect technology, the digital image symbolizes the self-contained and auto-referential character of postmodern expressions. What is at work here is not an organic retrieval of reality and the mythical aura clinging to it but rather a self-gratifying idolatry. The digital image might be perfect, but it represents precisely the kind of technological (as opposed to natural) perfection that Eszter abhors. It is the visual equivalent of the perfectly (in the sense of Werckmeister) tuned piano.

Organic Reality

In organic expressions, reality might be presented in the form of a circular movement of decomposition and evolution but is not deconstructed because it remains intact as a whole. In organic buildings, novels, and films, there is *one* reality, which remains ontologically founded in a relatively conventional fashion. This is true for Tarr's films and his adaptations of Krasznahorkai's writing.[5] A plot exists—Robert Boyers calls it "a rather elementary tale" (2005: 171)—and just like in organic architecture, the architect fully controls a clearly recognizable living space. In this sense, even Werckmeister's harmonies, abstract as they may be, are a metaphor for something that can be extracted from the text, though perhaps only with much difficulty. John Hodgkins's perception that Krasznahorkai "deploys postmodernist techniques" because he "takes on the role of the ultimate postmodern historian in his novel" (2009: 49, 52) is thus not sustainable. Nor is Elzbieta Buslowska's idea that there is "no storyline" (2009: 108). Conventional devices common for tales support the narrative structure of *Satantango* as it begins (even in the film) with: "One October morning before the first drops of the long autumn rains which fall on parched soil, which turn tracks into bog, and cut the town off, Futaki was woken by the sound of bells. The solitary chapel eight kilometers away had no bell and its tower had collapsed during the war. The town was too far away for its sounds to carry here" (2012a: 3). Jacques Rancière's observations are thus much more correct as he finds that "there are no games [*il n'y a pas de jeu*] in Béla Tarr's universe" (2013: 34; 2011: 41). In the end, everything is relatively serious and quite the way it is meant to be.

Tarr produces no postmodern universe, except perhaps in *Almanac of Fall,* where the film's imagery becomes dominating and expressionist. However, it is generally appropriate to present Tarr as the last representative of a disappearing school of European cinematic modernism, as was done in 2012 in the Tarr retrospective at the Lincoln Center in New York, which was cogently entitled "The Last Modernist." Or perhaps Tarr can also be called "meta-modern," as suggested by Sylvie Rollet (2011: 102). On the other hand, Tarr, Krasznahorkai, and Makovecz are "antimodern" if modern signifies rational, abstract, engineered, and centralized, but their skepticism toward those latter terms leads neither to a simple return to the vernacular nor to postmodern relativism. Instead of alienating (*verfremden*) or deconstructing understandable forms, their expressions tend to overemphasize selected components.

All this perhaps brings them closer to kitsch (see chapter 9) but not to postmodernism. While the postmodern tends to deconstruct all clearly established components and prefers random play, organic expressions employ processes of disintegration and evolution (both of which often appear together). This is how the organic image world differs from the marketable image world of postmodernism. The word "organic" relates to "organization," and organic expressions, despite their complexity, are always "well organized," which is one more reason the organic is incompatible with postmodernism. Krasznahorkai's (2012b) "disciplined madness" is simply too disciplined to end up as postmodern play, but the organization does not lead to modern enthusiasm about progress either. On the contrary, Eszter is the typical protagonist of this antiprogress attitude as he withdraws "in face of the pathetic stupidity of so-called human progress" (Krasznahorkai 1998: 99). The disillusionment with progress and development we encounter in Tarr's film worlds, paired with Krasznahorkai's "disciplined madness," will lead to melancholy. This melancholy, which is an ironic combination of disintegration and evolution, does not give way to relativism but rather represents a force able to resist postmodern relativism. As shown in chapter 4, for Kierkegaard and Lukács, melancholy is linked to irony, meaning melancholy is basically playful but still too serious to reemerge in the form of the serenity so typical for the relativist mindset.

The paradoxical nature of melancholy is emphasized by the fact that melancholy in Hungary signified not simply despair but also hope, as György Konrád explains in his text *The Melancholy of Rebirth*. Konrád finds that "switching to a new system of government is inevitably disenchanting, perhaps because of the eschatological expectations it is bound to raise" (1995: 40). In other words, great expectations produce great disappointments but also hope. Rollet notes that "no progress" exists in Tarr's worlds and immediately adds, "if the history of living organisms is that of its destruction, it is also the history of its resistance" (2013: 2). In this way, "melancholy of resistance" becomes a formula for the inherent procedure of organic philosophy in Central and Eastern Europe, and it can clearly be contrasted with the other type of irony, the serenity qua relativism underlying postmodern expressions. According to Boyers, resistance in Krasznahorkai's novel "has no active component, though it is vaguely discernible in an activity of mind that never threatens to issue in anything effectual" (2005: 175). Thus, Eszter's resistance to temporal tuning is a resistance to modernity that turns—necessarily—melancholic.

In *Damnation*, the film's hero, Karrer, says, "Every story is a story of disintegration." He definitely does not mean "deconstruction." Furthermore—and this makes the organic again distinct from postmodernism—organic disintegration has an almost religious undertone, as it affirms the supreme circularity of life and death. The organic is against construction, but this does not mean it automatically refers to deconstruction. The organic alternative of construction is organic growth proceeding from the seed of material. And the organic alternative of deconstruction is decomposition combined with evolution.

The detached attitude brought about by the alternation of growth and decomposition also produces the playful aspect of the organic. Frank Lloyd Wright wrote: "decoration should never be purposely constructed. True beauty results from that repose which the mind feels when the eye, the intellect, the affections, are satisfied from the absence of any want" (1987: 72). This differs from the spectacular playfulness of the postmodern that constructs while deconstructing. Organic thought is playful inasmuch as evolution is a playful undertaking. It does not want to hark back to a pre-Darwinian taxonomic system of classification and build certitude on factual resemblance and identity. It does not want to establish, as did classical modernism, the individual as an objective reality defined by the bearer's specific position in time, space, and a chain of generations. Contingency does exist in evolution in the form of accidental variability, overdetermination, and discontinuity (cf. Darwin 2004: 40), which is why any organic system can be seen as a game. Postmodern critiques often mistakenly attempt to describe organic development as causally determined and continuous, as René Wellek does in his critique of analytical philosophy of history (1982: 70–71; see also Neubauer 2009: 27).[6] True, the existence (of species) is not a matter of facts for organic thought, but existence does not dissolve into gamelike structures either.

Hugo Häring has provided an example that confirms these observations. Häring did not entirely accept Darwin's idea of evolution because he understood it as a purely functional concept. Classifications (Aristotle's, for example) distinguish the organic from the nonorganic and establish hierarchies, which is already against the spirit of organic philosophy. Consequently, for Häring, the term evolution did not express anything about the being, the identity, or the Gestalt of the phenomenon meant to evolve. He believed organic order presupposes a complex interrelation between form and activity but cannot be established by evolution alone. He joins here Friedrich Nietzsche's critique of Darwinist determinism, which is, according to the German philosopher, reductionist, as it cannot explain the extant biological diversity (see Nietzsche 1998: 14; Joullié 2013: 184).

Tarr, Krasznahorkai, and the Hungarian Tradition

Considerations of Hungarian organic architecture show that Tarr is rooted at least transversally in the Hungarian cultural tradition. Some people—for example, András Bálint Kovács—say Tarr's work is not much marked by "Hungarianness" and that "no Hungarian cultural or cinematic tradition would help in appreciating or understanding his particular stylistic universe" (2013: 97). This might be true in some sense. Tarr's films are not based, like Hungarian organic architecture, "on the traditional concepts of a particular people, their landscape and their mutual history" (Cook 1997: 6). However, Tarr (2004) himself has recently insisted that "fact is fact and *Werckmeister* is a very Hungarian film." The truth is that Tarr is not Hungarian because he indulges in the folklore of the Middle Ages or in the heroic ambiance of Turanian flatlands, just like organic architecture is not organic because it reproduces imagery from nature. Tarr's films are Hungarian because of an obsession with the organic process of production of a cinematic world, just like organic architecture is organic because it employs nature-like structures of space production.

The same problem arises with Krasznahorkai, whom Boyers does not find Hungarian at all because he offers nothing of "the tumultuous history of Hungarian communism" or of the "dispassionate, highly evocative documentary realism" typical for Central and Eastern European literature. Furthermore, Boyers finds it hopeless "to read this unfamiliar work as a typical product of the Hungarian imagination or as a reflection of peculiarly Central and Eastern European circumstances" (2005: 171). However, the organic—in all the dimensions in which it can be encountered—remains important. Béla Bartók has been considered a Hungarian "organic" composer (see Frigyesi 2000, chap. 1), and I don't see why Hungarian cinema and literature should not be discussed in similar terms. It is the organic that makes him Hungarian.

Notes

1. The case of Hungarian literature is different, as it embraced postmodernism relatively early. According to Beatrice Töttössy (1995) postmodernism started in 1979 with Peter Esterházy's *Termelési-regény* [A novel of production].

2. Andres Kurg writes: "Kahn, Stirling and Archigram, who in architectural debates had featured as paradigms for practice throughout the decade were now replaced by Rossi, Krier and Graves" (2009: 90; on Eisenman, see p. 109).
3. This is substantiated by the fact that in Socialist Hungary, images of Wright's and Goff's work, as well as texts about this American movement, had normally not been available to architects. Furthermore, only few Hungarians spoke English and could have read those texts at this time, even if they had been freely available.
4. In defense of the Pécs Group, they were forced by the authorities to limit their design to these exterior aspects (see Ferkai 1998: 291).
5. True, other Krasznahorkai novels, especially *War and War*, can be considered postmodern, as they produce kaleidoscopic constellations of narrative elements (see Töttössy 1995).
6. In general, Wellek does not oppose the metaphor of organism but thinks there is "a simple truth in the old view that a successful work of art is a whole in which the parts collaborate and modify each other" (1982: 94).

CHAPTER 7
Organic Harmonies

László Krasznahorkai's obsession with the organic speaks through not only his lengthy accounts of natural organic processes—"The nitrogenous compounds including the micro-organisms entrusted with the breaking down of albumin completed their task, which micro-organisms, soon reinforced by the front-line troops, then began their operation among the intestines" (1998: 313)—but also his general descriptions of architecture and space, as well as the kind of architecture made not of bricks but of sounds: music. For music, a universal order (harmony) is fundamental. As mentioned, the model of the organic is not math or logic but nature, and the musicological part of *Werckmeister Harmonies* explores this theme in music. The main topic of *Werckmeister Harmonies* is Eszter's obsession with the "falseness" of the harmonic scale introduced by the German organist and theoretician Andreas Werckmeister (1645–1706), though this, or similar kinds of scales, have generally been accepted in Western music.

Historically, music and math have often been linked, but the relationship between both is complex, especially in light of the questionable "naturalness" of math. Though music is an art and math a science, they share common origins traced to cults and mysteries. There are important commonalities: both display similar concerns with proportion and measurements that can easily be projected into the realm of space; both are abstract and independent of human language but tend to use metaphors and analogies to convey more general meanings; in combination with metaphorical language, both can become models helping to understand the world.

Eszter believes that since Andreas Werckmeister, "music, its harmony and echo, its unsurpassable enchantment, is entirely based on a false foundation." More precisely, the dissensus is not merely about music but about the general decline of humanity, as Krasznahorkai continues:

"Ever since he was young he had lived with the unshakeable conviction that music, which for him consisted of the omnipotent magic of harmony and echo, provided humanity's only sure stay against the filth and squalor of the surrounding world, music being close to an approximation to perfection" (1998: 112–13). As an alternative to Werckmeister, Krasznahorkai mentions Aristoxenus, the Greek theoretician of music who rejected the Pythagorean idea that intervals depend on arithmetic rules (in fact, the opposition of both theories does not become entirely clear in the film, where the musicological aspects are only delivered in an abridged fashion through Eszter's monologue). Instead of a system based on mathematical ratios imposed by the "Pythagorean demon" (114), Aristoxenus (1868) was looking for an organic whole based on human sense perception.

Eszter's philosophy of "harmony" is very similar to that of Aristoxenus: mathematical rules of music cannot grasp the object they pretend to embrace. Only an organic logic, which is truer and more fundamental than the logic of numbers and syllogisms, can provide the principle of harmony in music, in the world, and in space. This organic order is the logic of nature, which is incompatible with artificial logic used in technology, even though many people have pretended that both are the same. In Krasznahorkai's own description of the situation, Eszter is convinced that certain symmetries arising in musical sounds are due to "harmonies inherent in its basic physical nature" and that those sounds are linked within an organic system. Single vibrations thus comprise "a whole series of so-called periodic waves" (1998: 114).

"Is perfection perfect?" is Eszter's rhetorical question. The answer: it might be perfect, but even when it's perfect, it's not perfect for just that reason. Too much perfection will make things imperfect in return. In other words, something might be perfect from a natural point of view, but then again, it will be imperfect mathematically. And when it's mathematically perfect, it will be imperfect in terms of nature. Is Eszter mad? Even independently of the technicalities exposed by the Werckmeister problem, the idea is not as strange as it sounds. Eszter's question makes sense in several contexts, one of which is the contemporary digital image culture that reproduces reality almost "perfectly" in the eyes of some but appears cold and insipid to others. The question of whether this process should really be called "perfection" will always remain pertinent. Similar to mathematically perfect music, the digital image symbolizes a self-contained perfection claiming to be "real," though its perfection, as some will always claim, does not engage us in the same way art can engage us with reality.

This kind of "perfection" arouses Eszter's scorn. Can an "imperfect" Polaroid photo not be more real than the "perfect" digital one? Furthermore, should reality not always be understood as something "rougher" (more natural) than the merely perfect? Can the natural not be, for example, like a piano out of tune, while the "perfectly" tuned piano can appear less natural? Even if one does not entirely agree with this kind of cultural criticism, everybody must admit these are important questions. As civilization progresses, the problem becomes more generalized. In the future, computers will be able to think in relatively complex ways. Should their "thinking" be called more perfect than that of humans? Is it thinking at all? The vast natural versus artificial dichotomy linked to posthumanism arises transversally here and is exploited in the book/film by questioning the "natural" character of temperate music.

Organic architecture, however, never found these thoughts farfetched and even adopted them as the basis of its theoretical framework. Hugo Häring distinguished between shapes "that have been shaped by life and have a nature-like authenticity that is not due to human work" and "shapes that are created for the sake of expression, whose character can be traced to laws dependent on human knowledge" (Häring et al. 1964: 13). The author concludes that the former are eternal, while the latter, as they depend on human will and knowledge, are temporary. The most radical brand of organicism is unsatisfied with shapes established by human (mathematical) reason but constantly searches for the organic reason of nature. Radical organicists continue doing so even though (or just because) they know this "reason of nature" is incompatible with math. Eszter in his search for natural harmony also follows those organic guidelines.

Art Nouveau and the Twelve-Tone Technique

In order to show how radical this form of organicism is, it can be contrasted with its more superficial version represented, in the more recent history of architecture, by the Art Nouveau/Jugendstil movement that was also very important in Hungary. The Hungarian Art Nouveau movement is seen as a predecessor of organic architecture and sometimes even classified (for example, by Bruno Zevi) as a proto-organic movement (see chapter 2). However, essential differences exist between radical organicism and the philosophy of Art Nouveau. True, Art Nouveau also sees nature as a model, as its shapes are obviously organically evolving, and it often even attempts to see buildings as organic unities. However, too often the organic language of Art Nouveau remains self-consciously linked to mathematics. In certain cases, mathematics were even meant to produce Art Nouveau expressions, to the point that the engineer was seen as the most perfect "artist" because he could recreate the beauty (reality) of nature. This is what Art Nouveau architect Henry van de Velde believed when he wrote, "The exceptional beauty proper to the works of engineers consists in that this beauty knew itself, just like the beauty of gothic cathedrals had become self-conscious" (1901: 112). The line of mathematical aesthetics goes from here to constructivists and Bauhaus-inspired designers like Max Bill who believed art can be developed by following a mathematical logic (see Fabbri 2016). Eszter's philosophy of organic harmony is directed against this kind of mathematical aesthetics, and he expresses his thoughts in the realm of music. In music, van de Velde's ideas on math and nature exist in the form of Arnold Schoenberg's twelve-tone technique in which human subjectivity is subordinate to mathematics. In fact, both Schoenberg and Anton Webern have been declared "organic" composers. Webern explains in *The Path to the New Music* (in which he acknowledges his debt to Goethe) that "rules in the arts are based on laws in nature" (1963: 40–42; see also Frigyesi 2000: 25; Neubauer 2009: 30) and his twelve-tone technique is driven by a search for organic unity.

While the suggestions made by twelve-tone composers sound radical, they are not radical enough for Eszter. Schoenberg and Webern do not deliver the radical, absolutely perfect—or imperfect, for that purpose—organicism Eszter is interested in. The twelve-tone technique merely manipulates an ordered series of twelve notes in the chromatic scale. Obviously, this method solves the problem of temperate tuning that both Werckmeister and Eszter struggle with in a unique fashion. While in temperate tuning, some notes (usually the tonic and the dominant note) are declared more important than others; the twelve-tone technique gives equal importance to all notes because the system has no key. Logically, all problems linked to temperate tuning are now solved. However, this is no solution for Eszter because here the "harmony" has merely been achieved by submitting music to math, which is precisely what he wants to avoid. Interestingly, Krasznahorkai attributes the twelve-tone technique (or something very similar to it) to Werckmeister, which is historically unsustainable but forcefully underlines the above argument: "Werckmeister cut the Gordian knot with a cavalier swish of his sword and, maintaining only the precise intervals between octaves, divided the universum of the twelve half-tones—what was the music of the spheres to him!—into twelve simple and equal parts" (1998: 115).

The Infinite

The math versus nature theme appears in other places in Krasznahorkai's work. In Északról hegy, Délről tó, Nyugatról utak, Keletről folyó (From the north by hill, from the south by lake, from the west by roads, from the east by river) (2003), the idea of mathematically constructed abstract quantities (and with it, of abstractly constructed concepts of reality) are combated and deconstructed. While in Japan, the protagonist of the novel finds a two-thousand-page mathematical tractate written by an imaginary Sir Wilford Stanley Gilmore entitled "Infinity: An Error." The text was hidden in a Buddhist monastery. Though mainly composed of numbers, the text turns out to be a long rant against the work of the German mathematician Georg Cantor, who held that the infinite is part of reality and therefore does exist. Cantor is the inventor of set theory and proved that real numbers are more numerous than natural numbers. As the spiritual cousin of Eszter, Sir Wilford depicts the scientific push toward mathematical constructions of space and time as part of a conspiracy leading Western culture toward its inevitable decline. We find on these pages the same fanatic and paranoiac ambiance we know from Eszter's perorations on the decline of "real music." Both Sir Wilford and Eszter are fighting against the rest of the world seeing Cantor and Werckmeister, respectively, as the engineers of the occident's undoing. Sir Wilford holds that reality is finite and that Cantor's idea of the infinite is purely imaginary. By convincing the Western world that the infinite exists, this "lamentable Platonist" called Cantor has made himself guilty of bringing about the "scandalous intellectual limitations to which Western history of science has been submitted ever since." The tractate by Sir Wilford is supposed to be a "coming to terms with the infinite," demonstrating that "reality does not know a single infinite number because it does not know infinite quantities." Reality is "objective" while the infinite "can only be constructed by using sophisticated abstractions and by taking advantage of the properties of human consciousness" (74). As a proof, the author "stages" the reality of numbers by inviting the reader to read all printed numbers (which often have eighteen digits) aloud, showing that numbers are real and not merely imagined. In parallel with Krasznahorkai, Sir Wilford sticks to an idea of language as a concrete and "real" phenomenon unmitigated by grammar, punctuation, or any other abstract rules.

This project overlaps with Krasznahorkai's own obsession with the existence of an antigrammatical language. Sir Wilford is annoyed that scientists like Cantor simply do not recognize this reality but tend to see the whole world as a game. Math is also practiced as a game because those people are:

> unable to grasp this real though ungraspably large quantity and as a result they have the feeling that it is infinite, which is for them of course quasi identical with The Infinite, but not identical with the reality of The Infinite, which is not the case, because only very mean and devious so-called theoretical mathematicians, who are lost in a game and do not engage in the research of reality, have postulated all this with the help of abstract constructions ... (72)[1]

Krasznahorkai's aversion to abstract space and his quest for an organic reality also become manifest in the short book *Animalinside*, where he makes "the animal" say: "I hate all that is infinite, there burns within me an unspeakable hatred toward the infinite ... the infinite is a deception, the infinite is a deception in space, the infinite is a deception in measuring, and every aspiration to the infinite is a trap" (2014: 26). Much of the animal's ruminations are about the "conventional" logic of space and time that the animal, this representative of nature, finds impossible to live in:

> They have placed me inside this moment, but have also excluded me from the moment previous as well as the one to follow, so that I howl with one howl, expelled from time, trapped in one space ill-matched to my proportions, because the problem is the space, I have nothing in common with this space, in the entire God-given world I have nothing in common with this structure, with these perspectives, and these perspectives not even made so I can exist in them, so that I don't even exist, I only howl. (9)

As a result, the animal invents his own spatial order, which is, to say the least, very illogical, as it pretends to "extend from one city to another, I extend from one country to another, and if I want I extend all the way across the Atlantic Ocean" (12).

Music and Space

"The animal's" reflections on the logic of space represent the writer's general tendency to make space the protagonist of his writings. Most strikingly, Krasznahorkai's musings about music maintain a strong link with architecture. Given the fundamental similarities between music and space in terms of harmony, space (lived space as well as outer space) often appears in Krasznahorkai's books like an eternal realm in which objects and even moving bodies are organically linked to each other, as becomes particularly clear in this passage:

> He felt there was time to sink into the peaceful silence which hugged him as close as did the blanket his body, into the impregnable order of permanence where everything remains as it was, where furniture, carpet, mirror and lamp waited undisturbed to receive him, and where there would be time to take stock of the tiniest detail and discover every part of what now revealed itself to be his inexhaustible treasure trove, gauging, in his imagination, the distance between his current position and the hall, a distance that seemed to be constantly increasing, but one that would soon be entered by one person who would give meaning to all of this: Valuska. Because every element of this "beneficial sweetness" referred to him Valuska was the cause and subject of every process. (1998: 193)

Music is described with the help of spatial metaphors current in architecture, such as "symmetry" or the "proximity" of elements. Both architecture and music share a mathematical basis that must be transcended in order to find the organic structure of nature in both. Then the fusion between the space and the body will be so organic that the body is "hugged" by the space. This "space beyond time" (the "impregnable order of permanence") is simultaneously static and fluent: in *The Melancholy*, Krasznahorkai speaks of "a distance that seemed to be constantly increasing."

Some of these thoughts on music read as if they have been adopted from a handbook of organic architecture. The image of an organic space as it appears in the above passage from Krasznahorkai is reminiscent of Makovecz's project to "create a connection between the sky and the earth, while, at the same time, interpreting and expressing the movement and place of human beings" (Gerle 2010: 20). In films, the effect of an organic space can be obtained through the use of long camera shots. Béla Tarr reproduces Krasznahorkai's "organic time" through an aesthetic of slowness that concerns not only time but also—or even more, as we will see in chapter 12—space. Moreover, in Tarr's slow cinema, individual actions and the general framework within which they are carried out are fused into an organic whole. The effect, according to Tony McKibbin, is that "the characters don't act in the world so much as [they] seem to be acted upon by the world; a decision made is secondary to the forces compelling them" (2005: 1).

The Universal and the Cosmic

Decisions "are made," says McKibbin, but who or what makes the decisions? The formulation, "the forces compelling them," almost suggests that those decisions flow out of a cosmic framework. In other words, those characters follow not universal laws but cosmic laws. In *Werckmeister Harmonies*, astrophysical considerations pertain to almost everything. They are so important that Tarr decides to import the space-world parallel into *Satantango* as well. Though the doctor's existence in the novel bears no link with the astrophysical discourses that dominate *Werckmeister Harmonies*, Tarr installs an additional clue perhaps meant to connect *Satantango* to the film he would make six years later (in 1994, when the film *Satantango* was made, *The Melancholy of Resistance* had already been published). At the entrance to the doctor's house hangs a map of the solar system, though no indication of such a map appears in the novel. What does "cosmic" mean more precisely in this organic context? It certainly does not relate to the mechanical cosmology established at the end of the eighteenth century by Enlightenment thinkers who wanted to see the universe as a precise clockwork winding down. This is not the cosmic as a metaphor represented through the image of a living organism. Rather, the "living cosmos" is a typical image used in organic philosophy.

In discussions of Tarr's films, the word cosmic appears again and again. Peter Hames (2001) finds the images in *Satantango* "cosmic." Tarr himself said in an interview: "I have to recognize it's cosmic; the shit is cosmic. It's not just social, it's not just ontological, it's really huge. And that's why we expand" (McLaren 2012). David Bordwell also highlights Tarr's "cosmic perspective" (*Talking about Tarr* 2008, and Jacques Rancière draws on Marcel Proust's idea of the single moment born of "cosmological" pressure (Rancière 2013: 34; 2011: 41). Sylvie Rollet presents in the same context a passage from Walter Benjamin's letters to Max Horkheimer in which Benjamin puts forward the "cosmic vision of a society that projects this images of the cosmos against the sky" (Rollet 2013: 2).[2]

Important as they are, these allusions to the cosmic all remain rather suggestive and do not attempt to conceptualize the term. On the conceptual level, it is important to retain that the organic philosophies of Makovecz, Tarr, and Krasznahorkai reject the universal in favor of the "cosmic." Sometimes, even when they *say* "universal," they do not mean the scientific (or pseudoscientific) universality claiming to represent "the truth" for everybody and everything. Still, they are not relativists either, because they believe in and try to express some kind of truth, and this truth is called a cosmic truth, while the "universal" is always the "mathematically calculated" universal. Tarr (2008) makes his dislike of this definition of the universal very clear:

> "Universalism" is a very dangerous word. I don't like to use it. The universe is too vast and we're too small. But I agree with you, I'm not abstract. I prefer doing very simple movies, but with a different logic. If you are a filmmaker you have to show what's around you. And I see just simple human situations. And I see some real emotions. I see real human tragedies.

Tarr offers a definition of the cosmic as it is used in organic thinking. Makovecz, Tarr, and Krasznahorkai are critical of modern universal or totalizing concepts such as "progress," "race," or "rigor," but they do not believe a universal moral order should be obtained by imposing the rules of the universe established by science or religion on everything. In this sense, all three are antimodern and anti-premodern, but at the same time, they are too cosmically oriented for the swamp of postmodern relativism that refuses any universal order to absorb them.

Organicism is born out of the confrontation between the absolute and the relative. The pattern emerged with modernity in order to overcome classical ideas of the absolute. Einstein attacked the idea of the absolute and replaced it with the relative. Consequently, Peter Berger and Thomas Luckmann speak of a "vertigo of relativity" (1966: 17) created in the early twentieth century by new discoveries, especially in Germany, in science but also philosophy and anthropology. In this context, the notion of the organic arises as an affirmation of the relative that yet refuses to be absorbed by blunt (universalist) relativism. Therefore, organicism can also be understood as an overcoming of modern scientific paradigms, which is highly paradoxical. In any case, the first step toward the organic is most typically the engagement with relativism. In order to be organic, universal values need to be deconstructed. In this sense, Häring also wanted to push this universalism toward relativism, asking, is not everything relative in architectural history? How can there be absolute values? At the same time, the organicist does not stay within a relativism in which "anything goes." Organicism holds that good and bad do exist, if not universally then definitely in concrete situations, and these situations must find their place within an organic, "cosmic" order. Art, for example, develops organically by taking those concrete (and relative) situations as points of departure but, in the end, makes "cosmic" statements about what is good and what is bad.

The German philosopher Eugen Fink has called a "cosmic gesture" any philosophical attempt to interpret the totality of the world (1960: 22). What Fink has in mind are not universal rules but rather myths, aesthetic expressions, and organic philosophies able to provide a sense of the universe. Religions can also be used for this purpose, but empirical science is not up to this task. Makovecz's, Tarr's, and Krasznahorkai's arts reflect this cosmic philosophy. When W. G. Sebald (2000) writes in his blurb to the English version of *The Melancholy of Resistance* that the "universality of [the book's] vision rivals that of Gogol's *Dead Souls*," he definitely means cosmic, not universal.

Cosmic Architecture

In architecture, the cosmic is linked to the organic, and the organic is linked to the cosmic. Häring reflected on the cosmic ordering of ancient Chinese house foundations, while Krisztina Fehérváry (2012), in her article on Hungarian architecture, "From Socialist Modern to Super-Natural Organicism" (see chapter 9), is subtitled "Cosmological Transformations." Even one of the Pécs Group's manifestos was called "Cosmic Axes." This manifesto explained that in a house, "the infinite horizontal and vertical axes of the freely expanding cosmos are controlled within the sheltering concept of house where man then can blossom into fulfillment" (Cook 1997: 11). The aim was to reestablish the lost harmony between nature and man because "man has forgotten his organic constructive instincts." The word "harmony" appears at least ten times in this manifesto, meaning the Pécs Group does exactly what Tarr and Krasznahorkai are doing when contrasting the cosmic with the universal: "The natural unity of the REGION is created by organic processes through time, in a method that seems both timeless and universal" (from the manifesto "Only from Pure Sources," in Cook 1997: 12).

Peter Blundell Jones, in his book on Häring, writes that the history of cosmology "looks suspiciously like mankind's struggle to impose successive geometric systems on phenomena that remain largely resistant" (1996: 88). Blundell Jones means that while the universal can easily be established in the form of a rational structure independently of the individual, the cosmic constantly meets with the resistance of the individual. Unlike the universal, the cosmic maintains a tense relationship with the individual.

Moreover, "cosmism" as a cultural movement is present in Central and Eastern Europe more than anywhere else. In the nineteenth century, a blend of futuristic speculations, materialistic science of evolution, religious mysticism, and esoteric practices trying to define the human role in a cosmic development thrived particularly well in Russia. Cosmism revolved mainly around the works of Nikolai Fedorov (1829–1903) but has also been addressed by some of the philosophers presented in chapter 3 as thinkers linked to the notion of all-unity. The cosmism revolving around the works of Fedorov even has some "posthuman" connotations, as it emphasizes the necessity to overcome humanism (see Zavaliy 2012). The "overcoming of humanism" theme will be dealt with in chapter 8 in the context of Eszter's humanist (or posthumanist) projects.

Gestalt

Another concept that comprises the "cosmic" is closely attached to the phenomenon of architecture and is one of the main terms of Häring's theory: Gestalt. The German word is a hybrid of form and being or of the abstract and the concrete. Consequently, Gestalt appears whenever the individual and the general are organically connected: "Consciously ordering things in a way that allows their individuality to unfold, while this unfolding also serves the file of the whole. This whole is the Gestalt of our life" (Häring 1925: 4). Gestalt is an organic concept. The situation is similar to the method of Schlegel, who wanted to use the organic to describe how the mind translates indefinite pluralities of distinguishable parts "into an entire and perfect unity" ([1845] 1933: 335).

To delve into Gestalt psychology here is impossible, but I should at least point out that the most important convictions of this movement closely relate to the present discourse on the organic. Gestalt theory represents one more attempt at retrieving a totality within an apparently chaotic world, as Häring's quotation above illustrates. Gestalt psychology believes that the human mind, whenever it perceives something, automatically forms a global whole. In other words, the mind has organic, self-organizing tendencies. Frank Lloyd Wright's sentence that "the first principle of growth is that the thing grown be no mere aggregation" (1941: 185) reflects the famous phrase of Gestalt psychology's founder, Kurt Koffka, who said, "the whole is other than the sum of the parts" (1936: 677). For Koffka, the Gestalt formed by the human mind has a reality of its own that is not entirely independent of the parts but is still more than simply the sum of its parts. Like in organic philosophy, Gestalt psychology emphasizes not the abstract rules of cognitive processes but rather the organization of those processes. In order to appear as a Gestalt, each component must be considered a part of a system of dynamic relationships. In other words, the attention will shift from an interest in unrelated geometrical elements (points, lines, squares) to a principle of organic totality.

Goethe, in the context of his work on morphology, even considered the word Gestalt too static. His *Urphänomen* is explained as an image that will suddenly arise "between Gestalten." For Goethe, the *Urphänomen* able to hold everything together is floating and immaterial and cannot be fixed:

> Since we want to introduce morphology as a discipline, we should not speak of Gestalt; when we use the word morphology, we should only think of an idea, a notion, or something that can be fixed in experience just for a moment. What has been formed will be immediately deformed, and we ourselves should remain as flexible and imaginative if we really want to achieve an immediate intuition of nature. (1817: 55–56)

The Reality of Math

Krasznahorkai's discussion of the Werckmeister topic is clearly a typical example of organic philosophy. The organic in music concerns beauty. Can math be the arbiter of beauty, or is there something more fundamental about beauty, which the human ear can hear but which logic and math cannot grasp? Since the ancient Roman architect Vitruvius (c. 80–70 BCE–c. 15 BCE), humans have made many efforts to show that the organic logic of nature and the rational logic of the human do overlap "by nature." But what if all this is simply not true? The Werckmeister theme touches on one of the most important philosophical problems of humanity, as it questions the categorical distinction between the given (nature) and the constructed (culture) and asks whether culture (here designated as "math") has the status of being real.

Discussions about the "reality character" of math have never ceased to attract the interest of philosophers. In the twentieth century, Wittgenstein developed the same themes in his *Tractatus Logico-Philosophicus* (1921) when reflecting on the language/math–reality connection and the foundation of mathematics altogether. Is language (or math) really about the world? Wittgenstein holds that "mathematical propositions are not real propositions and that 'mathematical truth' is essentially non-referential and purely syntactical in nature" (Rodych 2008: 84).

Wittgenstein's statements about math are very similar to Eszter's quests surrounding music.

Edmund Husserl developed a similar line of thought in his inquiry into the origin of geometry and the meaning of geometrical truths. What is the status of geometry as an ideal object? In his seminal commentary of Husserl's text on the origin of geometry, Jacques Derrida points out:

> geometry's being is thoroughly transparent and exhausted by its phenomenality. Absolutely objective, i.e., totally rid of empirical subjectivity, it nevertheless is only what it appears to be. Therefore, it is always already reduced to its phenomenal sense, and its being is, from the outset, to be an object for a pure consciousness. ([1962] 1978: 27)

The question: is geometry real, or is it just produced by the human consciousness? We clearly recognize the Werckmeister theme in these reflections on the reality character of mathematical constructions. There is a gap between math (or mathematically established music) and reality (or real music), and this gap cannot be bridged. Is music merely "an object for a pure consciousness" (in Derrida's terms), or is music real and natural? These thoughts were prominent in Hungarian cultural discussions around 1900. They underlie Béla Bartók's questionings about what is really expressible in music. According to Judit Frigyesi:

> [Bartók] went through a crisis that made him question whether language was at all capable of expressing anything of the meaning of life. Bartók's situation is unique only in that he did not need to resolve this problem within the domain of language. His solution was simply to abandon language and concentrate on music as the sole medium for the expression of universal thoughts and great feelings. (2000: 8)

The difference in Eszter's position in *Werckmeister Harmonies* is that Eszter sees music as still too much determined by a mathematical grammar, which lets him doubt in a more radical fashion than Bartók whether this music can express something "real."

In Hungary, the question has preoccupied several more intellectuals, even Marxists. Georg Lukács, famous for his theoretical developments of realism in literary theory, asked whether language could be trusted "to bring about a coherent vision of an incoherent reality. What makes us believe that coherence in an artwork is the revelation of truth behind the fragmented everyday reality and not merely a matter of technique?" ("On the Ship of Tristan," quoted in Frigyesi 2000: 111). Furthermore, the Hungarian Marxist sociologist and art historian Arnold Hauser, another member of Lukács's "Sunday Circle," drafted a critique of Beethoven's

Symphony no. 9, highlighting the necessarily organic coherence of music just because music is not merely reproducing reality: "As the other arts are just reproducing life, in music, life manifests itself. Music has its own organic life, is liveliness in itself. Being unfettered by anything, it can't be an imitation of existing artifacts.... Music as the sole objectless art expresses nothing but the unconscious, unformed, tormented state of the sole" (1911: 1).[3]

When Wittgenstein, Husserl, and Eszter, as well as all the others, question the compatibility of mathematics/science with human experience, it is important to understand that its compatibility is not just a matter of either linear or nonlinear geometry (as some contemporary pseudo-organic architects facing the same problem today tend to think). The philosophical criticism is much more radical, as it addresses the "reality character" of geometry/math altogether. This means that computer modeling and fractal geometry rendering curved and spiraling objects in the form of mathematical fractals do not solve the problem. Nor does the postmodern "play with" geometry as long as this play remains unable to establish a holistic reality.

Werckmeister Harmonies presents all of the above philosophical problems by talking about music and astronomy. The same questions can be translated into an architectural language: is a building merely a mathematical, relational system, or is it instead a holistic reality? In the latter case, the building comes closer to a living organism. Of course, this assumption goes against the grain of all modern thinking. Descartes had already announced that even animals are mere machines, so how can a building be alive? We recognize that the choice of the dead/alive whale in *Werckmeister Harmonies* is not random at all but should be understood as a conceptual organic metaphor. Is architecture merely a mathematical science, or is it possible to conceive something like living architecture?

Musical Paradoxes

In *Werckmeister Harmonies*, Krasznahorkai chooses music because, more than any other art, it offers the clearest insights into these problems because, contrary to architecture, the musical system follows relatively simple mathematical principles. If one goes up seven octaves from an A (an octave defined as an interval that always doubles the frequency of the preceding note, thus $A3 = 220$ Hz, $A4 = 440$ Hz, $A5 = 880$ Hz, etc.), one should end up on exactly the note that the human ear identifies as a higher C. The problem is that one doesn't. After seven octaves, the note we land on will be a quarter of a semitone off if measured mathematically (the difference is called the Pythagorean comma). Is this an imperfection of the human ear, of mathematics, or of nature? The organicist will say it is an imperfection of mathematics. Ratios that appear to exist in nature do not necessarily overlap with mathematical order, which makes the organicist say that nature has its own laws. Natural laws hold the individual intervals together inside a harmonic system that might be irrational from a mathematical point of view but still must be accepted. This, at least, is the organic standpoint.

In music, the problem is intellectually intriguing to the point that several generations of thinkers and piano tuners have tried to solve it in their own ways. One approach suggests that because the keyboard of a piano is based on mathematical divisions, the natural order should be adapted to the mathematical one. This was Werckmeister's task. In the context of his seventeenth-century culture, Werckmeister did not see his duty as a merely technical or even scientific one but instead gave it theological or "cosmic" dimensions. Once math and music are enabled to overlap, music will be led to divine perfection, that is, to a truly universal order. Werckmeister believed to have achieved this task. The problem is that what he believed to be cosmic does not really deserve this predicate but rather looks—from Eszter's point of view—like a scientifically established universality. It might be perfect, but is perfection perfect?

Musical Theology

In his posthumously published work *Musikalische Paradoxal-Discourse* (1707), Werckmeister explains that his decisions were influenced by religious considerations drawn from "natural theology" (Felbick 2012: 115). Natural theology, which was current in early modernity, derives knowledge about the existence of God not from the supernatural realm through revelation but from nature. This is precisely what Valuska is doing when he interprets the whale exposed in the marketplace as a manifestation of "how great is the Lord's creative impulse and power, and how omnipotence is reflected in that animal." Since God has created the world, science *must* find God by looking at nature.

Natural theology is not limited to early modernity but has a much longer history. It can be traced to Plato, was popular during scholasticism, and has had Thomas Aquinas and Isaac Newton as its adherents.

Werckmeister also believed God can be revealed not only through the Holy Scripture but also through nature ([1707] 2007: 6), and he sought evidence for this in music. The fusion of natural theology with musical theory resulted in not natural theology but "musical theology" (*musica theologia*). For musical theology, music must reflect the realm of God. Why? Because its laws overlap with mathematical calculations. In other words, through its mathematical coherence, music becomes proof of God. Some decades after Werckmeister's death, the German philosopher Lorenz Christoph Mizler (1736) continued musical theology. Mizler was influenced by not only Werckmeister but also the German Enlightenment philosopher Christian Wolff (1679–1754), a foremost representative of natural theology.

The link between musical theology and the Enlightenment tradition shows that the tendencies described above to emphasize connections between math, music, and theology must be considered universalist. The searchers of universal harmony might have pretended to have cosmological aspirations, but in reality they were looking for universal mathematical rules. And once the mathematical ratios were established, they had to be reflected by the stars. If music reflects the realm of God, it must also reflect the entire universe, because everything created by God *must* obey the same mathematical rules. Is it possible that one plus one is two on Earth but in the heavens it adds up to three? If we want real harmony, we must describe the cosmos in terms of math; of course, this is a universalist approach, not a cosmological one. Eszter would say that here math has been imposed on the cosmos.

Is it really possible that in another solar system one plus one is three? Neither Werckmeister nor Eszter would affirm this, which makes this problem extremely complex. Chapter 10 will address the astrophysical implications of the Werckmeister problem. Now, it is only necessary to elucidate a few more facts about music. Though, superficially speaking, all of the above points on musical theology seem to be in perfect agreement with Eszter's ambitions, the more so since some of his own ruminations (see the quotation below) often sound truly (and confusingly) Werckmeisterian, in the end, Eszter *disagrees* with Werckmeister, and for one particular reason. For Eszter, the idea of joining math and nature simply by letting them meet—so to speak—in the middle is not a solution but a simplification. The bone of contention is that Werckmeister joined music to math and not the other way around. He should have joined math to music because music is more "natural" than math. Eszter is not irrational. He *does* believe in math, but he dreams of becoming a sort of "inverted Werckmeister" able to establish in music a natural principle that simply *is* compatible with math. Once he can establish "a whole series of so-called periodic waves," he hopes to be able to express them

> in terms of relations between whole numbers; then went on to examine the essential conditions under which two sounds existed in harmonious relationship with each other, and established that "pleasure," or the musical equivalent of such a sensation, was occasioned when the two above-mentioned sounds or tomes produced the maximum number of harmonics and when the fewest of these were within critical proximity of each other; all this so he should be able, without the least tinge of doubt, to identify the concept of musical order. (Krasznahorkai 1998: 114)

The project sounds truly fascinating. The problem is that Eszter seems unaware of one important fact: the music he is looking for is so ideal that it cannot exist in reality. On a scale on which all octaves have a frequency ratio of 2:1 and all fifths have a frequency ratio of 3:2, it would mathematically follow that major thirds have a frequency ratio of 5:4 and so on. However, such an ideal tuning is impossible in practice. Eszter forgets that, by definition, tuning is a matter of pragmatism, not of spiritual elevation. The primary purpose of tuning is to find pragmatic solutions to practical problems. We tune instruments because we want to play music. Eszter does not seem to understand this.

Eszter's search for purity is reminiscent of the geometric-abstract suprematist painter Kazimir Malevich, who designed the *Black Square* as an expression of nothingness in the sense of a disintegration of Aristotle's divine Logos. Similar to what Eszter is looking for in music, Malevich thought the *Black Square* had given him access to a vision of the pure materiality, that is, to nature itself (see Groys 1992: 71; Petrova 2003: 3). Through its nonobjective purity, the *Black Square* was supposed to represent the absolutely divine. In the end, for this avant-garde artist working at the time of Stalinism, like for Eszter, the purity of artistic feeling became a religion. Eszter also shares these characteristics with Russian avant-garde artists who—at least at some point in history—sincerely believed they were initiating a new age of cosmic regeneration.

Despite all the obstacles these logical paradoxes produce, Eszter continues looking for "real" music, as opposed to music that math has calculated and distorted. His approach remains unconvincing. What would be "real" about this music? Why would this music be more "real" than Werckmeister's? Should we instead say that everything Eszter is doing remains based on just some other kind of fiction (similar to that of "mathematical music") and *not* on reality, simply because the kind of music he is looking for does not and cannot exist? What does "reality" mean in this context anyway? Suppose after years of fine-tuning, Eszter can unite music and math in a way that they will meet not just "in the middle" through Werckmeisterian manipulations and compromises but that music and math will meet because a "real" music that *is* compatible with math has been found. But how "real" would this be? How can anybody be sure this is real music (and real math) and not something else? How can anybody be sure this is the "thing itself" and not a simulacrum? Eszter refuses to see this problem. He wants to find real music, and then, most "naturally," this music will also overlap with math. Eszter's approach is extremely idealistic, more idealistic than that of Werckmeister; of Eszter's ex-wife, Tünde; and of the Prince. Eszter is pursuing a dream of perfection that simply cannot exist in the real world. His is similar to other major dreams of thinkers in the history of philosophy: the dream of the perfect overlap of nature and civilization, of morals and technology, or of our desires with the limits of our desires. These concepts are fascinating, but they can exist only as theoretical constructions. Accordingly, Lukács has described this attitude of "abstract idealism" in a way that fits Eszter very well:

> It is the mentality which chooses the direct, straight path toward the realization of the ideal; which, dazzled by the demon, forgets the existence of any distance between ideal and idea, between psyche and soul; which, with the most authentic and unshakeable faith, concludes that the idea, because it should be, necessarily must be, and, because reality does not satisfy this a priori demand, thinks that reality is bewitched by evil demons. ([1920] 1971: 96)

Krasznahorkai's "Grammatical Realism"

Krasznahorkai's own aversion to what James Wood has called "grammatical realism" (2012: 280) duplicates Eszter's opposition to mathematical rules. As mentioned in the case of the imaginary mathematician Sir Wilford Stanley Gilmore from Északról hegy, Wilford attempts to prove the reality character of math by inviting readers to read large numbers aloud. He believed the "linguistic reality" of numbers could make those numbers "real," as opposed to the abstract unreality of signs. People who believe in the abstract unreality of signs are bound to make gross mistakes about reality. For example, by seeing math as an accumulation of signs, they will create the illusory concept of infinity.

The pattern of "linguistic reality versus reality of signs" continues into Krasznahorkai's own writings. Similar to Sir Wilford, Krasznahorkai insists that the reality of language (or any reality for that matter) cannot be grasped with the help of abstract grammatical rules. We have seen that this is in perfect accordance with Eszter's ambitions, but it is also in accordance with Krasznahorkai's own aesthetic approach. According to Wood, Krasznahorkai is "at odds with grammatical realism, whereby the real is made to fall into approved units and packets. This grammatical antirealism is not necessarily hostile to the real; in fact, all of these writers, according to Wood,[4] could be called "realist, of a kind" (2012: 280). The same can be said about Eszter and Sir Wilford. In the case of Krasznahorkai, the full stop and the comma are declared artificial conventions, distorting "real language" in the same way temperate tuning distorts real music, while real language should evolve organically, slowly, and phrase by phrase.

There is only one problem with the appellation "attitude grammatical *anti*realism." Why should this attitude be called such when language is supposed to grasp reality as it really is? Should it not be called "antigrammatical realism," following Eszter's guidelines postulating "the unique realization of *non*-music" as an example of music that is "*more* real"? In fact, Krasznahorkai's reality is not "anti-real" in the sense of being nonsensical like the reality of absurd literature. Krasznahorkai never challenges "regular" language by fracturing his narratives' verbal communication. His works are very different from that of classical absurd art in which, according to Lilla Töke, "the illogical, the nonsensical, and the ungrammatical are symptoms of an overall distrust toward the 'fossilized debris of dead language'" (2011: 104, partially quoting from Martin Esslin's 2001 book on absurd theater). Krasznahorkai is never absurd in this sense because a strong sense of an organic coherence subsists in his antigrammatical realism. Organicists rarely have mere absurdity on their agenda. The Hungarian champion of realist aesthetics, Lukács, even declared to not like absurd art because it "does not provide a comforting feeling of organic unity" (Töke 2011: 104). Krasznahorkai follows this Hungarian organic tradition by producing an antigrammatical, organic flow of language whose aim is not to make his text arbitrarily absurd but to make it more "real."

Antigrammatical Realism and Neorealism

A parallel can also be drawn between Krasznahorkai's antigrammatical realism and André Bazin's neorealism. Similar to Krasznahorkai, Bazin held that our imagination should always be fed "by a reality that it will soon replace" and that "the fable is born of the experience that it is supposed to transcend" (2005 1: 47). This, as well as Eszter's curious mixture of idealism and realism (finding the real in the realm of the ideal), comes close to the kind of antirealist realism Wood suggests when analyzing Krasznahorkai. In cinema, so Bazin thought, reality is "found" the moment it is overcome. Eszter's ideas about the reality character of music follow a similar pattern.[5] The scope of the "reality problem" Eszter discovers is large and covers aesthetics, science, and politics.

For centuries, European artists copied reality more and more perfectly because they believed nature to be an organic expression of the whole that is, most importantly, of God. The artist able to imitate this reality of nature most perfectly was believed to have divine gifts. In the modern age, the intrusion of technology into art has caused dramatic changes, most obviously in music, architecture, and the pictorial arts (in the latter through cinema and photography). As a result, the authority of a godlike nature/reality had to be revised (this task became extremely urgent because God also appeared to have been murdered). Bazin's focus on the (often paradoxical) interplay of idealism and realism must be understood in this context. The same is true for the "socialist realism" discussions of the Russian avant-garde. Finally, relationship between idealism and realism is also relevant for the above Werckmeister discussion and Eszter's idealistic ambition to find real music in the unique sense of natural music.

Romanticism

Eszter still takes up another fight, one that the German romantics fought two hundred years earlier against Immanuel Kant's skepticism toward the existence of a priori elements in the real world. As mentioned in chapter 3, Kant did not believe in a priori elements existing in the real world but instead thought that these elements are simply "put into it" by the human mind. For Kant, nature itself was not more than "blind material." What nature really *is* can only be understood by the intellect (*Verstand*). Only the intellect (which is, of course, constantly subject to critical self-examination) will let nature appear "as nature." In the preface to the second edition of *Critique of Pure Reason,* Kant characterizes the method of previous scientists who once examined nature and believed it really exists. These scientists had to change their attitude: "A light broke upon all students of nature. They learned that reason has insight only into that which it produces after a plan of its own, and that it must not allow itself to be kept, as it were, in nature's leading-strings, but must itself show the way with principles of judgment based upon fixed laws, constraining nature to give answer to questions of reason's own determining" (1929: 20; 1781: 23).

The atomic character of nature that leaves the "real world" divided into the tiniest elements (though the intellect can still reconstruct it) is what post-Kantian philosophers like F.W.J Schelling strove to call into question. They thought that nature *itself* should be coherent. A hundred years before Kant, Werckmeister had been doing to music what Kant's scientist did to nature: he divided music "artificially" into tones based on the piano's keyboard (and thus on math). And unlike Schelling and Eszter, Werckmeister did not see this as a problem. For him, the temperate system was not artificial but merely natural, which is why he believed he could establish an organic harmony between music and math, between science and the universe, and between humans and God.

The Circle Closes

Eszter the idealist wants to find "real music." The inspirational source of this peculiar approach ("the last straw") is a piano tuner going by the Hungarian-German name Frachberger, who is even quirkier than Eszter. Eszter's organic universe is supposed to be based on truth, not on a lame compromise between music and math à la Werckmeister. However, is there really such a big difference between the two? Unfortunately, the answer is no, which plunges Eszter into an enduring existential crisis. According to Eszter, Werckmeister's system has made us entirely deaf to the organic order of music that is so much more magnificent than the artificial one. He believes Werckmeister never solved the main problem: even in temperate tuning, math continues to produce subdivisions that mean nothing in the real world (in nature). According to Eszter, Werckmeister's approach remains based on the pretentiousness and "unhinged arrogance" of science that pretends to know the world but, in reality, constructs the world according to its own rules. By basing science on nature (that is, math on music), Eszter hopes to reinstall "the most wonderful harmonies and most sublime mutual vibrations" (Krasznahorkai 1998: 114). We understand perfectly well why he directs those reproaches against Werckmeister. The problem is that Eszter himself sounds so amazingly Werckmeisterian that some critics (James Wood, for example) could believe he simply wants to reestablish

Werckmeister's old system. Of course, the line dividing both projects is thin, a fact that is the main topic of the book, as well as Eszter's personal problem. Even if he had succeeded, would he not "merely" have inverted Werckmeister instead of deconstructing him? Would he not have continued his old system by other means?

In any case, Eszter does not bring his plan to the end, probably because he realizes his approach is still more or less equivalent to the Werckmeister project. Basing music on math or math on music—what's the difference? The circle closes. At the end of the novel's "Werckmeister Harmonies" section (as well as at the end of the film) and after many struggles, Eszter abandons his organicist ambitions and tunes the piano back to the temperate mode. In both the book and the film, this decision comes rather surprisingly. For the longest part of the text, we do not even know what kind of tuning Eszter actually chose for his piano in the first place. In the middle of the "Werckmeister" section of *The Melancholy of Resistance,* Eszter lauds both Pythagoras and Aristoxenus, who were living in "ages more fortunate than ours" (117) and relates "the brilliant insight of Aristoxenus, who trusted the genuine musicanship and instinctive inventiveness of the ancient player and relied entirely on the ear" (114). Only on the last page of the section do we learn that Eszter had effectively tuned his piano to Aristoxenus's system "a few years earlier" (282) and that he is now going to tune it back to the Werckmeister system. Eszter seems to understand that pure organicism is not possible and that we *do* need a compromise. Resulting minor dissonances (especially of major and minor thirds) must be accepted. Furthermore, the pure and mathematical keyboard can now be perceived as "consoling" (282). The idealist metaphysician turns into a pragmatist, even though only a halfhearted one. The "Werckmeister Harmonies" section in *The Melancholy* is thus suitably subtitled "Negotiations."

However, like all negotiations, this one does not lead to perfect results. A compromise has been reached and a "negotiated" center accepted, but the rejection of an "ideal organicism" in which elements overlap simply because they are the same in reality comes with a dear cost. In the end, Valuska, the person able to see most clearly through the nothingness of both Eszter's and the Prince's projects, is sacrificed in a Dostoevskian manner. Why? Because life can obviously go on only without him. Valuska was the only person who would stick to some general, pantheist belief but who also, paradoxically, would never believe in anything particular, not even in Tünde's pragmatism. He followed Tünde's instructions only hesitatingly. He, not the Prince, knows the whole truth just because he knows nothing. An eternal "in-betweener," Valuska does not even take the concept of infinity, by which he is so fascinated, for what it really is, but instead reconfigures it through a compromise: at the beginning of the opening scene in *Werckmeister Harmonies,* he asks the villagers to "step with me into the boundlessness where constancy, quietude and peace and infinite emptiness reign." This means infinity is not an abstract concept for Valuska (as it is for Cantor and Sir Wilford) but rather a concrete experience he attempts to stage with the villagers: "And just imagine that in this infinite sonorous silence everywhere is an impenetrable darkness."

After the "negotiations"—which clearly reestablish the center of the world, nature, and authority—people like Valuska will be declared persona non grata. The new regime interns him in the local mental asylum for his beliefs, or rather for his nonbeliefs. He cannot be accused of having actively offered resistance. He has probably been put on the black list Tünde established. The film actually states this as a fact, while the book points out that the immediate danger comes not from Tünde's regime but from the soldiers who might take revenge on Valuska (243). Of course, his complicity with the Prince is an invention. His only mistake was being in the wrong place at the wrong time. In other words, he had been undecided for too long. Valuska's internment should be read as a paradox coming close to a sacrifice. Paradoxically, though Valuska is the most innocent person in the entire narrative, he must be sacrificed. This sacrifice makes it possible for all other characters to continue their lives in a realm that contains no absolute truth but which is not entirely ruleless either. On the other hand, Valuska has been driven crazy by a world in which too many people insisted on knowing the absolute truth and where even relativism as a refuge was no longer permitted.

From now on, all people will live under the mild tyranny of Tünde's matriarchism and the rocambolesque aggressiveness of her all-too-human police chief lover. Tünde's existence symbolizes real pragmatism, which Krasznahorkai manages to stylize into a caricature. By default, the caricature of pragmatism is always Machiavellianism: if law-enforced order can stop the Stalinist Prince, then that's the way to go. Who cares about the "cosmic" rules of organic harmony? Who cares about the stars? Property is confiscated, and social organizations named "Tidy Yard" and "Orderly House" (306) are created. Eszter does not sympathize with this, but he has no choice.

Relativism and Pragmatism

The constellation opposing the pragmatist Tünde to the organicist Eszter needs to be analyzed more closely. In general, pragmatists are not organicists, not because they tend to be universalists but because there is simply no need for them to know the relation between the individual and the whole. Most pragmatists are pluralists, which is why William James took care to combat any holistic concept of cognition: "I left off by asserting my own belief that a pluralistic and incompletely integrated universe, describable only by the free use of the word 'some,' is a legitimate hypothesis" (2008: 46). James does not opt for an organically integrated universalism, because this organic model would be antipluralist.[6] Tünde embodies that kind of pragmatism. Why does the only important woman in *Werckmeister Harmonies* show such pragmatic tendencies? We can speculate. Tünde is willing to accept "anything" as long as it makes sense in the way of a pragmatic paradigm compatible with order and cleanliness. Her power is not that of masculine, pistol-swinging strength but rather the soft power of a female type, and she also cunningly uses other people's power for her own interests.

According to Richard Rorty, pragmatist pluralists tend to be content with patchworks and will denounce any striving for final vocabularies as metaphysical aberrations. As explained in chapter 5, Rorty sees the organicist as a "liberal metaphysician" who "wants a final vocabulary with an internal organic structure, one which is not split down in the middle by a public-private distinction, not just a patchwork" (1989: 92). Pragmatists are happy with patchworks as long as they "make sense," and what makes sense will be decided on the spot. Tünde has decided order and cleanliness make the most sense right now. The problem with her pragmatism is that it seems to work too much for her own benefit and is probably not pluralist enough.

Valuska, however, embodies wise and enlightened relativism, or perhaps he embodies the somehow indistinct and superficial harmony seeker described more closely below. In fact, his position is not entirely clear. He has some pantheistic beliefs (which make him a visionary), but they are not strong enough to turn him into a really religious person. Krasznahorkai writes, "he had no sense of proportion and was entirely lacking the compulsive drive to reason" (1998: 80). Unlike Andrei Tarkovsky's *Stalker* (1970), Valuska's actions are not motivated by any belief. He is even so undecided that he cannot proceed to real actions. At the end, Valuska has lost everything, but maybe he is the winner. Did he not convince Eszter that relativism is the only viable position? Eszter's last words when leaving the asylum are "nothing counts, nothing counts," repeated many times like an echo. Is Eszter trying to find absolute harmony in absolute relativism?

As pointed out at the beginning of this book, the confrontation of universalism and relativism in today's world has become an important issue. Valuska's peculiar interest in the stars shows that he (just like Eszter) is looking for cosmic harmony. However, unlike Eszter and Werckmeister, Valuska sees this cosmic truth as being contained in relativism. Perfect harmony is achieved when everybody has the right to claim to be right at least in some way; the world is probably most harmonious when nobody is entirely wrong. Are democracy and egalitarianism the ultimate principles of harmony? To nail down Krasznahorkai to such clear assertions would be simplistic. In any case, Valuska is the opposite of the Prince. While the Prince believes there is no truth, Valuska believes everything is true. That's why he is everybody's friend and, at the same time, almost everybody's enemy. Even his relationship with Eszter is not entirely unequivocal. Valuska's interest in infinity must clash with Eszter's philosophy, which does not admit the existence of abstract concepts that can only be grasped by math. Or think of Sir Wilford's (Eszter's double in Északról hegy) aversion toward infinity.

However, in the end, Valuska's position is unsustainable. Other characters adopt similar positions in other Krasznahorkai novels, and they all must be sacrificed. There is Estike (Erika Bók) in *Satantango* and Korin, the hero from Krasznahorkai's *War and War*. Krasznahorkai explains in an interview: "These are the very important figures who allow us to be in the world, this kind of people who are sacrificed, who are victims of this world. They are the price we pay for the possibility to live with compromises in the world" (Cardenas 2013).

One other option has not yet been considered: the possibility that Valuska is right simply because, empirically speaking, there really is no absolute truth—only many relative truths. This interesting line of thought deserves to be examined more closely. Stalin, Eszter, Werckmeister, and the Prince are all looking for an absolute truth. The Prince might be different because he is looking for an absolute nontruth, but in the end, even this is the same. At the same time, everybody is looking for harmony. At the other end of the spectrum is the relativist, but he is also looking for harmony. In this sense, Valuska's harmony-seeking relativism might come closer to the superficial philosophy that Allan Bloom has so famously characterized as the ideology of the "Nietzschean left." While "Nietzsche sought with his value philosophy to restore the harsh conflicts for which men were willing to die, to restore the tragic sense of life at a moment when nature had been domesticated and men become tame," Nietzsche's "value philosophy was used in America for exactly the opposite purpose—to promote conflict-resolution, bargaining, harmony" (1987: 228). Harmony is indeed perfect when all distinctions between good and bad have been erased. However, in the end, the "Nietzschean left" project does not work out for Valuska because programs that are more pragmatic prevail.

Does this disqualify relativism completely? Not really, at least not in music. The reality might indeed be that *everything* is simultaneously true. Recent experiments with music have shown that most humans are prone to adapt to any tuning they are exposed to over a longer period, as long as the tuning is not completely false. Afterward, they find the just intonation "weird" (see Ohio State University, School of Music n.d.). What does this tell us about Aristoxenus's "natural tuning"? None of the aforementioned men—except perhaps Valuska—would sympathize with this kind of relativism. There must be *some* kind of truth (or nontruth) in music and in the world. The idea that the public is ready to accept anything it is accustomed to as "true" remains unbearable for most serious searchers of truth. These people are degenerate, that is, they are alienated from nature. One person, however, would contradict: the pragmatist. Could the musical experiments made at Ohio State University not simply show that humans are pragmatic by nature?

The positions of the different Krasznahorkai characters can be limited to the types presented in this chapter. Apart from Tünde, nobody is really "conservative" in a political or cultural way. Neither Eszter nor anybody else in the film strives for fixed identities, steady locations, and binding moral ties. Valuska is constantly moving around, and the Prince is living in a trailer. What all have in common is that they want harmony, which is even true for the Prince. Another common trait is that nobody dares to engage in a utopian project. The Prince is delirious and outlandish, but he makes no utopian suggestions that could be linked to Stalinist ideas and Russian futurism. Here, it becomes particularly clear that Central and Eastern Europe is the exact contrary of North America: it is the territory of failed utopianisms. Therefore, the only options worthy of discussion are organicism, pragmatism, relativism, and deconstruction, and in an atmosphere of failed utopianisms, all of them will be wrapped in melancholy.

Notes

1. I cannot reproduce here the whole sentence, as it runs up to 1,339 words.

2. The sentence can be found in *Briefe II* (Benjamin 1978: 741–42), though Rollet attributes this passage to Benjamin's "Paris, Capital of the Nineteenth Century" (French edition by Cerf 1989, p. 137).
3. I thank Deodath Zuh for pointing this out to me.
4. Wood names, among others, representatives of experimental fiction since the 1950s like Claude Simon, Thomas Bernhard, José Saramago, W. G. Sebald, and David Foster Wallace.
5. In fact, both Bazin and Eszter have been called idealists. Walter Curt Behrendt, in his book *Modern Building: Its Nature, Problems and Forms* (1937) — lengthily analyzed by Bruno Zevi — calls organic architecture "realist" and inorganic architecture "idealist" (in Zevi 1950: 67). The idea is that the former is natural and the latter is producing style.
6. I am aware that not all pragmatists sound as anti-organic as James and Rorty. John Dewey was actually looking for an organic unity in art, as will be shown later in this chapter.

CHAPTER 8

Back to Humanism?

During all of the reflections on the organic character of music that have been presented, architecture has remained on the horizon. Clearly, architecture and music are particularly close because of the love–hate relationship they both entertain with math. They turn out to be even closer when both are examined from the angle of harmony. Aristoxenus's musicological conundrum concerning mathematical ratios that cannot overlap with an organic whole based on human sense perception is precisely the conundrum Frank Lloyd Wright recognized in the realm of architecture when concluding, "it is the first principle of growth that the thing grown be no mere aggregation" (1941: 185). In other words, math cannot sum up the logic of nature.

Still, Eszter has not given up the hope of harmonizing both. Is it possible? At this point, Eszter's reflections enter into conflict with Enlightenment thought but even more with the intellectual heritage of the Renaissance. The clash with Renaissance thought could be expected, given that the basis of Eszter's philosophy is organic and that modern organicism has often considered Renaissance geometrism and rationalism as prime enemies. Bruno Zevi, for example, opposes the organic striving for free expression emergent in Gothic architecture to the Renaissance's geometrical culture because the latter was not free but functioning through "arranged, predetermined canons" (1950: 67). Although, as Zevi admits, such oppositions can lead to gross simplifications, the philosophy of the organic does not only go against the grain of a certain form of rationality issued by eighteenth-century Enlightenment thinkers known for their worship of reason and their naïve optimism. The philosophy of the organic also finds fault with a rational movement preceding the age of Enlightenment that revolved around the idea of harmony inherent in Renaissance philosophy and art, but not the harmony Eszter—and with him, Goethe and a whole string of nineteenth-century philosophers—advocates.

What is wrong with Renaissance harmony? First, it is not as harmonious as it looks. After all, the unitary human ideal became fragmented during the Renaissance. According to Agnes Heller, the awareness of man's own dynamism in a dynamic world that emerged in the Renaissance marks the beginning of modernity. In the Renaissance we find, for the first time, "competing logics, values and norms," and the modern thinker "chooses from among them and makes judgments accordingly" (1982: 104). Eszter, the antihumanist searching for harmony beyond fragmentation is certainly antimodern in this sense. On the other hand, given the Copernican cosmological baggage Eszter is dragging around, Renaissance humanists would have never accepted him because, according to Thomas S. Kuhn, "the work of Copernicus and his astronomical contemporaries belongs squarely in that university tradition which the Humanists most ridiculed" (1957: 126). For humanists, astronomy, which is so important in *Werckmeister Harmonies,* was more of an art than a science. Is astronomy for Eszter an art or a science? As usual, Eszter floats between art and science, just like he floats between music and math.

Leonardo da Vinci's drawing of the *Vitruvian Man* is based on the rational principles laid down by Vitruvius in book 3 of *De architectura (Ten Books on Architecture)*. Notes on Vitruvius's work accompany the drawing. From Eszter's point of view, both Leonardo and Vitruvius are on the other side of the organic spectrum because the overlap of math and natural harmony is for them not a problem but a solution. Leonardo believed math could be the arbiter of beauty, which is precisely what Eszter is fighting against. When Vitruvius described architecture as a harmonic and naturally proportioned organism, he drew on not only the abstract formulas of geometry but also nature, that is, on the human body. A hundred years before Werckmeister and a hundred fifty years before the Enlightenment, Leonardo could spell out the relationship between nature and science/math in relatively simple terms. What could be more perfect than the mathematical rendering of natural proportions in art? The symbolism is clear: a human body had been put into a perfect square and a perfect circle. Eszter's response would be: yes, it's perfect, but is perfection perfect? Even Werckmeister, operating at the end of the Enlightenment, can no longer take those Vitruvian equations for granted. However, *he* will engineer a "perfect" theoretical framework for music that permits nature and math to overlap through "negotiations." Eszter, like any real organicist, abhors those negotiations.

Strictly speaking, Vitruvius's views of the human body are not that unusual. Since ancient times, the human body has been a model for architectural proportions. The golden section or the golden ratio represented a holistic principle, making this thought clearly organic. The problem is that in the Renaissance, the golden ratio developed into an analytical tool. At the end of the Roman Empire, proportion had entirely lost its divine, cosmic significance and was reduced to a purely technical phenomenon. Only Byzantine culture maintained some of the mystique and spirituality of the golden ratio in the context of a Christian tradition. Thus, for Hugo Häring, Leonardo's "golden ratio is like a musical scale," which means it is nothing but an empty rational system or a "frame on which to work—the music has still to be written" (Blundell Jones 1999: 89).

Leonardo draws the Vitruvian man as a rational animal endowed with language, which does not signify much in terms of this man's individual culture. For Häring, who fought (in an almost "Eszterian" style) throughout his lifetime against Latin and Greek influences in modern architecture and their "degenerated extension at the hands of humanists" (139), humanism is just as obnoxious as it is for Eszter. The rigid standards of perfection expressed by the Vitruvian man (who is also called *homo quadratus*) have brought about typical Enlightenment ideals such as individualism, autonomy, and self-determination. While some of those ideals are still worshipped today, others have been contested by postwar philosophy after World War II. Three hundred years after the Enlightenment, criticism of Vitruvian harmonies has become more powerful than ever. Humanist ideas have been almost totally rejected by the most recent postmodern philosophies.

In general, humanism has had a bad reputation among philosophers in the later twentieth century. Most "progressive" postwar philosophy perceives humanist thought as a prime example of a universalism in need of deconstruction (see Lyotard 1991). An important point inscribed into the postmodern and posthuman agenda is the conviction that the binary opposition of nature and culture needs to be deconstructed. Here, organicism and postmodernism tread common ground. Organic architecture shares this deconstructive spirit at least partly, as it is fighting Vitruvian academic classism with its formal, rational planning attitude relying mainly on symmetry and axes. In this sense, organic thought is antimodern and perhaps even postmodern to some extent.

Despite all this, Eszter is no postmodern man. At first sight, his explicit outbursts against "Platonism" and the metaphysical tradition sparked by this rationalist way of thinking (outbursts he shares with Sir Wilford in *Északról hegy*) might look like classical postmodern statements. However, in the end, Eszter's torturous reasoning remains incompatible with postmodernism. In postmodern contexts, this obstinate search for organic harmony definitely has no place. True, like postmodern philosophers, Eszter believes the "natural" harmony suggested by Leonardo's drawing is merely a cultural construct. Why should this "white male" represent the principle of universal harmony? Humanism wants the harmony it calls "natural" to be universal, which postwar postmodern philosophy—just like Eszter—perceives as an inacceptable authoritarianism. Still, Eszter is no postmodernist but a modern organicist critic of modernism. There is no way to relate Eszter's cosmic aspirations to the fragmented contemporary network culture marked by multilingualism and cultural diversity. Eszter would look out of place in any poststructuralist, post-Marxist landscape. He is similar to the elderly Johan in Ingmar Bergman's last film, *Saraband* (2003), who isolates himself in his country cottage and delves into classical music as if it were a source of ultimate truth (though, different from what happens in *Saraband*, Eszter's quirkiness does not lead to dramatic ego trips and explosive family disasters).

In any case, this aging scholar locked in his Central European village will never be a defender of a world of "postmodern d's": deconstruction, decolonization, decentralization, desexualization, and so on. His worldview comes too close to Goetheian and anthroposophical thought holding that art is not subjective or illusory but that the artist should reproduce laws hidden in the "depth of nature," a nature equated to the expression of a cosmic world spirit (see R. Steiner 1883: 11). Nothing can be more opposed to postmodern culture. Therefore, Eszter's position is rather that of a humanist in the sense of the "humanities" as they once were—and sometimes still are—practiced in universities, which are distinguished by being inefficient in the modern sense, narcissistic, old-fashioned, and out of touch with contemporary technology. Some readers and spectators might associate this brand of humanism even with "Eastern European culture," which had not only free health care and education but also a high amount of lending libraries full of classics and "good" literature. Eszter represents a modernism with humanist (perhaps nineteenth-century) roots. It is a culture Gáspár Miklós Tamás has described like this: "Everywhere in the Soviet bloc there existed a strange combination of high modernism and—looked at from today, or from the West—an incredible and tradition-laden cult of Letters, of the Arts, of Science and Philosophy.... Hundreds of scholars worked on translations. These were extremely bookish nations" (2013: 11).

Though Eszter's aim is definitely not to destroy as many binary dichotomies as possible, he still does share one important feature with poststructuralism. He is convinced at least one binary opposition needs to be deconstructed: the rigid opposition of the particular and the universal. In this sense, Eszter's curious musical ambitions represent a truly deconstructive project. And the deconstruction of the particular and universal can only happen based on the dualism that distinguishes the particular *from* the universal. From both an organic and a deconstructive point of view, humanism is wrong because humanism is always either universal or particular (often deriving one from the other). The clash of different "universal" values by which our present époque is marked (see the introduction) is thus a heritage of humanism. Humanism produces ethnic pride and nationalism and has often attempted to universalize those arbitrarily established particular values. In this sense, "McDonaldization" is a consequence of humanism just as much as Stalin's undoing. What can be more "humanist" than claiming, as Stalin did, that reality is Caucasian and authentic? In fact, Stalin's new "Soviet individual" was once defined in terms of a "superhuman, transcendent, transhistorical new humanism" (Groys 1992: 50; see chapter 9).

Organicism and Deconstruction

Similar to poststructuralists, Eszter claims that individualism is not an intrinsic part of human nature but merely a historical and cultural construct. Purely individualist, creative expressions should never be the highest aim of music. In this sense, Eszter is the contrary of a humanist. However, instead of heading straight toward a world of "postmodern d's," Eszter's "deconstruction" of humanist universalism leads to an organic world in which individual elements are "cosmically" justified.

Here, his position becomes that of a critical modernist. The moderns tended to neglect the cosmic order. Hans Blumenberg has shown in *The Legitimacy of the Modern Age* that since the seventeenth century, humans have been preoccupied with security, survival, and the acquisition of all kinds of means but are generally unwilling to rely on a cosmic order, providence, or a promised salvation in the next world (1983: 3–15). Therefore, in Eszter's opinion, the moderns need to be criticized. Eszter's cosmic ambitions are—at least to some extent (see chapter 10)—incompatible with modern thought and even more so with poststructuralist, deconstructive thought. For Eszter, reality (real music) and truth *do* exist, not in the form of arbitrary cultural, mathematical, and humanist constructions but rather cosmically or "in reality." Despite his apparent skepticism toward almost everything, Eszter remains a realist since he believes in only one reality that is, in principle, independent of human communication. This reality has a cosmic validity. Therefore, Eszter is neither a constructivist nor a deconstructivist. Both constructivists and deconstructivists deny the existence of independent realities, while reality *does* exist for Eszter: leaving the Vitruvian framework supported by math does not mean everything has now become merely relational and relative.

In film theory, Eszter's approach can be likened to neorealism, which attempted—for the first time—to grasp reality "out there" by moving out of the studio, restricting the script, and being spontaneous. This purely modern (not postmodern) approach attempts to "reveal" reality in the form of the artistic expression it already is. This vision of realism is that of André Bazin and is well known in cinema theory. However, seen from a modern (perhaps Western European) point of view, Eszter is an odd case the moment we evaluate him as a philosopher. Like poststructuralists, he denies the validity of centralized, geometrical universalisms of which the scientifically minded Renaissance thought remains the symbol. He opposes the self-centered attitude that makes "man" the sine qua non of the entire world, enabling him (often with the help of math) to universalize these individual standards in the name of "nature." Eszter also shares with postmodern thinkers a general skepticism toward the equation of "naturalness" with "obviousness" and does not believe scientific analysis can make everything transparent. As a result, he opposes all reifications of culture.

However, while the poststructuralist and postmodernist critique of nature highlights the local, temporal, and individual context specificity of truth, Eszter wants "reality" or, to choose a word from the metaphysical tradition, immanence. This immanence represents a self-sufficient "natural logic" absent in the form of empirical facts or abstract rules. Still, it is not merely individual. In other words, it is not universal but cosmic. Apart from that, this immanence is a reality best discovered by means of contemplation. Immanence as it is used in the Western philosophical and theological tradition will be explained later in this chapter by contrasting it with transcendence.

What is Eszter? He does not favor positive, scientifically proven universal rules either. The answer: Eszter is an organicist. He wants a "cosmically" justified kind of authenticity and reality, which seems to be a big task if understood as a philosophical project but in concrete terms the task is rather straightforward. All Eszter wants is authenticity in the form of old-fashioned core qualities like embodiment, sexuality, affectivity, empathy, and desire, none of which are products of deconstructive activities. Moreover, none seem sustainable within a complex, liquid web of global social relations where identity permanently shifts toward difference. Still, Eszter wants to inscribe those core qualities in an organic spatial context where they can simply "make sense," which basically means they are supported by the unity of space and time as governing principles.

What does Eszter disapprove about the modern age more precisely? Eszter is frustrated with a world in which digital photos are "perfect" to the point of being boring, with a world in which the piano is so perfectly tuned (think of a digital piano) that we must ask ourselves the absurd question of whether perfection is really perfect. Sometimes Eszter appears as a reincarnation of the Viennese critic Karl Kraus, who wrote in an essay ironically entitled "In These Great Times": "Where all energy has been expended to make life frictionless, nothing remains that still needs such care.... The tyranny of necessity grants its slaves three kinds of freedom: opinion free from spirit, entertainment free from art, and debauchery free from love" (1914: 8). Like Kraus, Eszter speaks out against a world of fake comfort. To play on a temperately tuned piano is certainly more comfortable, but is this superficial comfort not an illusion barring us the way to "real" music? We constantly solve problems in order to maximize pleasure. But is a life without problems really the highest form of pleasure?

All these are reasons why Eszter adheres to the organic—not because he wants to reestablish binary oppositions but because he wants to unite those oppositions within one cosmic framework. This unifying activity is not fed by totalitarian ambitions. Eszter does not want to impose concrete identities on cultural matters and level all ambiguities, contradictions, and discontinuities. Doing so has been the humanist project to which both Eszter and postmodernists are opposed. Furthermore, Eszter favors a multifaceted appearance of music, culture, and human values, but he wants to de-link those human values from universalistic postures. Here, he is in line with a long organicist tradition that has mostly favored ambiguity and paradoxes and has opposed totalitarian concepts of universality but always strove for an "organic whole." The Russian "all-unity," for example, had already attempted to represent an organic "unity in multiplicity" of all beings. Even Gilles Deleuze admits, "the organic representation, it is true, retains its final ambiguity" (1986: 152). While poststructuralism clings to a "difference" that prevents consciousness from reaching meaning, the organicist Eszter is well aware that an eternal gap between ideology and reality will always exist, but he still thinks authenticity, presence, and individuality are possible and can be spelled out philosophically through the concept of organic harmony. In other words, Eszter wants to quit universalism and totalitarianism without succumbing to relativism. Aesthetics and ethics should remain founded on concrete actions endowed with cosmic dimensions. Who is "mystical": the organicist, the humanist, or the poststructuralist? Is not humanism clinging to the constant identification of individual truth with a quasi-mystical universal human nature? And poststructuralism is hypnotized by the negativity of the gap created by difference. Eszter practices none of these techniques. Like organic architects, he merely wants to be certain that an internal force has engendered the whole.

To say Eszter has a process-oriented vision of the subject is also possible. He rejects moral and cognitive universalism but does not abandon the ambition to link the subject to some cosmic meaning. Everything is interrelated but not to the point that social accountability ceases to exist. The spider web might be decentered because no Vitruvian framework can establish its coordinates in a mathematical fashion. At the same time, the spider web is more than merely a relational network connecting the individual to multiple others. It creates collective bonds, as well as a new affective community or polity, which is how the spider web metaphor challenges the traditional equation of subjectivity with rational consciousness.

Derrida's Harmonies

The relationship between deconstructionist poststructuralism and organicism is clearly very complex. Chapter 6 explained that postmodernism's reliance on geometrical form, as well as a certain iconic conception of the image, is responsible for a clash between the postmodern and the organic. However, in the preceding section we saw that, despite this clash, there are parallels between deconstructionist poststructuralism and organicism, and Eszter embodies those parallels. He refuses centralized, geometrical, and "natural" universalisms but does not abandon the search for an organic immanence. This strategy, which has been called "odd" above, can indeed be seen as constituting the deepest layers of not only organic but also some sort of deconstructive thought.

Of course, the detection of organicism in deconstruction is surprising given that postmodernist theory is famous for its fierce attacks against all kinds of organic models. Normally, for the deconstructionist, the organic structure symbolizes systematic Western thought's ambition to establish unity for its own sake. Poststructuralism opposes Aristotelian metaphysics, philosophical ideas exploring the possibility of a unified cosmos, linguistic systems, musical harmonies, and Hegel's idealism. It is even possible to contrast European poststructuralist thought with analytic philosophy on this point, because the latter has very often been striving for some sort of unity, especially in the realm of aesthetics. Richard Shusterman (1989) names the analytic philosophers G. E. Moore, John Dewey, I. A. Richards, Harold Osborne, and Monroe Beardsley, as well as the New Critics, as defenders of organicism. Paul de Man, Michel Foucault, Roland Barthes, Richard Rorty, and Stanley Fish should be named as representatives of the nonorganic, continental camp.

Jacques Derrida is one of the foremost critics of organic thought. However, despite this nonorganic outlook, something makes us doubt whether the deconstructive spirit in Derrida's philosophy has really abandoned any search for "harmony." In his famous text "Structure, Sign, Play," Derrida declares that once the anthropologist has adopted a consistent play perspective, totalization becomes impossible:

> But nontotalization can also be determined in another way: not from the standpoint of the concept of finitude as assigning us to an empirical view [*empiricité*], but from the standpoint of the concept of *freeplay* [*jeu*]. If totalization no longer has any meaning, it is not because the infinity of a field cannot be covered by a finite glance or a finite discourse, but because the nature of the field—that is, language and a finite language—excludes totalization. (1978: 260; 1967: 423)

By using the play metaphor as a deconstructive device, Derrida seems to go against the grain of the entire Aristotelian metaphysical tradition determined by the search for totality. At first sight, nothing can look more nonorganic than Derrida's procedure that has become a principal inspiration for much of deconstructive and postmodern culture. But what about the totality of the game? To conclude that the game metaphor cancels all aspects of the total is premature.

The fallacies of this supposed nonorganicism become obvious in Paul de Man's attacks against organic totalities. De Man claims that semantic richness and a plurality of significations cannot be sustained within any totality. In *Blindness and Insight*, he ridicules New Criticism for reissuing outmoded nineteenth-century organic premises by asking, "Is not this sense of the unity of forms being supported by the large metaphor of the analogy between language and a living organism, a metaphor that shapes a great deal of nineteenth-century poetry and thought?" (1971: 27). De Man's attacks against New Criticism are meant, in the first place, as attempts to move forward beyond formalism, which he sees—in accordance with Derrida—as too organic.[1] However, as Shusterman (1989) also points out in his essay on organicism, why an organic unity should be unable by definition to embrace radical oppositions is not entirely clear. The history of metaphysics actually teaches us that this is very well possible.

Deconstructionists confuse the living organic totality with a monolithic—and often formalist—totalitarian and centralized concept of unity and as a result they see the organic as an entity unable to embrace oppositions. According to Shusterman, the organic totality also comes closer to what Anglo-American aesthetics believes unity is (1989: 94), while deconstructivist thought—and Derrida in particular—suggest another model. On one hand, this model, which is based on not total systems but *differences* between concrete items, is supposed to be nonorganic. On the other hand, this model can be seen as intrinsically organic in its own right. Ferdinand de Saussure's idea of language as a network in which everything is relational without manifesting any foundationally positive essences can very well be understood as an organic concept (see Saussure [1916] 1995). Of course, by understanding it that way, we put the poststructuralist-organic controversy upside down. We imply that Derrida combats formalism not by "wildly" deconstructing but by designing an anti-system that still is a system.

The problem is complex because the line separating organic systems based on *différance* from totalitarian organic structures is thin for the simple reason that living organisms can easily become rigid. This has been the eternal problem of the organic. At the end of the eighteenth century, organic metaphors were already mixed into the progressive discourses of the Enlightenment. Through this fusion, the organic became rigid, ideological, and, strictly speaking, nonorganic because it excluded the metaphor of disintegration from its evolutionary vocabulary. The same is true for populist searches for native "organic" roots. What is lacking in all those fake organicisms is the irony or the melancholy able to resist straightforward and formalist schemes of evolution. Vice versa (see chapter 4), fluent networks can very easily become too liquid, which means the purely relational will become relativist. In other words, the meaning of Derrida's assumption that the world is nothing other than a "systematic play of differences" ([1972] 1981: 26) depends on how much "system" is still contained in the play. How much does coherence (even if sustained through *différance* and not through solid "present" rules) subsist beyond the differential network of language?

In any case, Derrida's concept of play as a self-sustaining system *is* conclusively organic, which makes the cascade of nonorganicist invectives launched from the deconstructivist side look rather peculiar. Shusterman finds Derrida's model organic even in Hegel's sense because in Hegel's idea of unity, everything is precisely constituted by what it is not. Of course, Hegel is not understood here as a "naturalizing" philosopher, that is, one who turns history into an organic narrative by applying principles of nature to society. Shusterman is right in concluding, "although deconstruction opposes organic unity in aesthetics, we shall find that beneath this aesthetic surface, at a much deeper logical level, it is itself fundamentally committed and inextricably wedded to one central (originally Hegelian) sense of the principle of organic unity" (1989: 94). Derrida's type of deconstruction wants wholeness by establishing an organic, and not a totalitarian, idea of wholeness.

Gilles Deleuze and Felix Guattari's notion of the rhizome represents an alternative system able to synthesize free development and unity within one organic expression. The rhizome model looks very much like what Eszter is looking for: it is not mathematically-systematically structured, though still coherent and organically grown. Rhizomes are not determined by evolutionary linearity, hierarchy, or geometrical orientations but are made of processes of variation and expansion. Therefore, they are compatible with gamelike evolutionary models that can be causally overdetermined and discontinuous and thus organic. Rhizomes have no beginning or end: they begin in the middle and rely on neither transcendental laws (roots) nor abstract models of unity. In music, architecture, and film, rhizomic structures become combinations of spatial-temporal "undifferential entities" in which acts of territorialization and deterritorialization, of organization and rupture, form a *chôraic* place that is stratified but without precise limits. In the above sections, allusions have been repeatedly made to two kinds of organicism: the rigid, humanist, totalitarian, evolutionary one and the ironic, melancholic, organic one. The difference is well reflected by Deleuze and Guattari's distinction between the arboreal and the rhizomic, the former being stable, centered, and hierarchical and the latter being nomadic, multiple, and decentered. A rhizome is similar to a structure but different in that it develops nondichotomous configurations in which profound, "metaphysical" structures are absent. Rhizomes expand from the middle and rely on neither transcendental roots nor abstract, mathematically calculated models of unity, but still they are natural: "Every rhizome contains lines of segmentarity according to which it is stratified, territorialized, organized, signified, attributed, etc., as well as lines of deterritorialization down which it constantly flees. There is a rupture in the rhizome whenever segmentary lines explode into a line of flight, but the line of flight is part of the rhizome" (Deleuze and Guattari 1987: 9; 1980: 16).

Derrida, Rousseau, and Eszter on Harmony

Derrida's writings contain even more evidence of a pro-organic attitude, which is strongly linked to his thoughts on music. Derrida's well-known attacks against Jean-Jacques Rousseau are also directed against the latter's dismissal of harmony and his call for a return to melody. In *Of Grammatology*, Derrida (1976: 210–17; 1967: 298–306) interprets these statements about music in parallel with Rousseau's subjection of writing to speech. The primacy of nature over culture, speech over writing, and passion over civilization motivate Rousseau's primacy of melody. In the chapters "On Melody" and "On Harmony" from *Essay on the Origin of Languages and Writings Related to Music* (*Essai sur l'origine des langues où il est parlé de la mélodie et de l'imitation musicale*), Rousseau explains that harmony signifies a decline in music because musical writings like the counterpoint could develop out of harmonic music. According to Rousseau, this musical writing is not natural but decadent and artificial. Instead of submitting to the tyranny of written notation very much corrupted by civilization, Rousseau suggests a return to the more "natural" melody. Melody is nature because it imitates "the inflections of the voice, expresses complaints, cries of sadness or of joy, threats, and moans," while harmony "shackles [*donne des entraves à*] the melody, it deprives it of energy and expression, [and] it eliminates passionate accent in order to substitute the harmonic interval." In other words, harmony is totalitarian because it "effaces and destroys multitudes of sounds or intervals that do not enter into its system" (1998: 322–23; 1781: 154).

Rousseau's writings on music are curious, as they contradict his general idea that language (which could be likened to melody) is *not* natural. In the preface to *Essai*, Rousseau argues, "men must have used, for the establishment of society, enlightenment which only develops with great difficulty and in very few people in the midst of society itself" (1781: 285). There is no natural language, just as there is no organic state of society that would antedate all existing social structures. This is actually what de Man finds so appropriate in Rousseau's philosophy of language: language is not natural but merely a temporal medium.

Thus, indirectly, by contradicting Rousseau's nonorganic anti-harmonism, Derrida contradicts de Man. For Derrida, melody is a present and natural expression, while harmony is an "absent" system—which still is a system. This enables Derrida to present Rousseau as a metaphysical fanatic afraid of the supplement called "harmony" or "scale" (*gamme*) only because it runs counter to Western ideas of presence and naturalist innocence: "From then on the dangerous supplement, scale or harmony, adds itself from the outside as evil and lack to happy and innocent plenitude" (Derrida 1967: 306; 1976: 215).

How much Eszter's quest relates to Rousseau's searches for harmony becomes clear. First, both Rousseau and Eszter intend to liberate music from a fake concept of harmony. Both dislike the intellectually established counterpoint, which Eszter renders unplayable on his piano through Aristoxenian tuning. Second, Eszter immediately discovers when delving into the history of music that the "natural tuning" is not natural at all but merely a social convention initiated by the musical ideologist Werckmeister. Third, both Rousseau and Eszter are devoted followers of the premise that real music must be free, and both will agree that only free music can be called natural music. "Harmonics" (*l'harmonique*) is for Rousseau a cold, weak, and calculating science that loses sight of music's living content (see also Derrida 1967: 304). Both Rousseau and Eszter see the freedom of music as restricted through harmony. While Rousseau thinks harmony "shackles the melody," Eszter believes music has been shackled for centuries because "the performance of their works of genius entailed some teensy-weensy departure from absolute purity of pitch" (Krasznahorkai 1998: 116). In both cases, the restrictions imposed on music are due to an overvaluation of mathematical, scientific thinking.

There is still another resemblance between Eszter and Rousseau. Rousseau's two chapters on harmony and melody in *Essai* relate to polemic discussions between Rousseau and Jean-Philippe Rameau. We find traces of this discussion in Rousseau's *Dictionnaire de musique* (1768), as well as in one of his entries in the *Encyclopédie* (1755).[2] According to Rousseau, Rameau excels in an "artificialist exuberance and an illusory or abusive recourse to nature." Rameau's calculations are entirely arbitrary, as they are "merely" grounded in the physics of sound and nothing else. Furthermore, Rousseau attributes the debacle of music to the moderns and to European ethnocentrism in general: only Europeans can conceive of a system based on harmonies as "a succession of following the laws of modulation" (Derrida 1976: 210; 1967: 299) and even dare to call this scientific system natural. Derrida's own attribution of Rousseau's anti-harmony discourse to a typically Western metaphysical machine always eager to implement presence and natural innocence (in Rousseau's case, in the form of melody) appears ironic here.

The above parallels between Rousseau and Eszter are stunning. Rameau is Rousseau's Werckmeister because he passes off "as natural what is purely conventional." Like Eszter, "Rousseau wishes to restore a natural degree of art within which chromatics, harmonics, and interval would be unknown" (quoted in Derrida 1976: 214; 1967: 305). Indeed, in the *Dictionnaire de musique,* Rousseau writes: "I ought however to declare, that this system, as ingenious as it may appear, is not in any way founded on nature, as he incessantly repeats it; that it is established only on analogies and conveniences [*convenances*], which one, who is tolerable at invention, might over throw tomorrow, by others much more natural" (Derrida 1976: 210; 1967: 299).

However, not everything works in parallel between Rousseau and Eszter, because the suggested remedies are not the same. Rousseau wants to return to melody, and Eszter dreams of inventing new harmonies more perfect than Werckmeister's. Eszter searches for harmony in the form of a divine system, which is something Rousseau's enlightened spirit would not aspire to and certainly never express in such terms. Though both agree that (certain kinds of) harmonies represent totalitarian restrictions to our free musical spirit that must be overcome, they disagree on *how* they should be overcome. For Eszter, they will not be overcome by simply abandoning harmony and concentrating on the more "natural" melody (as Rousseau suggests). Eszter chooses a different path: he is looking for a cosmic sort of harmony that is supposedly both "real" and natural. The irony is that he will never find this "natural harmony."

Nietzsche

Once again, what is Eszter? In this chapter, he has been characterized as an antihumanist organicist without postmodern ambitions. I believe the label most fitting for this quixotic searcher of truth is "Nietzschean." Nietzsche challenged accepted moral systems by announcing that those systems flow out of the pettiness of humanism inspired by Christian values. In the same way, Eszter challenges a common conception of culture (or of common, temperate music) by declaring this culture a mere construction. Like Nietzsche, Eszter is fighting against hypocrisy, corruption, and the narcissistic pathos of so-called scientists, and like

Nietzsche, Eszter wants to break up traditional and venerable but ossified knowledge. Too often cultural destruction has been disguised as scientific progress, and this cynicism needs to be revealed. A similar theme goes through *Satantango*.

No Art for Art's Sake

Nietzsche and Eszter share another ambition: the rejection of Art Nouveau's "art for art's sake" (*l'art-pour-l'art*) aestheticism. This philosophy was current at Nietzsche's time and is still weighing on Eszter in the form of an ideology able to issue "natural tuning" fueled by the implicit idea that art should imitate nature. Having started as a revolutionary movement, Art Nouveau degenerated into a movement of merely decorative art and even became reactionary. This is not the organicism Eszter favored but rather the organicism criticized by René Wellek, who accuses the entire metaphysical tradition—reaching from Aristotle through Kant to the New Critics—of an aestheticism, claiming, "the aesthetic experience is set off from immediate practical concerns." Wellek sees here a "lineage long preceding the art-for-art's sake movement" (1982: 93). Once again, Eszter is too antimetaphysical to engage in this pseudo-organic movement.

There is another reason radical organicists refuse the *l'art-pour-l'art* variety of organicism. Linked to the *l'art-pour-l'art* concept is the work of the biologist Ernst Haeckel, who encouraged artists in 1899 to imitate the natural forms contained in *Kunstformen der Natur*.[3] Here, art is reduced to nature or to the visual composition of natural shapes. Similar shifts took place in architecture. As shown in chapter 7, Henry van de Velde believed engineers are the real specialists of beauty. All this amounts very much to a belated reinstating of Renaissance thought that believed, like Leonardo, math could be the arbiter of beauty. Both Nietzsche and Eszter see this kind of aestheticism as insufficient for the existence of real art. Music is not natural if "being natural" means being determined by natural sciences or math.

The Übermensch

Through Eszter's obsession with the "falseness" of the temperate harmonic scale, Krasznahorkai reformulates in a metaphorical fashion the above Nietzschean strategies. For Eszter, Werckmeister's approach remains based on the pretentiousness and "unhinged arrogance" of science that pretends to know the world but in reality knows nothing.

Indirectly, Eszter speaks out against humanism's anthropocentric ideology that justifies man's glorious role and Eszter does so by referring to the "universe" in the most ostentatious fashion. Overcoming the Werckmeisterian harmonic system is thus the equivalent of Nietzsche's claim that "man must overcome himself."[4] Like Nietzsche, Eszter aims to inscribe the human in a radically new situation, which makes of him the Übermensch (Overman) dismissing the traditional "scientific" distinction between truth and falsehood with all the fake moralisms this distinction includes.

At the same time, Eszter remains distinct from the Prince and "the people" also fighting for nature and against civilization. Their "nature" is rather equivalent to the "centralized" concept of nature used by Catholics and religious evangelists for whom nature is provided by God. They pretend to have received knowledge about what nature is from some mysterious source. Eszter's approach is different. He is the scientist constantly searching for an ideal he names "nature" only for lack of a better word. Both Eszter and the Prince oppose an instinctive concept of nature to that of civilization, but this similarity is superficial. Eszter does not pretend to know what nature is, but he suspects it is very different from everything designed as "natural" by humanism.

The Religious and the Metaphysical

Something must be said about the status of religion in Béla Tarr's films, as the present book compares Tarr with (the more religious architect) Imre Makovecz. The topic is also important because discussions of resemblances or dissemblances between Tarr and Andrei Tarkovsky often revolve around religion. First, the status of Tarkovsky's religiosity has often been exaggerated because of the recurring Christian iconography in his films. In reality, Tarkovsky's religiosity is more on the line of non-sectarian mysticism and general spirituality, similar to what also appears in Tarr's films and László Krasznahorkai's writings. In Donatella Baglivo's documentary *Andrei Tarkovsky: A Poet of the Cinema*, Tarkovsky announces that he is "almost agnostic." Traces of dogmatic religious belief do not seem to be in his films and writings. Overall, Tarkovsky appears most plausibly as a secular humanist.

Tarr (2004) adopts the antihumanist organicist position when claiming he and his collaborator Ágnes *Hranitzky* "think it's best to go back to nature. We are really not religious. We don't believe in any kind of religion." The plan is of course not to imitate nature but to prepare, in parallel with the philosophy underlying organic architecture, for the "symbiotic embrace" of nature, an expression taken from Maggie Toy's (1993: 7) article on organic architecture. The organicism that wants to go back to nature is not religious simply because it does not accept any religious conception of heaven or hell. Still, nature *does* exist, and from the organic point of view, nature is not necessarily religious but metaphysical. In *Damnation*, Karrer reverts to a natural state when walking on four legs and barking like a dog. The pouring rain is a metaphor for nature, and Yvette Bíró comments on the weather conditions in *Satantango*: "And yet, the inclement weather is not the punishment of nature. It is as indifferent as the vegetation itself." In an organic world, people do not suffer from nature in the same way they would suffer in hell simply because nature is not hell. Those individuals are thrown into the void of vegetative life, creating "merely" an ontological condition of emptiness: "Our characters exist in this open prison, a cage without bars, in the total uniformity of space, subjected to the pressure of motionless or extremely decelerated time" (2008: 169).

The lack of religious solemnity à la Tarkovsky in Tarr's films, as well as the fact that his films are simply "viscerally naturalistic" (170), has made many commentators inclined to deny Tarr any metaphysical motives. However, nature as seen by organic philosophy does not expulse all metaphysical aspects but rather tends to depict them as immanent. To negate any metaphysical potential regarding a Central and Eastern European work is always a risky approach. Next to dynamic paralysis, fragility, and the search for identity and harmony, metaphysical ambitions remain typical motivations of the intellectual life in the region. Several scholars have highlighted the fact that the Central and Eastern European intellectual tradition attempts to redeem the metaphysical (Blokker 2013: 41; Szakolczai 2005; Szakolczai and Wydra 2006: 151). According to Arpad Szakolczai, "while Western thought is increasingly trapped in an ever more desperately radicalized critique of metaphysics, in East Central Europe—ironically, to a large extent in the footsteps of Nietzsche—the most important intellectual figures have sparked a return to metaphysics" (2005: 417).

Eszter represents those Central and Eastern European intellectuals Szakolczai describes as having "escaped from this blind alley much earlier than their Western colleagues, and also often in a completely different direction" (421).[5] Most importantly, these thinkers' interpretations of Nietzsche differ radically from contemporary Western views. Their Nietzsche is not the Nietzsche of the (postmodern) Western left meant to promote "conflict-resolution, bargaining, [and] harmony," possibly ending up highlighting Nietzsche's most questionable aspect—relativism—as the most important mission. The Central and Eastern European Nietzsche is rather the "organic Nietzsche" eager to "restore the tragic sense of life at a moment when nature had been domesticated and men become tame" (Bloom 1987: 228). This approach can also be called organic: in organic philosophies, nature is often understood as an unknown, metaphysical element whose organic rules do not necessarily overlap with the rules expressed by mathematics. As a result, far from attempting to radicalize the Western criticism of metaphysics, Central and Eastern European intellectuals "ended up returning to [metaphysics]" (Szakolczai 2005: 421).

Despite the metaphysical (though nonreligious non-religious) tendencies of Central and Eastern European intellectual life, many critics decided to deny Tarr any metaphysical potential. I believe that this is not sustainable. Bíró thinks that Tarr is "without metaphysical prospects," (2008: 170) and András Bálint Kovács (2008) writes, "it is a mistake to use the concept of metaphysics in connection with Tarr's films." Unlike Robert Bresson and Tarkovsky, Tarr wants "to evoke the *lack* rather than the presence of the metaphysical dimension of the world" (Bíró 2008: 239). The truth is that while Tarkovsky uses the metaphysical in the sense of religious transcendence, Tarr uses it in an organic sense of immanence. What does this mean more precisely? While Tarkovsky's images often do not represent anything as such but are "tied to the concrete and the material, yet reach out along mysterious paths to regions beyond the spirit" (Tarkovsky 1986: 114), no such transcendence occurs in Tarr because he is organic or, better, *more* organic than Tarkovsky.

In the Western philosophical and theological tradition, transcendence and immanence have always been used as opposites, most typically referring to two alternative models: God is either beyond the world or manifested in the world. As a result, organic philosophies contradicting the metaphysical (Aristotelian) view of God have often been defined through the concept of immanence. Stoicism and Spinozism are arguably the most famous examples. The opposition has also entered film theory. Paul Schrader describes the transcendent as "beyond normal sense experience, and that which it transcends is, by definition, the immanent" (1972: 5). Organic models, on the other hand, would hold that the immanent itself can contain elements like beauty, the good, and even God.

What about Tarr? Logically, no transcendence can occur in Tarr's (or in Krasznahorkai's) aesthetics of the eternal recurrence of the same. Even "beauty" in the conventional aesthetic sense cannot occur, and we definitely find no Tarkovskian transcendental beauty, which usually depends on the aesthetic value of one single element. For what beauty could transcendence "reach out" the moment the spiritual and the mundane are contained within the same organic expression? However, to conclude that metaphysical considerations are simply absent is like throwing the baby out with the bath water. The organic universe denies any transcendence, while metaphysical considerations *do* subsist. Similar to the romantic principle of "unity in the many" Samuel Taylor Coleridge formulated in *Theory of Life* (1965: 1, 174), the organic expression of the whole *can* contain metaphysical values.

This is also precisely what Kovács's most pertinent observations of the difference between Tarkovsky and Tarr mean to convey. Kovács (2008) analyzes the effects of slow cinema and concludes, "Quite contrary to Tarkovsky, who uses slowness to build a transcendent experience, Tarr uses the same technique to rid us of the illusion of transcendent experience." For me this means that despite striking differences, an important similarity exists: while Tarkovsky leads us to the contemplation of sublime metaphysical beauty, Tarr leads us to the contemplation of the "recurrence of the same" in the world of everyday life. The metaphysical is discovered *there*, in this recurrence of the same, and not through an act of transcendence. Thus, instead of establishing the divergences about slowness as an instance of insurmountable difference between Tarr and Tarkovsky, it is more consistent to infer a parallel distinction from the constellations Nietzsche had already held dear. This is the distinction between the dramatic and the tragic. That there is nothing "dramatic" in Tarr, as Kovács (2008) also rightly states, should not lead to the conclusion that the tragic has been eliminated with one sweeping gesture. Organic life (especially as depicted by this art) *is* tragic, even constantly tragic, simply because life itself is a matter of constant disappearance (of death), and the melancholy with which this tragic sense of life can be approached does not exclude but produces metaphysical questions about life. In other words, Tarr touches on metaphysical questions not through Tarkovskian transcendence but by deconstructing them along organic models. In this way, he is similar to Nietzsche.

Notes

1. De Man had listened to Derrida's paper on structure and play in 1966 in Baltimore, where it was delivered at a conference.
2. The entry is called "l'Examen de deux principes avancés par M. Rameau dans sa brochure intitulée 'Erreurs sur la musique'" (see also Derrida 1967: 298).

3. Characteristically, Haeckel's ambitions had been driven by a universalism, as becomes clear in his subsequent attempts to explain the meaning of not just earthly nature and art but of the entire universe (see his *The Riddle of the Universe,* 1900).
4. Nietzsche declares this repeatedly in his *Thus Space Zarathustra* ([1883–1891] 1978).
5. Szakolczai mentions in particular Jan Patočka, Béla Hamvas, Károl Kerényi, and Karol Wojtyla.

CHAPTER 9

Politics of Harmony

Eszter is an organicist, but he is not a fundamentalist organicist: he does not even consider waging war against the Prince or the pragmatic Tünde and her pistol-swinging companion. Fundamentalist organicists tend to be not liberals but dictators. And as is well known, dictators tend to be obsessed with harmony. One such harmony-seeking fundamentalist was Stalin. Boris Groys begins *The Total Art of Stalinism* with a description of the Stalinist project eager to replace "the unordered, chaotic life of past ages … by a life that was harmonious and organized according to a unitary artistic plan." For the totalitarian nation planner, the entire "nation was totally subordinated to a single planning authority commissioned to regulate, harmonize, and create a single whole out of even the most minute details." For Groys, the Communist Party leader is "a kind of artist whose material was the entire world and whose goal was to 'overcome the resistance' of this material and make it pliant, malleable, capable of assuming any desired form" (1992: 3). Resistance was not allowed in the Stalinist work of art, even in the form of melancholy and nostalgia. Again, we see that implicit in any "melancholy of resistance" is a potential "resistance of melancholy." Since the Russian formalists, it is well known that raw material *can* offer resistance. This resistance, even if only a playfully resisting melancholy, needs to be broken. For Stalin, in a truly harmonious state, melancholy cannot be permitted. It is surprising that even here, in this Stalinist context, the main subject of harmony is God. We hear the echoes of nineteenth-century organic philosophies in Stalin's ideas about aesthetics as much as we hear them in Kazimir Malevich, who designed the *Black Square* as an expression of nothingness in the sense of a disintegration of Aristotle's divine Logos. Groys explains that the art of the Stalin period, as it strove to extend art into life, "aspired to resurrect by technological means the wholeness of God's world that had been disrupted by technology; to halt technological progress and the march of history in general by placing it under complete technological control [in order] to conquer time and enter into eternity" (Groys 1992: 72).

Nowhere else does Stalin's obsession with harmony become clearer than in his attitude toward music. Hungarian composer György Ligeti (2001) reports how under Stalin's dictatorship:

> even folk music was allowed only in the "politically correct" form, in other words, if forced into the straightjacket of socialist realism: major-minor harmonizations à la [Isaak] Dunayevsky were welcome and even modal orientalism in the style of Khachaturian were still permitted, but Stravinsky was excommunicated. The "peculiar way" in which village bands harmonized their music, often full of dissonances and "against the grain," was regarded as incorrect. In the fourth movement of my Romanian Concerto, there is a passage in which an F sharp is heard in the context of F major. This was reason enough for the apparatchiks responsible for the arts to ban the entire piece.

Stalin adheres to the ideology of unimaginative organicism, the blandest kind of universalism one can think of. Unimaginative organicism believes everything on Earth (major and minor harmonies) *must* be universal and that any divergences from this natural order should simply be ignored.[1] In other words, for Stalin, there is no need to bring together—in a Werckmeisterian way—the individual and the universal or the scientific-mathematical and the natural, simply because they are already the same. Anybody who disagrees attempts to establish a new, "nonnatural" order and must be punished. This attitude can also be called "naïve realist organicism" because nature (harmony) is believed to be real, "out there," and understandable for everybody. Modernist experiments (even when inspired by science) can only distort this simple reality.

The idea of a harmonic reality as a model for art is based on a certain conception of history implicit in socialist realism. For socialist realism, reality does not emerge from history, but it "simply" appears. We encounter this reality like a fata morgana at a point zero of history in the form of an absolute beginning. This is the only reality that exists, and Bolshevik ideology would establish the precise location of this point zero. Consequently, realism (in art or elsewhere) could never be an imitation of an existing reality. How could the Bolshevik reality, which is supposed to be both pristine and ultimate, be imitated? In the end, this artificially constructed relationship between history and reality creates a particularly twisted relationship with nature. On one hand, "Stalinist aesthetics distances itself no less emphatically from naturalism, associating it with the repudiated 'ideology of bourgeois objectivism'" (Groys

1992: 52), and thus is very different from nineteenth-century realism. On the other hand, as paradoxical as this sounds, artists *had* to imitate nature because what can be more real than nature? "Formalism" of any kind was rejected precisely because formalists and the avant-garde are against nature. The avant-garde was "subjected to police coercion intended to suppress in art anything not encountered in Nature, or which, if encountered, does not correspond thereto and which without particular necessity is by certain persons employed solely to demonstrate disregard of the rules" (89).[2] Finally, Stalin will become the only "real creator of reality" and therefore also the unique authority in matters of both nature and harmony.

This kind of realism is obviously incompatible with not only the nineteenth-century concept of realism but also the realism this book has addressed: André Bazin's "transcendent" neorealism. Stalin's realism, just like abstract idealism, lacks any transcendental sense of time and space. It is a highly unimaginative "fundamentalist realism" because it firmly believes nature is real, logical, and ultimately harmonious. This is the only concept of nature and reality compatible with scientific socialism; it is the only concept of reality compatible with the mathematical way of tuning the piano by believing the system simply *is* natural. Nature must be math because how could it be otherwise? Once this premise has been established, everything can work toward an all-encompassing, harmonious solution: in the Stalinist eternal empire—an empire that exists entirely beyond human history—"the artistic and unartistic, traditional and new, the constructive and the everyday (or kitsch)" (Groys 1992: 71) will entirely overlap. When nature and math are one, we will obtain total harmony and the most perfect perfection.

László Krasznahorkai's treatment of the Werckmeister problem clearly reflects such thoughts on harmony, realism, and fundamentalism. Eszter also wants harmony, but, contrary to Stalin, he thinks the totalitarian harmony of perfect perfection is imperfect. Stalin tunes the piano in a mathematical way simply because he believes it is the most natural tuning possible. This is the worst option of all, much worse than Werckmeister's and Eszter's. Stalin's favorite folksong was "Suliko," which begins with the line "long I searched for your grave." It's kitsch, but if kitsch can exemplify the natural beauty of organically grown folk songs, then science and math must try to reinstate such beauty—and nothing else. If math really is scientific, it cannot and will not counter those natural-organic expressions.

Moreover, Stalin's program is also clearly "humanist" in the sense established in chapter 8. Stalin's aesthetic program attempts to establish a universal order based on particular ("scientific" or ideological) observations. Therefore, many of his more organically minded contemporary opponents, especially in architecture, have criticized it as "humanist." For example, the Association of New Architects (ASNOVA) found the Stalinist criteria of natural harmony too vague and instead attempted to derive architectural principles from ecological, technical, and ideological factors. Finally, it declared that those principles are "not to be found in Marxian philosophy which completely exposed the vague criteria of 'universalism,' of abstract humanitarianism and of 'eternal values' and which indeed regarded them as the philosophical values of the bourgeois" (Zevi 1950: 37–38).

The gist of Stalin's ideas about music is that he wanted music to be "realist," not formalist. Dmitri Shostakovich's satirical cantata for four voices, *Rayok*, ridicules the Zhdanov decree of 1948 and Stalin's antiformalism campaign[3] by making politicians say absurd sentences about what "reality" is supposed to be: popular, Caucasian, and authentic. Of course, it was also meant to be natural. In the Stalinist rhetoric, formalism is contrasted with naturalism. According to Solomon Volkov, the predicate naturalism was "applied to the excessively frank passages," while formalism "was usually used for complicated works that were too smart by half, in the opinion of the critics" (2004: 104). *Rayok* is played to the tune of "Suliko," and under Stalin, Shostakovich was forced to write music for Soviet kitsch propaganda films, which was difficult for an artist opposed to kitsch by nature. Shostakovich's symphonies usually never finish with pompous and rejoicing chords, as the symphonies are quasi-noncentered. Constantly struggling between good and evil, the music has no resolution, though it might radiate some "cosmic truth." Stalin did not appreciate Shostakovich's cosmic approach but dismissed it as "an intentionally unharmonious, muddled flow of sound" (Volkov 2004: vii). In 1936, the communist party newspaper *Pravda* issued the following judgment in an article about the opera *Lady Macbeth of Mtsensk*: "This is music intentionally made inside-out, so that there would be nothing to resemble classical music, nothing in common with symphonic sounds, with simple, accessible musical speech … This is leftist muddle instead of natural, human music" (Volkov 2004: 121).

Organic Nihilism

The Prince in *Werckmeister Harmonies* represents another kind of fundamentalist organicism, obsessed not with harmony but with nonharmony. He too adheres to an organic philosophy but sees it merely as a basis for destruction: "The Prince alone sees the whole and the whole is nothing."[4] This is organic nihilism. Waiting with his destructive whale in his prefabricated house, the Prince mocks scientists and Werckmeisterian harmonizers alike. Logic, math, rules—this is all useless because nature has its own anti-order. Logic and language do not matter. In the novel, the Prince speaks gibberish (which the film amends to Slovak). *This* organicist camp believes only in chaos. Despite its resemblance with what many people today might identify as the ideology of the Islamic State or Daesh, the Prince does not merely symbolize hooliganism and pseudoreligious brainwashers. Contrary to those religious fanatics, the Prince does not point to a central, metaphysical truth received from some gnostic realm. His truth is rather that there is no truth. Chaos theory, which is the scientific and philosophical study of randomness, represents the more elaborate and most recent branch of the organic philosophy of the Prince, though, admittedly, the latter have never brought havoc, ruin, and violence.

The theme of "the whole has no meaning" recurs in Krasznahorkai's writings. The interpreter in "Nine Dragon Crossing," who seems to have strong affinities with Krasznahorkai himself, sympathizes with the statements a speaker makes from a Hong Kong radio station: "the whole has no meaning because there is nothing beyond the whole from which something could lead from there to here, because there is no 'from where' and no Beyond, and we ourselves cannot be the aim, because the aim must always be beyond that what the aim desires" (2015b: 145).

For organic nihilists like the Prince, compromises are impossible. For David Auerbach, the whale "is the symbol of addressable nature, the leviathan, coming to crush us all without explanation or logic, to show us the utter failure of *our* logic" (2013: 159). In the eyes of a chaos organicist, the whale's purpose is to destroy *everything*—logic, science, and God—because all three are the same to him. Supporters of this philosophy are rumored to have come into town on the evening train to see the whale, says the porter, adding that even their mathematical number cannot be established: "Some say it's three hundred of them, some say it's only two ..."

The Prince's position should not be defined simply as nonorganic but is indeed related to organicism. In the end, the Prince doesn't stop talking about "the whole" and about nature. Thus, he *does* see nature as an organic whole, but this whole appears ruleless only to the one who has the right vision (which is him). This is a sort of inverted Gestalt theory. Ordinary people might still expect to find rules inside this chaos, but in reality, the only rule of the organic is that there is no rule. That's the Prince's wisdom.

Four Types of Organic Harmony

Organicism can be defined in four ways: (1) we tune our piano according to purely mathematical rules, which makes the music sound awful; (2) we play music in the natural way, which makes both science and the use of pianos impossible unless we stick to a very limited range of intervals (the Prince); (3) we meet in the middle and apply temperate tuning (Tünde does precisely this for purely pragmatic reasons, while Werckmeister for idealist reasons); or (4) we ignore all of the above problems and naively hold that math and nature are the same. Stalin is an example of this last option, as he took the temperate tuning for both as naturally and mathematically justified.

Initially, even Eszter was tempted by the Prince's position because both men want nature. In his long monologue dictated into a tape recorder, he suggests to research not music but rather "a unique realization of non-music which for centuries has been covered up." This cover-up is "a dreadful scandal that we should disclose." Nature might be "impure" from the mathematical point of view, but how can it be "impure" from nature's point of view? This paradox must be discarded because it is simply absurd. If the stated "impurity" is natural, then we simply have to put up with it. Nothing is worse than the artificial purity of math. As mentioned in the discussion of Rousseau, musical geniuses like Mozart and Brahms were once shackled because "the performance of their works of genius entailed some teensy-weensy departure from absolute purity of pitch" (Krasznahorkai 1998: 116). The organic reality is that "truly pure musical intervals do not exist," as says Eszter in the film. Aristoxenus's music might have been simple because only a few intervals could be played, but an organicist will always view simplicity as positive. Nevertheless, Eszter returns to the good old Werckmeisterian compromise in the end (most probably under Tünde's influence). He recognizes that the purist pursuit of truth—even of the most "natural" kind—leads nowhere. Somehow, Kant was right: nature does not exist "as such" but is always what we make of it.

In the town, the Prince's followers practice their radical organicism by smashing the city to pieces and beating up patients in the local hospital. The Prince, who is responsible for the ransacking, represents the typical organic being "whose excessive magnetic powers" are based on nothing. The circus director points this is out very clearly: "I invented the Prince for commercial reasons. He is a born freak who knows nothing about anything." The Prince is not even physically present: we see only his shadow. His equivalent in *Satantango* is Irimiás, the fake messiah who adopts a central position in the simple village people's lives without providing any justification for what he is doing. Both characters might be inspired by the charismatic charlatan Lajos in Sándor Márai's novel *Esther's Inheritance* who "lies the way the wind howls" (2008: 10). Krasznahorkai wrote his master's thesis on Márai, so to see this character as a recurrent inspiration is not far-fetched. The Princely organic power system is self-sufficient. The origin of the Prince's power remains unexplained, just like the final object those powers are directed against: "We punish them, we will be pitiless, the day has come," proclaims the Prince. Who is "them"? Radical organicism has no direction. The Prince's power is based on his knowledge of the organic. In the end, the Prince's nihilistic actions are identical with those of harmony-seeking dictators.

Of course, the actions lead nowhere, but this does not matter. The revolution did not take place, but at least it has been televised. What matters is to smash a few items: "We could not find an object for our disgust and despair, and so we attacked everything in our way with an equal and infinite passion" (Krasznahorkai 1998: 231). It is impossible not to see in this behavior the sinister and lunatic logic of Communist totalitarianism. However, the lightness of Krasznahorkai's narrative style leaves no space for any feeling of grimness or humiliation, a fact that Béla Tarr even reinforces with the extreme stylization of the hospital scene. The lightness becomes clear when we compare the ransacking spree with other literary accounts of Stalinist absurdity. In Ismail Kadare's *Chronicle in Stone*, for example, people are deported because they "spoke against." Someone asks, "Against what?" "I'm telling you, they spoke against" (2013: 37). Here, the lack of a referent makes the narrative dark and cynical. True, Krasznahorkai's voices are also dark, the more so since he might evoke not only Stalin but also some sort of Balkan super chaos: after all, from Hungary it's just a six-hour drive to Kosovo, Sarajevo, or Mostar. However, Krasznahorkai's darkness remains "darkness light," as nothing seems to be too serious here. Robert Boyers correctly points this out: "Like all of the ideas summoned in Krasznahorkai's novel, Eszter's ideas are entertained without real seriousness, and we feel that they can be dropped or renounced as abruptly as they are taken up" (2013: 176). In this postcommunist rhetoric, the world appears like a playful, carnivalesque spider web of polyphonic voices—and nothing more.

Dictatorial Harmonies

Harmony-seeking dictators with nihilistic outlooks are also well known in Central and Eastern Europe. To some extent, they have even contributed to the aesthetics of "absurd realism"—long before the absurd became a literary genre. Fyodor Dostoevsky's character Smerdyakov from *The Brothers Karamazov* (1880) is a good example. Costica Bradatan (2014) has named "Smerdyakovism" a brutal behavior having no other motivation than being coherent within its own system of brutalism. Smerdyakovian organicism is engraved into the collective memory of all Central and Eastern Europeans. As a child, Smerdyakov liked to hang cats and then bury them with ceremony. Why did he kill the cats? Just because! "Eventually Smerdyakov develops this into a systematic, coherent behavior. He kills Fyodor Pavlovich without any clear motive; he plans the murder to the last detail and commits it in cold blood, but we don't know why. He kills just because" (Bradatan 2014).

Stalin brought Smerdyakovism to perfection by decimating the Russian elite without providing any rational justification for his deeds. Did he need such a justification? No, nihilist organicists do not need justifications for anything. For the same "reason," Stalin starved the Ukrainians to death. His absurd acts can make sense—if they make sense at all—only as parts of a harmonious, organic system of terror. Therefore, despite the pompous optimism such dictators usually display, their acts will most likely appear bluntly nihilistic to the following generations.

The Prince's nihilistic machine functions like Stalinist Smerdyakovism. Eszter's compromise or "negotiations," on the other hand, can be read as a political metaphor establishing Hungary between East and West, between Smerdyakovism and scientifically engineered democracy, between barbarism and civilization, or between nature and culture. Compromises and "harmonization" can indeed be seen as the particular task of the entire Central and Eastern European region, as Julia Sushytska points out:

> Eastern Europe is the in between: neither civilized nor wholly barbaric, neither orderly nor entirely chaotic, neither cultured nor in the state of nature. It is rather the movement that underlies these dichotomies. Neither familiar nor exotic, or both familiar and exotic, it embodies the oneness of the West and its Other and becomes a source of their possible harmony. (2010: 61)

More than any other Central and Eastern European country, Hungary has been attributed to a "state of perpetual liminality or 'in-betweenness'" (sociologist Elemér Hankiss, quoted in Boromisza-Habashi 2012: 13). Though harmony is important for both the Prince's nihilistic machine and the "negotiations" Sushytska describes, the latter will opt not for the forced harmony of dictators but rather for the Werckmeister type of harmony: the harmony of a compromise. Hungary is better positioned here than any other Central and Eastern European nation. Historically, Hungary has pursued a liberalized approach to communism based on an ideological mixture; therefore, Hungary can represent an ideal case for experimental "negotiations" or harmonizations between East and West. Furthermore, Hungary's far-reaching "Easternness" and simultaneous integration into Europe can be considered unique. Composer Zoltán Kodály wrote: "one of our hands holds the hand of the Nogay-Tartars, the Votyars and Cheremiss, the other that of Bach and Palestrina. Can we bring those two distant worlds together?" (Schneider 2006: 9). Other dichotomies that needed to be harmonically fused in the course of modernization were the rural versus the urban or the peasant versus the bourgeois. The Pécs Group of architecture claimed to create "harmony in new works, with the old, with the region, with nature, with man, and with human settlement" (Cook 1997: 7). Today, a new challenge has appeared on the horizon: more than most other Central and Eastern European countries, Hungary seems to be stuck "in between" democracy and totalitarianism.

How relevant is Stalin's search for harmony for Hungary today? Some historians hold that Hungary's entire political history from the Hungarian Revolution of 1848 to the present has been a continuous civil war. The legitimacy of those in power was constantly challenged, and "to be in political opposition in Hungary meant wishing for the extinction of the rulers, or at least their exclusion from the public sphere. To be in power, on the other hand, meant desire for complete control and ownership of the nation. Such control included ostracizing the opposition from the public sphere" (Tamás 2007). In other words, minorities and majorities alike wanted power and nothing else. According to the Hungarian Marxist philosopher Gáspár Miklós Tamás, this "deeply antidemocratic historical and political legacy prevents today's Hungarian political system" from obtaining a consensus of any sorts (Boromisza-Habashi 2012: 15).

Folkloristic Organicism in Hungary

The harmonies established by Werckmeisterian compromises do not satisfy everybody, but this is not a new state of affairs. Since the day

Werckmeisterian harmonies were proposed, other, "better" organic philosophies—often with fundamentalist and purist implications—have been lurking around every corner. Some people simply believe compromises are fake by definition, and they prefer to go for the "real thing." At present, Hungary is partly subjected to a folkloristic kind of nationalism, the most picturesque one being Turanism (or Pan-Turanism), which proclaims an ethnic/cultural unity for the dispersed peoples of Central Asia, of which Hungary is believed to be a part. Political Turanism has existed since the nineteenth century, and the Iranian term Tūrān refers to a particular region in Central Asia (Vági et al. 2013: xxxiv). Turanism has also been a serious topic for architectural theories, at least for the national historicism that survived World War I. Those architects speculated about Turan as a mysterious country. Initially, the German linguist Max Müller coined the term "Turanian" in 1855.[5]

Though nationalists link Hungary to Turanian culture, the origin of the Hungarian people is in reality not clear at all. It has been traced to the Huns but also—in the past—to the Sumerians and Scythians. Today, only the Hungarian far-right party seems to support the Scythian thesis. The rejection of Europe in favor of Turanism played a role at the beginning of the twentieth century, when Hungary was to acquire the profile of a military nation. Finnish connections (established through common Finno-Hungarian linguistic roots) were considered less desirable because neither the Finns nor the Estonians can be perceived as impressive warrior nations, while Asian horsemen terrorizing Central Europe were much more inspiring. Today, Csanád Szegedi, former deputy chairman of the right-wing party Jobbik, openly advocates for a Turanian alliance of Hungary with Central Asian states (Ungváry 2012). Imre Makovecz also attempted to retrieve the spirit of the "Celtic and the Scythian cultures," which he believed to have roamed Central Europe (1993: 15). However, he does not state that Hungarians are related to these peoples. His attempts to retrieve their spirit are less direct and much more sophisticated. Makovecz looks for nonliteral traces of a metaculture in its most universal (cosmic) form or for a genius loci; he never looks for (imaginary) folkloric fossils and genetic links.

An example of folkloristic pseudo-organic architecture is the Hungarian pavilion presented at the Expo 2015 in Milan (architects Attila Ertsey, Ágnes Herczeg, and Sándor Sárkány). The pavilion is called "The Garden of Life" (Életkert) and dubbed "Scythian Boat" by its opponents. The title of this Expo project, "From the Purest Source,"[6] is also telling, as it shows how much this architecture is supposed to relate to the manifesto of the Pécs Group of the 1970s. The 2015 project is surprisingly identitarian if compared with earlier Hungarian Expo pavilions, for example, "Corpora" from 2008, which aimed at the realization of autonomously forming architecture and tried to incorporate new methods of spatial notation. The ecologically inspired building from 2015 draws on Hungarian vernacular farm architecture with silos, granaries, and sheds. All material used is organic. The most striking elements are huge shamanic drums, attached to each extremity, on which "tree of life" (életfa) symbols have been drawn. Those drums "refer to ancient roots as well as the mystical connection of the man and nature" ("Életkert Pavilon" Facebook page). The tree of life (also called "sky-high tree" or "world tree") is an element of Hungarian shamanism and folk art and also exists in Central Asian cultures. According to shamanistic beliefs, shamans can climb up the tree and wander in the seven or nine layers of the sky (see Hoppál 1984, 2007). The similarity of the building with Noah's ark (the ship will contain thirty-three different species of plants) underlines Hungarian's mystical relationship with nature, as well as with Christianity. At the same time, the pagan tree of life is praised as a link between heaven and earth. The plants are also supposedly able to transform minerals into life through cosmic energy.

This project—supported by Viktor Orbán's center right-wing party, Fidesz, and praised by former Minister of Defense Csaba Hende—is a naïve synthesis of different traditions and an example of nationalist kitsch. On one hand, the point of view is identical with that of the far right who, rather curiously, expects the conservative Christian electorate to embrace the anti-Christian propaganda of Turanism and celebrate Hungary's non-European, Asian heritage. On the other hand, the project also contains Christian elements. Noah's ark and pagan shaman drums are combined without any further thought about possible contradictions because both supposedly symbolize Hungarian identity. The easiness with which Christianity and paganism are confounded is not new: Hungarian Nazis (contrary to German Nazis, who were against Catholicism) had already attempted to develop a synthesis of Catholicism and pagan culture.

After the Milan Expo 2015, the pavilion will be reassembled in the small East Hungarian town of Karcag. Its earlier planned attribution to a future "Centre for Creative Heritage Protection and Value Development" in Hende's conscription met with obstacles ("Milan 2015 Expo"). The choice of Karcag is not random. The town has strong connections with a Turkic tribe called kipchak, a Eurasian tribe related to the kun tribe, which settled in Hungary in the Middle Ages but was also a predecessor of modern Kazakhstan (see Vásáry 2005: 6). The small town of Karcag has a Kazakh consulate. Furthermore, the next World Expo will be held in Kazakhstan and Karcag represents a connection between Milan and the 2017 venue.[7]

Once again, we must ask how far the resemblances with Makovecz are going. Some might object that Makovecz has produced similar mixtures of Christian and pagan iconographies all throughout his career. Strong resemblances even exist between this ark and Makovecz's draft of a floating pavilion from 1992 for the Seville Biennial, which had a tree of life as a mast. However, in general, the purpose of Makovecz's intercultural creations is not to present Hungarian identity in terms of nationalism but rather to evoke a more general type of spirituality. His Biennial buildings, for example, were for him "dead ciphers of [a pantheist] God," as he writes in his foreword to the catalog. He simply wanted "to erect buildings that make us remember our origin and ancestry" (Cook 1996: 180).

Communism

There is still another way of reading the Werckmeister parabola. Werckmeister's math can be understood as a metaphor for communism, which would be one more reason Eszter dislikes Werckmeister. For Eszter, Werckmeister's rational system still contains too much artificial engineering and not enough "truth." Werckmeister believed he led music to perfection because he had enabled nature and math to overlap. Because his approach moves away from that of Central and Eastern European (East–West) negotiationism and brings his project closer to the patterns of Stalin's totalitarian universalist harmony, Eszter believes Werckmeister's system "is entirely based on a false foundation." *Werckmeister Harmonies* can thus be read as the story of the organicist Eszter fighting against scientific socialism and socialist materialism, just like Hungarian organicist architecture fought against the socialist "rationalization" of architecture imposed on the country after 1956. Tarr's films and Krasznahorkai's novels should not be limited to such (post) communist interpretations, but some parallels are obvious. True, Tarr generally offers very few hinges on which critics can base political parallels. However, such parallels are relatively easy to establish in Krasznahorkai's novels. The disintegration theme is most obviously linked to the postcommunist collapse of values. Apart from that, Krasznahorkai, like Tarr and Makovecz, refrains from direct political statements. His organic spider web of philosophical options acknowledges Werckmeisterian,

Smerdyakovian, nihilist, and pragmatist positions, but it does not develop a clearer and more concrete political narrative.

Organic versus Material

Socialist materialism repressed the spiritual component of culture by privileging culture's material aspect. Though organic architecture could be practiced quite liberally from the 1970s onward, the postsocialist period after 1989 can appear as a spiritual awakening, with Hungarian organic architecture as one of its most important manifestations. In architecture, "postsocialist aesthetics" (which also began well before 1989) shifts from synthetic to "natural" materials. This is also when Krasznahorkai published *The Melancholy of Resistance* (1989) and *Satantango* (1985). While the aesthetics of the "socialist modern" believed in nonorganic materials like concrete and plastic, postsocialism, as well as the latest phase of Hungarian socialist culture, finds these materials oppressive and prefers natural and organic materials able to decay and decompose. In Hungary, which enjoyed more freedom under János Kádár's regime than any of the other Eastern bloc countries, the organic architecture movement began modestly formulating itself as early as the 1960s. Makovecz and architect György Csete were decisive in this development.[8]

The contrast between this organic procedure and socialist architectural principles has several dimensions. Marxism–Leninism had declared nonorganic materials liberating because they can overcome the vicissitudes of nature, which makes us free. At some point, the system was turned upside down: people expected to be freed from Marxism–Leninism's oppressive materialism, hopefully by using organic materials. For several decades, the "material versus living nature" dichotomy functioned as a political guideline in Hungary. As Krisztina Fehérváry explains, "man-made materialities in many ways mirrored the theory and practice of state socialism" (2012: 627). Industry and scientific knowledge had been the most powerful forces of socialism, and nature as a competing force was simply not permitted. In the 1970s, nature was brought back into architecture either through the aesthetics of the self-made rustic (which can easily end up as kitsch) or in the form of Makovecz's and Csete's sophisticated organic experimentations.[9] In this respect, the Hungarian aesthetic scenario is more dramatic than any other scenario in Central and Eastern Europe:

the Hungarian case brings into stark relief processes that are more muted elsewhere. It suggests that the superiority ascribed to "natural" materials—granite countertops, rich hardwoods, stonelike tile backsplashes, and leather furnishings—aids in discrediting modernist projects and generates the cosmologies that have replaced them. (619)

Organic architecture positions itself in opposition to repressive artificiality. Consequently, the mathematically "rectangular" is declared to be against nature, and round shapes and asymmetry are eagerly used to fight the "unnatural socialist system" (617). Later, this meant that organicism—not postmodernism—was to bring moderately anarchic freedom in the form of playfulness, openness, creativity, and improvisation. One might suggest that all those qualities are also typically postmodern, but they adopted an organic format in Hungary. Aided by the availability of new paints, materials, and technologies, organic architecture could be used to disguise socialist architectural misdeeds in prefab buildings and on civic squares. After 1989, the "organic makeover" became almost systematic. For example, in the small town of Fonyód, Makovecz students entirely transformed a school with a flat roof into "a humanized, character-filled building" (Cook 1997: 13). The school received hooded slate roofs, dormers, and gables.

While Stalinist architecture (practiced in Hungary only from 1951 to 1956) had forbidden all "modern" experiments with freestyle associations and had fostered "realist" expressions understandable to the common people, organic architecture provided experimentalism with an identitarian touch. As usual, harmony was organicism's main objective:

> Although organicist transformations were structured by opposition to a Socialist Generic, they were not a return to bourgeois materialities. Nor were they a return to premodern traditionalism. Instead, they were a concerted effort to generate a more "harmonious" modern lifestyle that fulfilled some of the dreams of socialist modernity while opposing others as heretical and unnatural. (Fehérváry 2012: 629)

Especially after the fall of the Berlin wall, organic architecture came to be identified as a Hungarian national style in and outside the country. In 1991, the Venice Biennale displayed thirty-eight "organic" architects representing Hungary, and Makovecz was chosen in 1992 to represent Hungary at the Universal Exposition of Seville. Makovecz's pavilion has widely been regarded by the international public as the most inventive structure at Seville Expo '92 (see Rockwell 1992). The conservative government of József Antall, in power between 1990 and 1994, had much impact on further pro-organic decisions, though their enthusiasm often clashed with local building politics in the public sector, which continued seeing organic architecture with a critical eye (Gerle 1985: 1561).[10]

The metaphysical connotations clinging to the organic since its philosophical beginnings remain important in the new postsocialist context, where they are repositioned against globalization and international homogeneity. Like so often in the intellectual history of Europe, the organic form is supposed to contain the eternally "unknown" mythical structure of nature that science (and math) will never be able to reveal. This brings organic philosophies close to religion because the organic draws not merely on "nature" as understood by the natural sciences but also on nature's "spiritual" component. Therefore, organicism in Hungary often comes dangerously close to mysticism, especially when combined with identitarian motives. On the other hand, this architecture is more removed today from mystifying nationalism than in the past, which becomes obvious when we compare modern organic architecture with what can be considered its equivalent before World War I. At that time, architects reveled in the straightforward mystification of Hungarian culture. At the Turin Expo in 1911, all Hungarian entries were to be variations on the theme of Attila's palace, announcing a revival of Hun culture (see Gerle 1998: 226).

Equipped with both aesthetic charms and philosophical arms, organic architecture would become, perhaps unsurprisingly, the most popular (and most radical) form of antimaterialism the postsocialist world had to offer: "You who took the role of God by declaring nature to be controllable by the socialist system will be impressed by nature's hidden powers, which are not material but spiritual." Organicism refutes socialism by eventually proving that spirit is stronger than matter. The "organic versus rational" dichotomy continues to make sense in Hungary today. According to Edwin Heathcote, "'the organic' counterpoised by 'the rational' has continued to provide such a rich dialogue for contemporary Hungarian architecture" (2006: 34). Many of Makovecz's followers continue to produce interesting buildings. Important names are Ervin Nagy, Dezsö Ekler, János Gerle, András Erdei, Agnes Kravár, and Ferenc Salamin. Regarding the future, there are reasons to be both optimistic and pessimistic. Heathcote is convinced "Hungarian architecture remains effectively defined by the reactionary and the progressive, but in the perverse atmosphere of postcommunism those positions are impossible to reconcile with any notions we may have in the privileged and long democratic West" (37). The "organic" Turanian antics of the far-right party, as well as of the center-right party, need to be understood through this prism.

This chapter has shown that Hungarian organic architecture (which might be called a belated Hungarian arts and craft movement) is unique. It differs from not only postmodernism but also Western European revisions of modernity (for example, the Scandinavian "natural" design) because it has, besides its metaphysical dimension, great political potential. This is probably why it could go farther than all other European movements and why it looks so different. Aesthetically, Hungarian organicism refers us back to the most radical expressions of Art Nouveau and ends up with shapes similar to those of Antoni Gaudí (who died already in 1926) and Rudolf Steiner. No equivalent exists in either Eastern or Western Europe. Some sort of national awakening has been staged in most Central and Eastern European countries during Soviet Perestroika from 1987 onward. However, nowhere did it look like it did in Hungary. In Estonia, "mass construction (now viewed as being more Soviet than modernist)" would rather oppose Estonia's own "neofunctionalism, carrying on local tradition" (Kurg 2009: 94). The flamboyant vernacularism framed by a distinct organic philosophy remains typically Hungarian.

One last question: is it really possible that "scientific socialism" had so profoundly misunderstood nature? If yes, these socialists were not worse than Werckmeister or the German Enlightenment philosophers preaching musical theology. While the latter replaced natural harmony with temperate tuning, the former replaced natural wood with PVC. This is at least what appears in *The Melancholy of Resistance*. Krasznahorkai's obsession with the decomposition theme in all its configurations lets his work appear as postsocialist, anti-PVC literature. At some point, the timeless future of the Marxist world needed to be reminded of the transitory state of all things material. Of course, this also has a religious (Buddhist) dimension of the kind dear to Krasznahorkai: "don't cling to things material." In the socialist realm, Krasznahorkai touches on a double taboo, as not only religion but also death could not really be dealt with in socialist countries. Fehérváry quotes Monica Black, for whom socialism "could not figure out how to deal with nature's ultimate triumph, or death" (2012: 628). The reasons are—once again—linked to the problems of the transcendent. Buildings related to death are always transcendent in the sense of transcending mortality. Makovecz solves the problem in his own uncanny fashion. His Mortuary Chapel in Farkasrét, Budapest, looks like the interior of Tarr's whale from *Werckmeister Harmonies,* and Heathcote comments, "The concept of being devoured in death has a rich history in architectural and artistic expression from the earth rising to devour mortals" (1997: 27).

Notes

1. This Stalinist aesthetic stance is different from what Marxist aesthetics would later often proclaim as an ideal of incompleteness that would oppose "consistency." French Marxist literary critic Pierre Macheray does this in *A Theory of Literary Production*: "Rather than sufficiency, that ideal consistency, we must stress that determinate insufficiency, that incompleteness which actually shapes the work. The work must be incomplete in itself. Not extrinsically, in a fashion that could be completed to 'realize' the work" (1970: 88).
2. Groys quotes V. Komar and A. Melamid, "A. Ziablov (Etiud dlia monogram," in *Russica-81: Literaturnyi sbornik* (New York, 1982), p. 408.
3. The cantata was performed publicly for the first time in 1989 under Mstislav Rostropovich.
4. *Werckmeister Harmonies*. The sentence does not appear in Krasznahorkai's book.
5. The Turanian linguistic group was supposed to comprise Finnic, Samoyedic, Tataric, Mongolic, and Tungusic (Müller 1855: 86).
6. See www.expohungary.com.
7. I thank Dr. Imre L. Szabó from Petőfiszállás for collecting some of this information for me.
8. Makovecz became the most influential person in Hungarian architecture, and the image of an underground artist that foreigners often want to stick to him does not correspond to the facts. After all, he was the founder and lifetime president of the Hungarian Academy of Arts and had much institutional power in the Hungarian state. The influence on his disciples was immense. Since the 1970s, hundreds of buildings identifiable as "organic architecture" have been built in the country.
9. The inclinations toward the rustic and the cozy might also have other roots. János Gerle points out that mass production began after World War I during an economic crisis that simply did not permit the construction of anything better (1998: 253). This might have created a certain taste in Hungary and other Eastern European countries.
10. "Ist die organische 'lebendige' Denkweise noch heute für Architekten und in der Bauverwaltung Beschäftigte eine ihrer Arbeit fremde oder gar feindliche Auffassung" (Gerle 1985: 1561).

CHAPTER 10

The Spiritual

Tarkovsky and Tarr

Chapter 7 explained that Andrei Tarkovsky uses the metaphysical in the sense of religious transcendence and that Béla Tarr uses it in an organic sense of immanence. Tarkovsky's images are "tied to the concrete and the material, yet reach out along mysterious paths to regions beyond the spirit" (1986: 114). He tends to highlight the sublime aspects of nature rather than the fact that nature is given to decomposition. As shown, though Tarr's organicism is not religious, it would be wrong to conclude that it contains no metaphysical potential. True, transcendence does not exist because no transcendence can occur in Tarr's recurrence of the same. Consequently, a transcendental beauty in Tarkovsky's sense is impossible. Tarr's aesthetic expressions have no spiritual climax simply because circularity has no climax. The circular narrative structures, the organic disintegration constantly affirming the circularity of life and death, the dances, Mihály Vig's repetitive music—none of this contains beauty we could point at and say, "This is a spiritual element in Tarr's film." At the same time, Tarr is neither a mud-inspired materialist nor a despiritualized version of Tarkovsky. Even without proper religious statements, the spiritual enters his art through the philosophy of the organic. András Bálint Kovács (2008) confirms this by writing, "Tarr had an eye for the same thing as Fassbinder: to see the spiritual source of the universal drama in the utterly banal figures determined by their environment."

Conventional religion appears in Tarr's films rather as a caricature, for example, in the form of the Bible-thumping bigot Mrs. Halics in *Satantango* or of Irimiás as the parody of Jesus. On the other hand, supernatural phenomena like the enigmatic whale as a symbol for a central cosmic order are just as spiritual as Tarkovsky's miracles. The same goes for the bar dance staged by Valuska, which he says is supposed to bring together heaven and earth or to "reconcile humans and God," a formula also very often used by Imre Makovecz when describing the architecture of his churches. Tarr's objects cannot be identified as "beautiful" in Tarkovsky's sense, because in Tarr's work, the spiritual and the mundane are contained within the same organic expression. Andreas Isenschmid (2015) writes that in László Krasznahorkai's stories "the forceful progression toward the moment when the sacred appears is masterly." To pass over these facts and declare Tarr simply secular and mundane is not possible. We find in the work of Tarr and Krasznahorkai the reinstatement of a certain self-contained concept of the organic-spiritual that has dominated large parts of the Western philosophical scene, especially since the nineteenth century.

Strictly speaking, all religions aspire to the organic because it can provide an overarching meaning to diverse fragmented and materialist existences. However, while most organic philosophies search for the spiritual, not all organic thought is religious. Most of the time, the "organic spirituality" is even incompatible with monotheistic religious traditions because it cancels the idea of a single creator as the "organizer" of the organism. The organic form simply evolves out of itself and in relationship with other forms. Any idea of a creator is contrary to the organic. Therefore, no transcendence leading toward "something" (a world of God, history, beauty, the nation, etc.) can be in the self-contained concept of the spiritual. In nineteenth-century philosophy, the circularity on which the organic is founded often has religious undertones. This kind of circularity is not merely absurd as meant in absurd theater; it does not lead to mere pessimism or sarcasm. The circular structures—which, in the eyes of many anthropologists, are reminiscent of rituals—are spiritual because they illustrate the circularity of the stars as well as of biological life cycles. Then, the spiritual is contained in neither the ecstasy of elements nor the beauty of the shot (both of which are Tarkovsky's strengths) but rather the organic coherence holding together the part and the whole. In this sense, "organic" equals "cosmic" because the organic not only decomposes but also expands infinitely.

Tarr interprets Tarkovsky's use of water in the unique sense of purification, pointing out that while water appears as purifying rain for Tarkovsky, water means mud for Tarr. This seems to be right to some extent. In Tarkovsky's films, even puddles of water are not merely puddles: they also reflect the clouds in the sky. In the best case, this could be interpreted as a "bringing together of sky and earth" in Makovecz's sense. However, the organic aspect of water should not be overlooked either. Tarkovsky's spiritual organicism is predominantly expressed via natural elements like water (*Stalker*) and fire (*The Sacrifice*). Water is mysteriously organic, as it conveys movement, growth, and change. The purification aspect of water is thus not the only function of water in Tarkovsky's films. Similarly, fire signifies not only purgation but also decomposition and decay.

Sculpting Time Organically

Tarkovsky was an Eastern European artist who, just like the Hungarian organic architecture movement, opposed Soviet rationalism by shaping his art in an organic fashion. His organic aspect is evident not just because he prefers organic matter, like earth and water, and insists on vitality and naturalistic genesis. The principle point is that Tarkovsky rejected editing as the "main formative element of a film" and announced that the "cinema image comes into being during shooting." He declares editing evil because it organizes the "unified, living structure inherent in the film" from the outside (1986: 114). This rejection announces an organic concept of film construction. From organic philosophy's point of view, the parallels between Tarr and Tarkovsky are thus more pronounced than most critics are ready to affirm. Critics often tend to find many differences in the contents of both directors' films. However, the resemblance concerns formal ways through which both directors achieve a similar aesthetic outlook. Tarkovsky's entire concept of "sculpting in time" is an organic metaphor that can oppose the technical treatment of time. According to Tarkovsky, a director can make, "like a sculptor," from a "lump of time ... an enormous, solid cluster of living facts" (63). Time here is presented as a fluent organic paste that must be handled as such and not rationalized with the help of abstract structures.

Tarr creates a water–mud dichotomy when explaining that water appears as purifying rain for Tarkovsky and as mud for Tarr. However, we should not forget that Tarkovsky's films also smell of earth. Tarkovsky is in love with the "Russian earth," though he never gives in to a Russian cult of the earth. In Tarkovsky's films, the mud and the earth are neither glorified nor seen as evil (as it happens in the Neoplatonic tradition); the earth simply connotes humility. To "love the earth" means to accept the life cycle and the fact that we all must return to the earth one day. Again, this reflects a premise of organic philosophy. Of Alexander Dovzhenko—one of Tarkovsky's role models—it has been said that his characters grew out of the earth, which should be understood as an anticonstructivist, organic metaphor. The only thing that is, is nature, and the cinematic space based on this idea will make all objects appear as what they are—just as if they have been growing out of the earth.

Are we still where Tarkovsky left us in the 1980s? His message was to abandon editing and start "sculpting time." Do the recent developments of slow cinema merely repeat this old Tarkovskian claim, or can we go beyond it? Benjamin Halligan (2000) thinks of Tarkovsky's rejection of rapid editing as "an attempt to reverse the history of cinema—to begin again, to rub shoulders with such figures from early cinema as D. W. Griffith and the Lumière brothers." The above thoughts on Tarr have shown that "organic cinema" with its renewed "editing revolution" is more radical than Tarkovsky ever was. The other reason we are not where Tarkovsky left us is that Tarkovsky was a Soviet film director, while we are living with Tarr in not only a post–Cold War situation but also a globalized world. Somehow, nineteenth-century organic thought has caught up with us as the scientific advances of molecular biology teach us (once again) that all matter is self-organized. The specialist of posthuman culture Rosi Braidotti writes, for example: "Living matter—including the flesh—is intelligent and self-organizing, but it is so precisely because it is not disconnected from the rest of organic life" (2013: 60). The "organic versus editing" controversy must be reflected against this new background.

Sacrifices

In *Stalker*, Tarkovsky depicts a postapocalyptic world, while the apocalypse is an ongoing event in Tarr's films or, in the words of Sylvie Rollet, "immanent" (Rollet 2011: 104). "Everything is over," sings Vali Kerekes in *Damnation*, but it continues forever. The end of the world is the world's permanent state. In Tarr's ruined villages, there is not even a mysterious chamber to discover. The doctor in *Satantango* walks through an abandoned factory similar to what we see in *Stalker*, but he only encounters miserable prostitutes.

In some way, Eszter is similar to Alexander in *The Sacrifice* (1986) because both men's ideals are incompatible with modern life: projects like sacrificing all of one's possessions through fire or discovering the system of real and cosmic music seem to come from another age. Alexander is also looking for harmony, the yin-yang symbol sewn on his kimono. Not very different from Eszter, he believes the loss of harmony between humans and nature has caused the catastrophe he is facing. *The Sacrifice* is a film about decay and the decline of human civilization.

However, decay is more radical here than in Tarr's films because at the end of the all-destructive war, neither civilization nor nature will endure. At the same time, the film is less radical because there is hope, which is the main message. Like in the case of Domenico in Tarkovsky's *Nostalghia* (1983), an extraordinary sacrifice is supposed to turn human destiny around. Domenico takes his life by fire to bring about a change in universal values. Alexander, when faced with destruction, is also driven to heroic spiritual acts bound to save humankind.

Even though an "everything is over" theme hovers above most of Tarr's films, the situation is never as bad as in *The Sacrifice*. Civilization and nature will not disappear. At the same time, there is no hope for improvement. A sacrifice also appears in *Satantango*: the peasants sacrifice everything when they want to start a new collective farm in another city. They hand over their possessions and destroy their own village. However, the story ends in a way Tarkovsky could never have imagined: the peasants are simply victims of a vicious con man and receive nothing in return. In *The Sacrifice*, the sacrifice gives hope, while people in *Satantango* have sacrificed everything only to later experience that this sacrifice has added to the fundamental absurdity of their lives. However, *Satantango* is not simply a film about misery and desperation: a minimal supply of hope seems to be maintained. According to Kovács, Tarr's objective has always been to show "how it was possible to preserve human dignity in the midst of the most miserable social conditions" (2004: 237). In that sense, according to Gáspár Miklós Tamás, who expresses his sentiments on the entire situation of Eastern Europe, the theme is rather "we are finished but at the same time the whole thing is a joke" (2013: 23). Apocalypse might be an ongoing condition, but we can get used to it, especially if we have a sense of humor.

At least the villagers have overcome socialism. A cynic might say they have still not passed the fundamental Stalinist test of the ultimate postapocalyptic culture. Stalinist culture was always meant to be postapocalyptic: once we recognize the truth of communism, we understand that the worst is over. Seen from this perspective, the *Satantango* people have chosen the worst option. While Stalinist culture was meant to be postapocalyptic, the villagers remain trapped in an apocalypse from which not even a sacrifice can redeem them. Within the logical construct of Stalinism, the ultimate truth of socialism has rendered its final judgment and declared everything that is "untrue" in the sense of "not realist" to be decadent and nonexistent. Everything "unreal" will simply be left behind in the apocalypse. According to Boris Groys, "only that which can endure this radiance [of socialist realism] will remain to bask in it—everything else will be plunged into a gloom from which only 'decadent' moans can be heard" (1992: 48). For socialists, socialist realism was showing a way out of the decadent state, but there is no such way for the villagers.

In *The Sacrifice*, there is also a tree of life—the shamanist element of Hungarian folk art. Here, it is not a device for wandering in the seven layers of the sky, though the meaning of the tree as a link between heaven and earth persists. The dried-up stem Alexander plants in the opening scene relates to the legend of an old Russian Orthodox monk named Pamve, who had planted a dead tree on a mountain and instructed a young monk to water it every day until it wakened to life. The young monk would ascend the mountain every day with his bucket and water the tree (see Green 1987). After three years, the monk's efforts were rewarded: the tree began to blossom. Such parabolic ways of expressing faith are clearly alien to the postsocialist universe of Tarr and Krasznahorkai.

Astronomy and the Spiritual

At least since Giordano Bruno's vision of the universe as an organism, the organic has been linked to astronomy, which creates another angle from which the spiritual can be approached. In *Werckmeister Harmonies*, the astronomical theme is predominant. As previously mentioned, the science-induced confusion about natural details and the loss of a center can make organicism attractive today. People in the sixteenth century must have felt the same way when Copernicus announced his astronomical revolution that changed mathematical astronomy. The loss of the center (the earth) also caused a deep crisis of religious belief that philosophers like Bacon, Montaigne, Pascal, and Descartes tried to amend in the sixteenth and seventeenth centuries. They could not really fix the problem. Since the earth could not be physically brought back into the center, all that could be done was to help "man to transform and to replace not only his most fundamental conceptions, but also the very structures of his thought" (Koyré 1962: 10). Enlightenment philosophers attempted to reestablish the center by means of "natural theology" (see chapter 7). They believed that the center (God) resides in nature. The problem is that even if the universe remains organic, it still has no "real" center (the earth) that could be taken for granted as something concrete. Philosophers can only provide metaphorical and conceptual centers to make good for the loss (see Botz-Bornstein 2007b).

"Happy are those ages when the starry sky is the map of all possible path," writes Georg Lukács in *The Theory of the Novel* ([1920] 1971: 29). In European culture, the idea of the perfect overlap of nature, math, and God has always been strongly linked to astronomy. This tradition was so sturdy that it even subsisted through the peak of the Enlightenment and was found compatible with the Enlightenment's rationalist aspirations. Hans Blumenberg (1983: 3–15) holds that neglecting the cosmic order has always been a typically "modern" disease (see chapter 8). However, not all moderns neglected the cosmos. The French nineteenth-century revolutionary thinker Auguste Blanqui developed a theory of eternal return based on astronomical speculations. Blanqui's theory is original in that it is subversive, just like Nietzsche's: the stars themselves show that there is no progress. In a preface to Louis Auguste Blanqui's *L'Eternité par les astres* (Eternity by the stars, 1872), Jacques Rancière explains that extracting knowledge about human matters from observing stars should not be seen as entirely opposed to Enlightenment thought.[1] A good example of this procedure is Pierre-Simon Laplace's *Exposition du Système du Monde* (The System of the World, 1795), in which the author attempted to transform the correspondence between the regularity of planets and political order into an allegory (Rancière 2002: 10). These Enlightenment philosophers would even discuss astronomical constellations with regard to utopias. Charles Fourier, in his *Théorie de l'unité universelle* (Theory of Universal Unity, 1822), soberly asks whether the laws of heavenly harmony cannot be translated into social order (Rancière 2002: 12). Even Auguste Comte strove to transform the power of scientific laws into a spiritual power guiding society. In the end, he attempted to create a new scientific religion (see Comte 1875–1877).

Krasznahorkai expresses his regrets that the cosmic dimension of human thinking has been entirely lost. In the story "The dark woods" he relates how he contemplated the stars during a trip to Beijing when "the sky beamed in the downright excessive splendor of an exceptional beauty" and where looking up to the sky meant recognizing that "I have no connection with the sky, because looking up means that for me like for the whole epoch that I am living in, the connection with the cosmos is terminated, that I am cut off from the universe, excluded, it has been taken away, perhaps permanently" (2015c: 52, 54). The ambition to present the universe as a mathematically coherent system goes back to Pythagoras and was particularly important for Johannes Kepler (1571–1630). For the "preeminent ancient theorists of the cosmos," Plato and Aristotle, physics was not fully mathematizable "because only whatever was perfect could be perfectly mathematical," writes Robert Wallace in his preface to Blumenberg's *The Genesis of the Copernican World* (1987: xxix). Eszter's peculiar relationship with "perfection" can clearly be traced to those fundamental facts of intellectual history.

Chapter 7 explained the principles of musical theology, which is the fusion of natural theology with musical theory that requires music to reflect the realm of God. This tradition influenced Werckmeister, and "musical theology" was directly linked to "astro-theology." The Werckmeister-inspired philosopher Lorenz Christoph Mizler was also influenced by William Derham, the English physicist who measured the speed of sound for the first time in history but also wrote a book called *Astro-theology* (1714). The gist of both Derham's and Mizler's ideas about theology and the stars is that since music and the universe both are God's creations, they must obey the same mathematical laws. Importantly, these philosophies are not organic but the contrary: they are mathematical. The mathematical obsession with counterpoint at the time of Bach was strongly connected to such "universalist" ambitions. Philosophers generally believed that if harmony is universal, it must also be mathematically measurable. Once music is composed according to strictly mathematical principles, it will be tied to the orderly movements of the planets Kepler established in his *Harmonice Mundi* (see Stauffer 2005: 711).

Werckmeister also believed the stars reflect mathematical ratios. Curiously, even Eszter, with all the animosity he has toward Werckmeister, wants the universe to mirror his natural "non-music." In natural tuning, the seven piano keys should be like "seven fraternal stars." The main idea is that once music is anchored "up there," it will be much more natural than anything Werckmeister produced. In the film, Eszter says, "We have to concern ourselves with the seven notes of the scale but not as of the octave, but seven distinct and independent qualities like seven fraternal stars in the heavens." In the novel, Eszter dismisses Werckmeister's option not because it is cosmic but because it is not cosmic enough. His choices are too arbitrary, that is, they are not reflected by the stars: "Maintaining only the precise intervals between octaves, [he] divided the universum of the twelve half-tones—what was the music of the spheres to him!—into twelve simple and equal parts" (Krasznahorkai 1998: 115).

Eszter speaks of the "heavens" as they exist in nature, not as astrophysicists have constructed them. In *Werckmeister Harmonies,* the piano is a metaphor for the universe, and the realm of astronomy reflects the tuning problems we face with the piano. Will the equation $1 + 1 = 2$ remain true in another solar system? Perhaps the sum would be 2.1. This is actually the case on the piano, where math does not match the natural reality known by earthlings. What can we do? If we opt for math, we become adherents to the false idea that the world simply *must* follow mathematical rules; in other words, we become Pythagorean-Platonic technocrats. There is another option: we can simply say math does not matter and that one should follow nature. In that case, we become radical organicists who submit to all fundamentalist temptations enclosed to this option.

Despite their caricatural presentation, these reflections on music and astronomy should not be seen as quirky topics occupying the minds of early eighteenth-century philosophers or crazy Hungarian musicologists. We make similar decisions on a daily basis when holding that art does not follow scientific rules or that certain aesthetic decisions cannot be explained logically. To say there is "another logic" in art and proper is not irrational. Art is neither math nor chaos, but it has a logic that can be organic. Apart from that, aesthetic theory has forged a typically "Werckmeisterian" compromise when inventing the notion of "style." In style, rational, statistically measurable rules join the "logic" of artistic creativity. Style, once understood in this sense, that is, as a unification of sense and spirit (not merely as an aesthetic choice), by definition is organic.

Notes

1. Rancière wrote this preface eleven years before his book on Tarr.

CHAPTER 11
Organic Places

The particularity of nature is that it evolves but also dies. The idea of the organic can thus stand for "vitalism" in Henri Bergson's understanding of the term, but it can also stand for death. Everything natural must die. In this sense, the buildings in Tarr's films are whalelike corpses whose existence is prolonged within a state of degradation, and the people have adapted their way of being to this environment. It's similar to what Giorgio Agamben has said about Venice: "Venice is not more than a cadaver. The city can continue its existence only in a state following death and the decomposition of a cadaver" (2009: 58).

The Truth of Myths

The organic tries to implement a structure derived from nature as well as the universe. Imre Makovecz expresses this idea when explaining that his buildings are situated "between Sky and Earth" or exist as a "continuation of nature" (Gerle 2010: 21). Makovecz actually talks a lot about the sky. At the same time, his astro-organic search for the universal is based on an interest not in mathematics but rather in a "natural logic" absent in the form of empirical facts or abstract rules. The logic can be guessed—very much like a Gestalt—when looking at places, which represents a strong parallel with László Krasznahorkai's astro-organic approach. When Makovecz says the world for him is "God's imprint [or] a place from which God has withdrawn" (2014: 5), he means that the organic order of this world has been temporarily forgotten and covered under formal, rational, and technical structures. But still, it exists. Makovecz's concept of the organic as a deep, preexisting structure is neither mathematical nor purely religious (it has neither a central point nor God), but it is mythical, as it refers to a "lost world in which all cultures shared a great knowledge" (Heathcote 1997: 20). Organic structures are not empirically present, but they can be "read" as signs or, perhaps most aptly, as traces of a Derridaean *écriture* present only through its absence.

Makovecz is also fascinated by traditional patterns of the Kalotaszeg (in Romanian, Țara Călatei) region of Transylvania. They are called "written" patterns even though they do not bear the slightest resemblance to letters. Makovecz "discovered that these patterns are essentially all composed of one basic symbol and its variations. [They are called] written patterns because they use this symbol in order to communicate vibrant, living messages and ideas about the structure of the world" (Gerle 2010: 8). The architect needs to reestablish this "lost world in which all cultures shared a great knowledge" and of which we can find traces: "We try to summon up the architecture of a mythical area. Our aim is to counteract the subsensible spell of technical civilization using supersensible imaginative power" (Makovecz in Heathcote 1997: 7). The approach is very similar to Michel Foucault's description of science as practiced in times of old: signs were scattered in the world and people believed the task of knowledge was to "uncover a language that God had previously distributed across the earth" (1973: 242). Furthermore, the organic view of history this science suggests, which implies seeing the past and the present as organically interlinked, can be understood as part of the neo-Kantian project of shifting scientific interest away from facts toward myths. Ernst Cassirer developed these ideas in his book *Language and Myth* (1946), which influenced organic architects such as Hugo Häring. Finally, the phenomenon is paralleled by what Sylvie Rollet finds in Béla Tarr's images and stories: they do not make statements about certain social situations but "carry the imprint of an immemorial time, the memory of all losses" (2006: 102).

A similar cessation to mythology appears in *The Melancholy of Resistance*, as human rationality is radically questioned. Correspondingly, David Auerbach (2010) writes: "philosophy's explanations, by which I mean *rational conceptualizations*, cannot sit next to chaos. It is only mythology that can make space for the chaos of the Prince." Truth is a matter of neither science nor God but myths. Valuska finds a "curious writing at the inside of the van that chiefly fascinated him; he had never seen letters or signs like it, and, having tempted to read it from both bottom to top and from right to left and failed to make any sense of it, he lightly tapped the shoulder of the person nearest to him and asked, 'excuse me—you wouldn't happen to know what it says here?'" (Krasznahorkai 1998: 86) In his "universal theseus" lectures, Krasznahorkai offers a more detailed description of the circus wagon, specifying that "its walls were constituted of blue corrugated iron sheets on which someone had roughly sketched—in yellow paint—enigmatic shapes" (2001: 11). The mysterious Trojan prefab trailer is equipped with strange messages. Again, the walls are silent, but the silence is the message. In this sense, the trailer also resembles Makovecz's church in Paks, whose inside is covered with mystical folk symbols that become smaller and smaller toward the end of the building. Krasznahorkai's obsession with walls covered with mysterious inscriptions is striking. In the story "Once on the 381," the protagonist finds deep in the thickets of the Serra de Ossa a ruined palace with

> marble slabs, painted tiles of enchanting beauty with sacred landscapes, scenes and inscriptions, of which Pedro could not understand a single one. And wherever he was, these wonderful tiled walls! At one setting he recognized Jesus Christ as he drags the cross.... Innumerable pictures had been painted on the tiles as if they wanted to tell him in this huge palace everything that had happened in the history of mankind from the beginning until then, everything, and he saw it, his eyes flickering because of all those landscapes and scene and inscriptions. (2015b: 167)

Yet another parallel exists between Krasznahorkai and Makovecz. Makovecz points out that Scottish dances create patterns similar to the Kalotaszeg. The "astro-dance" performed at the beginning of *Werckmeister Harmonies* might be precisely what Makovecz calls a "living message about the structure of the world." We will return to this dance later. Makovecz describes the Carpathian Basin as a stage for buildings "between Sky and Earth [which] exist as elements in a meta-nature, as a continuation of nature itself" (Gerle 2010: 21). This approach does not aim to imitate nature, nor does it have anything to do with ecology. Instead, it tries to retrieve a fundamental logic believed to be covered by a world that has become "techno-logical." The process is very similar, according to Makovecz, to retrieving "[a]n elemental strength [that] can be heard in the old, Hungarian songs sung on the pentatonic scale" (80). Those harmonies are real and need to be retrieved. Thus, Makovecz shares musical ambitions very similar to Eszter's.

One cannot emphasize enough that this project of retrieving the logic of nature has nothing to do with ecological approaches. At first, organicism and environmentalism seem to head in the same direction because both search for a "natural" totality. Rosi Braidotti has called environmentalism "a new holistic approach that combines cosmology with anthropology and post-secular, mostly feminist spirituality." Braidotti is right in pointing out that this movement deconstructs (paradoxically

Organic Places • 165

Figure 11.1. Interior of Holy Spirit Church in Paks by Imre Makovecz.

through its holistic perspective) Western humanism and "the West's investment in rationality and secularity as the precondition for development through science and technology" (2014: 48). A universalist way of thinking (such as humanist scientism) can be deconstructed through holism, and this paradoxical constellation indeed brings environmentalism close to organic thinking. The problem: ecology is a natural science that will necessarily reformulate its cosmological quests in terms of a new set of universalist ambitions. In the words of the French geographer Augustin Berque (2011), ecology is interested in the environment "in the form of an *object*, which is not supposed to contain human subjectivity. Even if it is relational (like ecosystems or trophic links), in its essence it is not supposed to depend on the point of view of the observer. Instead, it is detached from our existence, which is the only reason why it can be 'scientific.' For ecology, the environment exists in itself and can be measured." This means that even New Age–inspired "eco-spiritualism"—which is very often based on sources from Fritjof Capra and James Lovelock and by which some contemporary organic architecture is inspired—insists on absolutes and necessarily ends up as a universalism. Another problem is, of course, that eco-spiritualism's universalism is not even formulated in a scientifically rigorous fashion.

For Makovecz, objects must be "alive," an idea we already know from Krasznahorkai, whose organic spider web had turned the environment into a living organism. While Makovecz refers to Celtic legends in which trees once walked on earth as inspiration for his treelike architecture (Heathcote 1997: 73), trees become alive for Krasznahorkai through the workings of bugs. The villagers in *Satantango* hear "the ever more frequent *scratch-scratch* of the bent acacia trees outside, and the strange nightshift work of the bugs in the table legs and in various parts of the counter whose irregular pulse measured out the small parcels of time" (2012a: 89). Here, the world has been turned into a living universe. Krasznahorkai's approach also recuperates organic thoughts expressed in theories of *Einfühlung* ("empathy") Theodor Lipps and Wilhelm Worringer developed at the beginning of the twentieth century. Furthermore, the idea of the world experienced as a living universe also affected architectural theory, as Hans Schleicher (1987) shows in his *Architektur als Welterfahrung* (Architecture as world experience).

Organic Space

Contrary to geometrical space, phenomena in organic space are not mathematically constructed: they simply occur. Häring coined the word *Geschehensraum* ("event space"), which is not an abstract container of events but a space defined in accordance with processes and activities. Makovecz, Krasznahorkai, and Tarr also conceptualize space in a particular way. For Krasznahorkai, space is an eternal realm in which objects and even moving bodies organically connect. The spider web metaphor in *Satantango* reinstates this organically linked universe almost literally. For András Bálint Kovács, this metaphor represents the "eternity of natural laws" (2013: 130). A space is not merely a geometrical extension but is inscribed in an eternity of cosmic laws.

Makovecz's church in Paks is a collection of symbols and quotations whose holistic character is not at all obvious. Elements are often autoreferential and require individual interpretations. Still, one does not have the impression of postmodern fragmentation. The strange shape of the steeple seems to contain its own story; the round side chapels near the altar seem to be incompatible with the Gothic, upward-striving roof. However, a spatial fluency dependent on a continuous structure that permeates the whole interior maintains the organic coherence. The "rhythm" of this space does not seem to be predetermined by a plan but is "enacted" by the particular elements it contains. The phenomenon is similar to Tarr's concept of rhythm in cinema "that is not provided by the story but by the actors, by the play of the actors.... I understand the temporality without forgetting that this is a life and that it is happening" (Breteau-Skira 2010: 18, 22). The film's form or Gestalt is thus found in the simplest way through the play of elements. Consequently, similar to Makovecz, Krasznahorkai creates "pseudo-mysterious spaces" (Makovecz 2014: 112), which seem to be simultaneously natural and holy. In the novel, Krasznahorkai describes the scene unfolding in the ruin, where Estike dies and where her brother discovers her body, like a Tarkovskian image: "The corpse started to rise again, and some six feet above the clearing it trembled, then with incredible speed it rose and flew off, soon to be lost among the still, solemn clouds" (2012a : 217).

Krasznahorkai and Tarr almost literally implement Makovecz's "bringing together of Earth and Sky" when Valuska organizes the dance for the revelers at closing time in a tavern, a dance meant to demonstrate the

Figure 11.2. Holy Spirit Church in Paks by Imre Makovecz.

relationships between the sun, the earth, and the moon and, more precisely, during an eclipse. By linking bodies organically, Valuska attempts to fuse the universal with the particular and solemnly announces in the film: "All I ask is that you step with me into the boundlessness where constancy, quietude, and peace and infinite emptiness reign. And just imagine that in this infinite sonorous silence everywhere is an impenetrable darkness." We must understand Tarr's peculiar emphasis of the representation of the environment in this context. Kovács describes how Tarr "construct[s] the landscapes from little pieces, as in the case of *Damnation*, where the town in which the film takes place does not correspond to any existing location. Every street, every corner and every building is taken from a different place" (2013: 15). This alone is a remarkably organic approach to create a coherent whole out of parts. In *The Turin Horse*, the house had to be built at a certain place in the landscape directly opposite a lonely tree on the peak of a hill. The wintry tree is indeed planted like a Hungarian tree of life that Makovecz so often depicts. In ancient Hungary, spirits were associated with trees, which is why they were placed in cemeteries (see Cook 1997: 13). Jacques Rancière even notes that this house is "at once entirely real and entirely constructed" (2013: 70; 2011: 77), which sounds very much like an evocation of organic architecture. Perhaps Rancière means this is a "house prior to the appearance of man, in the world of beginnings, a radiant, real image, a real home, a living house of the Golden Age?" (Makovecz 2014: 5). Makovecz would perhaps describe the entire scene like this.

Furthermore, Rancière's "entirely real and yet entirely constructed" could also be an allusion to the ancient Greek *aletheia*, the "disclosed" truth that is simply revealed and not a state of affairs "true" within a logical system. Martin Heidegger (1969) has rediscovered the idea of *aletheia* for the purpose of his own ontology, but it has also been a keyword for Häring for whom it expressed "true createdness of the world as a creation of the spirit" (Blundell Jones 1996: 197). In any case, the house in *The Turin Horse* assuredly "grows out of the landscape as naturally as any plant; its relationship to the site is so unique that it would be out of place elsewhere." This sentence comes from nobody else but Frank Lloyd Wright, who wrote it in his seminal essay "Organic Architecture" (1941: 178). Its total correspondence with Tarr's approach illustrates one of the meanings of "organic space" in cinema. In *The Man from London*, space appears artificially produced: a look out of the fur shop window yields the view to the harbor. However, this is how people in the film seem to experience this space, making it not artificial but natural. The space of this small town is simultaneously claustrophobic and universal.

Figure 11.3. Still from *The Man from London* (2007).

Maloin can see all of it from his tower, which is how the individual and the general become fused.

Tarr often produces organic space through long walking scenes that are striking in *Werckmeister Harmonies, Satantango,* and *The Man from London*. *Werckmeister Harmonies* is a sort of road movie as we follow Valuska, who never gets tired of walking. In Krasznahorkai's and Tarr's works, the activity of walking creates space in a way similar to how Michel de Certeau believes the space of cities becomes "real" through the process of walking. The walker establishes the place by making the potential actual: "If it is true that a spatial order organizes an ensemble of possibilities (e.g. by a place in which one can move) and interdictions (e.g. by a wall that prevents one from going further), then the walker actualizes some of these possibilities. In that way he makes them exists as well as emerge" (1984: 98). For Walter Benjamin, the act of walking also constitutes the experience of the city as a place. Christine Boyer finds that with "each step the flâneur takes, whether in the city of Paris, Berlin or Moscow or Marseilles, new constellations of images appear that resemble the turns of a kaleidoscope" (1996: 51). In Tarr and Krasznahorkai, the organic spider web of trajectories holds those individual images together. In the walking scenes, time and space become fused. In other words, the walks function like spider webs, which, according to Ottilie Mulzet, "paralyzes and immobilizes, and yet, at the same time, like the extraordinary sentence, connects all of the characters' dreams, knitting them together into one thread" (Esposito 2013: 114).

We have encountered in this book the concept of "dynamic paralysis" in various contexts. Here, in the context of spatial creation in art, dynamic paralysis refers to a spider web of trajectories that holds the space together and makes it organic. However, other "strings" of the web should not be forgotten: the trajectories of the camera, whose movements are often autonomous, as the camera is not simply following the logic of the narrative or even of the subjects. (Chapter 12 will present more about these autonomous camera movements.) Furthermore, dynamic paralysis is also important for the style of acting. Though a lot of dancing and walking occur in Tarr's films, the actors often appear static and stiff. In general, there is much staring, posing, and standing about. Even in the astro-dance, the actors appear almost like the living figurines employed in Vanessa Beecroft's performances or like the blank, expressionless, waxlike figurines of the popular advertisement campaigns by the fashion brand Diesel. The swirling around of the (often drunk) people during dances looks mechanical. Lucie Wright and Eric de Lastens (2011: 89) find those movements "purified and frozen" (*epuré et figé*), and Josef Dabernig (2011: 72) even suggests that Tarr "visualizes the protagonists in an autistic way." This also becomes obvious in *The Turin Horse*, where human gestures appear particularly mechanic as the characters are enclosed in a universe that offers no beyond. Though the characters in all those films engage in entirely normal actions, agency is far from being free. This is the case not so much because their individual will has been submitted to constraints but rather because there does not seem to have been much will to begin with. Even people's libidinal instinctiveness (in *Damnation*, for example) lacks the usual will, desire, and passion. Overall, movements are predetermined like those of the stars the village people were asked to enact in *Werckmeister Harmonies*. This is not *real* action but it *symbolizes* action. Dynamic paralysis is therefore an appropriate term for this acting style. If we think of *The Turin Horse*, we might say that, in the end, characters become organically linked to the space they are acting in, which follows, once again, the principles of organic architecture. For Häring, a house is the organ of inhabitants (Blundell Jones 1996: 186).

Actions Harmonized

How can an acting style and a spatial economy based on dynamic paralysis be described more precisely? What matters in this cinematic aesthetics is not the objective toward which the action is directed but rather the "how" of the action. This flows from the aesthetics' imperatives of the organic. Like for all things organic, the most important quality in these films is harmony. For example, when trajectories make space organic, walking becomes an exercise in harmonization. The long shot of Eszter and Valuska walking side by side in *Werckmeister Harmonies* might appear superfluous when deprived of the theoretical context into which both the book and the novel are imbedded. However, Krasznahorkai's description of the scene provides an essential input in terms of philosophy of space. What we are asked to watch for a full two minutes is a "walking version" of the Werckmeisterian compromise reinforced through the sound of their synchronized steps.

In the book, matters are actually more complex, as the author will explain with the usual dedication to details. The long passage illustrates Krasznahorkai's vision of the paradox of space and time: both men are moving next to each other but at apparently different speeds. The description of this logical impossibility reads like a definition of organic space:

> They had to harmonize two ways of walking, two different speeds, and, indeed, two different kinds of incapacity, for while Eszter's every step across the suspiciously glimmering surface was taken as if it were his last, each appearing to be a preparation for a gradual but ultimately total cessation of movement, Valuska's acute desire to increase his own momentum was consistently frustrated. (1998: 134)

This space is organic because speed is "merely" experienced and not mathematically measured. In fact, it *cannot* be mathematically measured. In Bergsonian terms, we can say the speed is experienced in a "pure" way, the "trick" being that both men experience it in the same pure way, which makes the above paradox possible even though it remains a mathematical impossibility. If we follow the words of the novel, we discover that the paradox is made possible because the speed is not objectified but remains unobjectified. In other words, Krasznahorkai describes speed as it is experienced before it has been objectified in terms of miles per hour. The author is actually very eloquent when it comes to describing the desperate attempts at creating simultaneity in a situation where it remains mathematically impossible:

> One could perhaps sum up the situation by saying that their roles consisted of Valuska pulling and tugging and Eszter acting as an effective brake or that Valuska was practically running while Eszter was practically standing still, but it would be inappropriate to consider their progress severally, partly because the discrepancy between their strides

seemed to be resolved in some combined lurch forward, an uncertain, painful-looking progress, and partly because their clumsy clinging interdependence precluded their being individually identified as Eszter on the one hand and Valuska on the other: in effect they appeared to form a bizarre figure. And so they advanced in curious unitary fashion. (1998: 134)

Yvette Bíró concludes that Eszter and Valuska are walking in a circle, though I see no evidence of this. Bíró writes: "only after a while do we realize that they are going round and round, circling all around as if under a spell. The growing speed makes it foreboding and disquieting: we have to sense their doom" (2008: 171). In my opinion—and regarding Krasznahorkai's detailed description of the passage—the walking scene rather works toward the overcoming of all spatial notions, including that of circularity. The only "positive" result that can be retained is dynamic paralysis.

The continuation of the narrative shows more clearly than ever that harmony remains a very difficult thing to achieve, and even when achieved, it can easily appear contrived and not natural at all. Is this "bizarre figure" composed of Valuska and Eszter really the "natural harmony" so many people in this novel aspire to obtain? According to the author, they look like a "wandering shade, a demon that had lost its way." If this is harmony, it is still based on a compromise, and like all compromises, this one is not entirely satisfying. It is still not the "real" thing in the sense of "real music" Eszter wants to discover.

However, Eszter and Valuska are not the only ones practicing harmonized walking. There is also the crowd about to take over the town by creating an increasingly extended spider web of trajectories while walking through the city. Here, the coordination of speed, that is, the integration of individual speed into the overall speed of the crowd, is of utmost importance. Slowly, the masses advance in the form of a silent organic whole. Any individual consciousness has been absorbed by the consciousness of the unique mass, which is also why, afterward, no individual reason can be found for the actions committed:

> Just as would happen later in the square when their companions met with a noticeable larger crowd by the now burning chapel, the way they came upon them enabled them to maintain their rate of progress during whatever remained of their terrifying unfinished expedition, ensuring that their otherwise slow but menacing pace should chime in with the even tempo of the march, which had been previously maintained from the cinema through the entrance of the square and thence to the deserted silence of St. Stephen's street behind the place of wor-

ship. Not a single word passed between them now, only the odd match flared briefly with the answering glow of the lit cigarette, their eyes being fixed on the back of the man in front or on the pavement as they moved almost unconsciously in step with the others in the freezing cold. (Krasznahorkai 1998: 214)

Things change dramatically toward the end of the film/novel, when everything has been destroyed, a new pragmatic order has been established, and Valuska is fleeing the city. In this new environment, walking is no longer a matter of spider web making but of mere confusion. As Eszter walks away from the whale, he looks profoundly disturbed because he recognizes what Valuska suspected from the beginning: there might be a web, but it has no center. Valuska pointed this out very early in the novel when suggesting "the ramshackle truck" might contain only "a stinking corpse" (86).

Valuska is a classic example of the enlightened idiot. His knowledge of science is far superior to that of the herdlike village people. Valuska explains the event of a solar eclipse, which has historically been seen as a mysterious and unexplainable occurrence, in purely rational and scientific terms while organizing the curious bar dance. During the rare occurrence of an eclipse, two organically centralized systems—the geocentric and the heliocentric orbit—overlap. In this spider web of orbits, the main center (the sun) is temporarily covered, which lets the universe appear temporarily uncentered when seen from a particular angle. Still, the sun exists. This is different from an uncentered universe with only

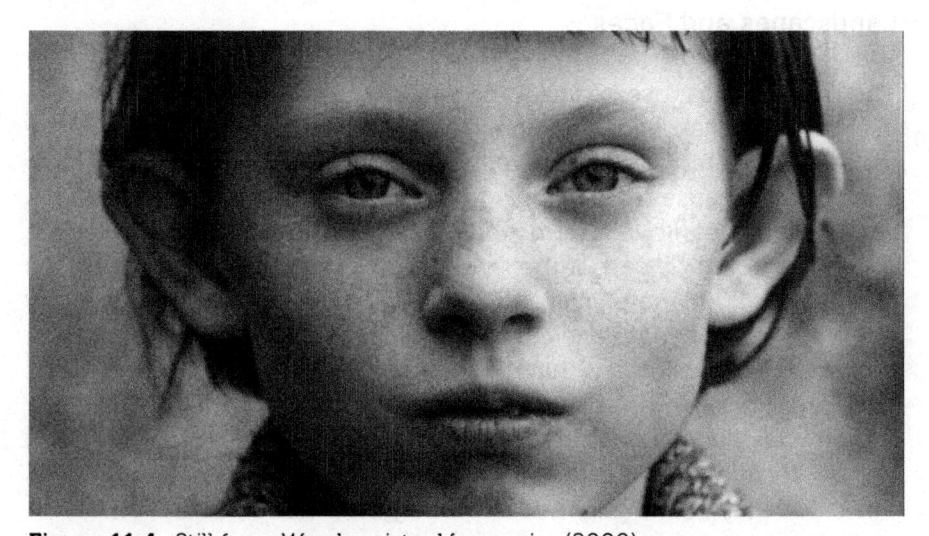

Figure 11.4. Still from *Werckmeister Harmonies* (2000).

a decaying whale in the middle, which is the universe *in reality* that all protagonists are living in.

Overall, the village idiot scores better than the scientist and humanist György Eszter, though in the end, a similar destiny awaits both. As Eszter walks away from the whale, a no less confused and aimless Valuska is fleeing the city, desperately following railroad tracks, though he should know straight lines have no meaning in this uncentered universe. Eventually, he will run into his enemy's arms:

> He had no "ultimate destination" for he did not think he was fleeing from anything behind him; in other words he fully accepted the paradox implied in the conclusion that his movements had direction but no aim. And he had absolutely no intention of deluding himself in this respect but accepted the necessity of all such things in so far as all such things existed in their own natural state of chaos, that is to say he too must act on necessity. (240)

Again, Krasznahorkai's description of Valuska moving in a certain direction, simultaneously affirming that his movements have "no aim," is strange, to say the least, in terms of spatiality and time. Captured inside the organic spider web, Valuska still believes to go somewhere, though in reality there is no place to go. Finally, his actions become random, just like those of the Prince and his people who have been smashing things randomly the night before.

Landscapes and Faces

The metaphorical use of facial morphologies establishes another parallel between Makovecz and Tarr. The approaches are different but the results similar. Tarr's and Makovecz's approaches toward space are also analogous because their spatial creations are often organic formations resembling faces. Kovács notes that in Tarr's films "bodies and faces are of the characters as part of the material environment" (2013: 63). In his article from 2008, he explains: "In *Damnation,* the past was carried by the outer and inner surfaces of buildings; here history is condensed in human faces." This means that bodies and faces form landscapes. About *The Turin Horse,* Tarr has said the location is one of the main characters: "When you're doing a movie, you don't do theories. I just look for locations. A location has a face. It's one of the main characters. So I found this little valley in Hungary and the lonely tree" (Jaffe 2014: 160).

Figure 11.5. Church in Siófok by Imre Makovecz.

Faces become integrated into the space as the camera "slowly pans through a certain space at a monotonously slow pace, not stopping or slowing down when it reaches a human body or face, just passing it by as if it were another object in the environment" (Kovács 2013b: 63). What occurs is thus a curious fusion of human faces and space. Here, the face is not as it was for Béla Balázs: a window or a gateway to the human soul. But it helps to make space organic, the more so since the faces are not integrated into the landscape as dispassionate, inexpressive objects. Instead, "faces and postures always carry certain expressions, which are also articulated in the position of the landscape." Tarr asserts that the real protagonist of *Damnation* is the landscape and "that characters were part of the landscape" (60). He admits he began seeing cinema differently through this film. *Damnation* is a "landscape film," he says, which means landscape has replaced narrative. What is more important than narrative is "the rain and the most banal event" (Tarr in the "La Rochelle interview," quoted in Breton 2011: 100). It is also here, while working on this film, that Tarr became interested in walls. Filming a wall like a painter paints a panting while the narrative continues, clearly visible though not central to the film—this is precisely the strategy of organic cinema.

In *Werckmeister Harmonies,* the camera pans around on a huge bleak and foggy market square, moving in circular motion with Valuska. The square is very bleak, just like the whole town in which streets have only generic names like Jokai Street, Arpad Street, Petöfi Square, and Honvéd Passage. Finally, the camera rests on the faces of people, similar to what Tarr did when filming people in a long queue for his short film *Visions of Europe* (2004). This sequence in *Werckmeister Harmonies* lasts a whole two minutes, at the end of which the faces have become part of the square. Faces also become important when Valuska is "face to face" with the whale. What came as a prefab building becomes highly personal because, in the end, it has a face. In the last scene of *Werckmeister Harmonies,* Eszter looks at the whale's face, too. The whale, which had so far been the center of the town, as well as of the whole universe, is not only decaying, but even the glassy essence of its eye remains expressionless and metaphysically meaningless. Obviously, this cannot be the center of the universe.

Several other critics have noticed the importance of the face for Tarr's spatial economy. Susan Doll finds that "places in Tarr's cinema are faces and characters, each of which Tarr chooses most carefully" (*Talking about Tarr* 2008: 12). "Regarding Tarr's belief in the near equivalence of location, face, and character, Doll has noted that besides saying "a location has a face," Tarr has stressed—to David Bordwell, among others—that "the face is the landscape" (Jaffe 2014: 160).

Tarkovsky's Landscapes

Of course, this treatment of space is not so different from Andrei Tarkovsky. In *Sculpting in Time,* Tarkovsky declares that one should watch his films "as one watches the stars, or the sea, as one admires a landscape. There is no mathematical logic here, for it cannot explain what man is or what is the meaning of life" (1986: 9). Above the organic "math versus nature metaphor" this statement implies, Tarkovsky suggests one should refrain from deciphering his films by locating symbolisms. A film is an organism, not a mathematically organized collection of signs. Like Tarr, Tarkovsky points to the "landscape" as a conceptual means to express what cannot be conceptualized otherwise, because the organic coherence is not an empirical fact.

There are not many landscapes to see in Tarkovsky's films, but the landscape concept remains important. Tarkovsky's landscapes are not geological but "mental landscapes," like the "zone" in *Stalker,* which represents organic space par excellence. In the zone, there are no straight lines that could be followed to arrive in "the center" in the shortest time possible. When the Professor is lost, the other men continue, but as they emerge from the tunnel, they find themselves back at the spot where they began. They see the Professor sitting on this same spot eating his lunch. Apparently, the center is reached via long, circular trajectories and by taking the longest way possible; once we arrive, we discover that the center is a noncenter. There are also purely mental landscapes like the "cosmic ocean" or the space station in *Solaris* (1972), where people live only through their own memories. These landscapes are not Euclidian, geometrical spaces, but they are purely spiritual/mental.

Makovecz's Landscapes

Makovecz's face concept is similar to Tarr's, the only difference being that it is literal, not metaphorical. For Makovecz, "organic" means a house should be humanlike and have the structure of a face: it should have eyes, eyebrows, and a nose because a house is a being (see Figure 11.5). The face morphology is actually one of the most striking features of Makovecz's buildings, and it also occurs in those of Bruce Goff, who influenced Makovecz. However, not only can faces be integrated into space, but landscapes can also become faces. Makovecz points to the "landscape" as a conceptual means to express what cannot otherwise be conceptualized. The landscape is a typical example of an organic space and a can be recognized in a way similar to how we recognize a face. This is why landscape language is most often visited by anthropomorphisms ("brooding mountains," "dancing streams," etc.). In Makovecz's view, landscapes have organic structures because they are not just nature, but they also contain cultural elements: there is "something in the shapes of nature, the arrangement of the mountain that attracts us like the vague memory of some ancient city" (2014: 112). This is not the natural landscape of the geologist but the cultural landscape of the painter. In both cases, in that of the landscape and that of the face, individual elements are unified by a universal concept that can be given various names according to the philosophical approach pursued: culture, God, myths, spirit. Makovecz actually prefers the word spirit: "The location of a village, the route of roads—these are nothing less than the thought-out world's language, as spoken by the peoples' spirit" (Gerle 2010: 56).

Importantly, spaces in Makovecz's works do not become faces through mere "folklorization." This is also true for Tarr. Despite the recurrent tactile evocations of the past, no idealization of tradition or nostalgia appears in those films, but the depictions of run-down town halls and restaurants are simply "realist." In the best case, they evoke a (post)socialist charm. As Kovács notes, "this landscape evokes a strong social milieu without being specific to any particular city, nation, region" (2013: 61). Tarr shares precisely this idea with Makovecz for whom folk arts are not a celebration of nationalism but vehicles to reveal "the structure of life of old towns, trees, tectonic forces and natural materials" (Gerle 2010: 103). Nothing could be further removed from the new Hungarian right-wing architects' "The Garden of Life" pavilion, which is an objective, environmentalist statement imbued with not cosmic spirit but nationalist ideologies.

Finally, Krasznahorkai also seems obsessed with the anthropomorphic character of landscapes. In *The Bill,* Krasznahorkai analyzes a painting by the sixteenth-century Venetian Palma Vecchio. The author insists on the existence of a "valley in Seriana" from which this painter has descended and where Krasznahorkai believes the anatomy of the women painted is located: "That what you wanted was, beyond any doubt, precisely the same thing each time, that's to say, that valley in Seriana, you filthy reprobate, that is to say the valley between a whore's shoulders and her breasts, that is, the valley where you were born" (2013b: 14).

Dreams

The last sentence of János Gerle's important book on Makovecz refers to the cultural content hidden inside the world not in the form of a mathematical, calculable structure but as a dream. He believes "only that architecture is justifiable, which is capable of discovering and comprehending from within the mental powers that create the dream-image, and that is able to evoke and visualize this in the outside world" (2010: 217). Through his association with dreams, Makovecz's architecture becomes cinematic. Andor Wesselényi-Garay (2008) believes the difference between regionalist and organic architecture is that the former is designed while the latter is dreamed. Given this quest for a visualization of mental states through dreamlike images, the parallel question for cinema theory, which aims at the core of organic cinema, must be: what is the inner structure of a film and how do we comprehend the mental powers that create a film image "from within"?

CHAPTER 12

The Organic Camera Shot

The Materiality of the Shot

This last chapter aims to finally show that the long take and the landscape are conceptually linked. Imre Makovecz's buildings have faces. What is relatively easy to establish for an architect is a tricky task for a film director. To produce organic environments with facial expressions is obviously much more difficult in films. A priori, this should be even more difficult for Béla Tarr because—paradoxically—his films excel in the "faceless" uniformity of space represented by run-down villages given to postcommunist depression.

The main tool for obtaining an organic space in cinema is the long take, which can transform space into a coherent and respectable entity, similar to the stable entity of a face. Tarr is the modern master of the single shot. David Bordwell finds that for Tarr "the long take is ... a token of respect for the integrity of the person.... I think there is something about this idea of the long take either on a face or even on an entire city or street" (*Talking about Tarr* 2008: 10). Similarly, Jacques Rancière (2013: 34) sees a film by Tarr as an "assemblage of these crystals of time in which the 'cosmic' pressure is concentrated" ("assemblage de ces cristaux de temps où se concentre la pression 'cosmique'" [2011: 41]). And Sylvie Rollet speaks of the "quasi-tactile, sticky sensation of a time, first of all produced by the extreme stretching of camera shots" (2013: 2). In those long takes, time is not liquid and abstract but rather obtains the more tactile, organic, and "sticky" fluency of a paste. Both Rancière's and Rollet's statements can be passed on as descriptions of organic cinema. Rancière goes even further by saying those films contain "no pieces, no demiurge of montage. Each moment is a microcosm. Each sequence shot [*plan-séquence*] has a duty to the time of the world, to the time in which the world is reflected in intensities felt by bodies" (2013: 34; 2011: 41).

Organic architects refer to the shots and moments that are microcosms in their own right as "materiality." The semifluid, long takes follow a rhythm based on the inherent qualities of the filmed material, not on editing. This is a characteristic of organic cinema. In Tarr's films, not only do the walls have textures and patterns, but each sequence shot also has a texture. Since our attention cannot be captured in those long scenes—predominantly—by psychological states, social questions, or motivated actions, we do not concentrate on narrative elements, and our attention shift to objects, micro-events, and darkness. This is also precisely the kind of "realism" André Bazin aspired to when emphasizing the importance of "depth": "That depth of focus brings the spectator into a relation with the image closer to that which he enjoys with reality. Therefore it is correct to say that, independently of the contents of the image, its structure is more realistic" (2005 1: 35).

The principle of this kind of viewing, which is more hypnotic than the one determined by following a story line, is the metonymic shot, Andrei Tarkovsky's specialty. In Tarr's cinema, the metonymy is purified and emptied of any narrative sense, which is made possible through the length of the camera takes. The material makes us dream as we—in a way of speaking—bump into it. Consequently, Rancière describes Tarr's films as a universe in which we are confronted with the "inertia of things, and the breaches that can create the obstinacy to follow an idea, a dream, a shadow.... There is the *huis clos* where one turns in circles, bumping up against furniture and other people" (2013: 42; 2011: 48). Though Rancière provides no reference to Marcel Proust, this passage strongly reminds us of Proust's description in *Swann's Way* of how Swann is waking up at night feeling that "everything would be moving round me through the darkness: things, places, years." Swann attempts to construe the form of the room and "to induce from that where the wall lay and the furniture stood, to piece together and to give a name to the house in which it must be living." In the end, the spatial experience becomes one of organic composition: "While the unseen walls kept changing, adapting themselves to the shape of each successive room that it remembered," Swann attempts to make sense of the space he has been thrown into (Proust 1922: 5).

Rhythm and Harmony

Swann's experience comes very close to viewing a long take by Tarr. Like in organic architecture, the material organizes the space and not the other way round. When I say "material," I do not mean the "raw material" of Sergei Eisenstein, who attempted to organize material in a futurist manner mainly through *ostranenie* (alienation, estrangement, or *Verfremdung* in German). Eisenstein's procedure relates to Russian constructivism, which produced art through the combination of *faktura*, that is, the particular material properties of an object (see Lodder and Benus 2012). All this has nothing to do with the organic creation of space and time through material. "Constructed" is the contrary of organic. The difference is that Eisenstein attempted to install a conflict between the object shown and its spatial nature, or a conflict between an event and its temporal nature. Moreover, his main aim was to combat "intuitive creativity." Like futurists and formalists, Eisenstein wanted to overcome any temptation of what early twentieth-century philosophers like Theodor Lipps had established as *Einfühlung* ("empathy") in the theory of perception. Chapter 11 showed that *Einfühlung* is an important part of organic thought recuperated by László Krasznahorkai. It is also important for organic architectural theory. Paradoxically, in formalism, the "raw material," that is, the object or the micro-event in question, has no "material" value in itself. Even time is meant to be only an abstract structure, not real time. Rhythm is considered equally dangerous because it still relies too much on "artistic feeling." In "The Montage of Film Attraction" (1924) Eisenstein writes: "A rhythmic schema is arbitrary; it is established according to the whim or the 'feeling' of the director and not according to mechanical periods dictated by mechanical conditions of the course of a particular motor process" (1988: 48). Neither material nor time is supposed to be concrete.

Tarkovsky attempted to overcome this formalist aesthetics of film. In a famous page in *Sculpting in Time*, he describes how he "once taped a casual dialogue. People were talking without knowing they were being recorded. Then I listened to the tape and thought how brilliant it was 'written' and 'acted.' The logic of character's movements, the feeling the energy—how tangible it all was. How euphoric the voices were how beautiful the voices" (1986: 65). Tarkovsky derives everything he appreciates in this dialogue *from* this dialogue by means of observation. It is a little like Tarr filming the long dancing scene in the bar. Both examples contradict what Eisenstein and the formalists would propagate as the "capturing of raw material." For Tarkovsky, this scene contains an "inner time," which means not only that time exists through the relationships between different shots but also that a fascinating rhythm and a brilliantly "acted" scenario occur in this scene. For formalists, on the other hand, a single shot remains static and mechanical because it contains no time (see Botz-Bornstein 2007a: 4–5), and the rhythm will be installed through a mathematical structure. In other words, dynamics is for the formalist not an organic phenomenon produced through the relationship between two different times (the individual time of the scene, which can also be called "mood" or "atmosphere," and the general time of the film), but dynamics is constructed by fitting individual shots into an overall structure. Tarkovsky, however, when speaking of the "unusual combinations" and "conflicts between entirely real elements" (1986: 72), describes a principle of organic cinema. Here, the proper rhythm is rather the *différance* between the two rhythms or the movement restrained by nothing other than itself, which is again highly evocative of "dynamic paralysis." In the *Werckmeister Harmonies* scene in which Eszter and Valuska are walking next to each other (see chapter 11), Krasznahorkai takes much care to describe the "rhythm" of their movements and the evolution of time. By doing so, he creates a paradoxical vision of space and time: both men are moving next to each other though at apparently different speeds. We have already concluded that the underlying principle of this phenomenon is dynamic paralysis. The concept of dynamic paralysis can thus oppose the formalist idea of dynamics. The latter is merely constructed by fitting individual shots into an overall structure.

The keyword is "restraint." On his blog, *Unspoken Cinema*, devoted to "Contemporary Contemplative Cinema," Harry Tuttle (2007) suggests that in Tarr's films "the rhythm is constructed and based on restraint. Everything has its proper rhythm, nothing can be hurried nor slowed down." Once again, the situation is paradoxical: on one hand, the "harmonized walking" practiced by Eszter and Valuska, which is supported by the rhythmic sound of their synchronized steps, is a logical impossibility since both are moving next to each other though at apparently different speeds. On the other hand, readers and spectators in the text and the film can experience the walking scene. The organic time-space is created as each step appears "to be a preparation for a gradual but ultimately total cessation of movement," which cannot be measured but only "lived." This experience is, according to Krasznahorkai, based on a "painful-looking progress," which is, once again, nothing other than restraint. The dynamic paralysis of the protagonists' roles consist "of Valuska pulling and tugging and Eszter acting as an effective brake or that Valuska was practically running while Eszter was practically standing still" (Krasznahorkai 1998: 134). We are strongly reminded of Béla Hamvas's genealogy of the great artist who knows the secret of restraint and that winning cannot consist only of winning, victory, and triumph. As shown in chapter 4, Hamvas's (2007) aesthetics of resistance, in which the evolution of the ego must always be—melancholically—restrained by the anti-egoistic powers of humility, advances the paradoxical (Buddhist or kenotic?) truth that strength must always be linked to the "weak, fragile and incomplete."

Furthermore, the pattern also connects to the main topic of *Werckmeister Harmonies*: nature (reality, space, and time) cannot be summed up by math. Here, this same conundrum is reiterated in the philosophy of time through which it also extends into the philosophy of film. The walking scene shows that time (cinematic time or just any time) cannot be rendered through mathematically calculated structures even when time is rhythmic. While a formalist will look for the right balance of scenes by applying a mathematically calculated (geometric) model in which movement and time make logical sense, an organic film director will choose another path: she will let one scene (one "real element") grow out of another element, exactly as it happens in this walking scene (each step appears "to be a preparation for a gradual but ultimately total cessation of movement"). In other words, the movement creates its own temporal logic that can be called an organic rhythm. While conventional films let "life" appear within the logic of a story, an organic director attempts to show life itself. Correspondingly, Tarr (2004) says in an interview: "The people of this generation know information-cut, information-cut, information-cut. They can follow the logic of it, the logic of the story, but they don't follow the logic of life."

Fluent Space and Long Takes

The fluent space produced by the long take is also the space most appreciated in organic architecture. One of the most important principles for all generations of organic architects is that the boundaries between parts should be not closed but open: "Gardens never end and buildings never begin," wrote the organic architect Alden Dow in 1935 (Robinson 1993: 11). Similarly, Rollet finds that in Tarr's spaces "the border between inside and outside is fading (*s'efface*)" (2006: 102). For Frank Lloyd Wright, "" (1975: 32). Purely geometrical divisions of space should be avoided because space is always lived and never mathematically calculated. How does Wright want this organic space to be experienced? The experience comes close to the vertigo produced by a long take in a film: space should "never [be] fully comprehended when viewed from one point but must be slowly experienced as one moves through the space" (32).

Wright's insistence on the "slowness" of the experience is interesting in its own right. For the same reason, Makovecz sometimes "destroys the viewer's ability to navigate" in some of his buildings (Gerle 2010: 199). The result is an amazingly similar spatial experience offered by Tarr's films and Makovecz's architecture: "The unsettling experience of being uncertain is gauged toward forcing the viewer to rely on his own consciousness and inner self instead of unthinkingly accepting what his senses tell him" (199–200). This should not be confused with the postmodern type of disorientation because the entirety of the spatial experience is maintained here. The state of disorientation is very similar to Krasznahorkai's description of the arrangement of the monastery buildings in Északról hegy, where the extraordinary architectural complexity enables the relationship between the whole and the parts. As shown in chapter 11, the organic coherence in the Paks Church is maintained by a spatial fluency dependent on a continuous structure. The "rhythm" of the space is not predetermined but rather "enacted" by the particular elements.

Perspective

The fluent spatial experience that avoids geometrical divisions comes close to a negation of perspective. We encounter here (after the Vitruvian proportions that were meant to be universal) another Renaissance paradigm that organic architecture and cinema are trying to overcome: perspective. The one-point perspective construction was fundamental in Renaissance art and architecture in the fifteenth century and considered an important progress in both science and art. The nonperspective way of seeing the world before the Renaissance, on the other hand, would be equated with a time in which the individual as a social entity had not yet been discovered. Lack of perspective means to be unconscious of both the surrounding space and one's own individual position within this space. Perspectival seeing aimed to reconstruct the world within a unique geometric system, which provided new possibilities for science and art. At the same time, this new mathematical rationalism confined artistic imagination to relatively narrow limits. Is reality really geometrical, and can the whole of reality be grasped from a single point of view? The criticism that Eszter directs against Andreas Werckmeister in music reappears here in the realm of optics.

In philosophy, a critical attitude toward Renaissance perspectivism has been most efficiently formulated by the German organic philosopher Jean Gebser, who found that in the Renaissance:

> although man's horizon expanded, his world became increasingly narrow as his vision was sectorized by the blinders of the perspectival worldview. The gradual movement toward clearer vision was accompanied by a proportionate narrowing of his visual sector. The deeper and farther we extend our view into space, the narrower is the sector of our visual pyramid. (1985: 23)

In Byzantine paintings before the seventeenth century, which were not yet influenced by linear perspective, the point of view from which an object was seen could appear to be constantly moving and changing. We can say those painters attempted to grasp the essence of reality in a more organic fashion, independent of a single point of view. Of course, Renaissance painters and theorists would attribute the old nonperspectival way to a kind of drunken mysticism. Gebser, on the other hand, believes nonperspective viewing can grasp an "integral reality" and represents an "intensive awareness of the world's transparency, a perceiving of the world as truth" (5). Hugo Häring found Gebser's ideas supportive for his own architectural theories and accepted his claim that in the history of humanity "human evolution moved from pre-geometric to a geometric state before it could finally move on to enter the organic" (Blundell Jones 1996: 186).

Krasznahorkai's Organic Space

Krasznahorkai's prose directly connects to these reflections on space and perspective because he attempts to recreate an organic spatial experience through language. Krasznahorkai's sentences can be experienced as spatial, as becomes clear in Janice Lee's (2014) observation that Krasznahorkai "uses these long sentences that sort of cycle through. You start off in one place, and somehow, through the succession of his dense language and phrases, seem to pass through eternity and end up in another place altogether." However, though the world might be animated by an "unknown power," a certain rhythm evolving in an organic fashion always firmly holds the world together. This organic rhythm is the rhythm Eisenstein abhorred because it enables empathy. In *Satantango*, Krasznahorkai describes this phenomenon of "empathized rhythm" in a curious passage where the night is said to have its own rhythm in the form of an atmosphere or a mood: "The entire October night was beating with a single pulse, its own strange rhythm sounding through trees and train and mud in a manner beyond words or vision: ... in the slow passage of darkness ... ; in the working of tired muscles; in the silence, in its human subjects" (2012a: 89). Out of the "rhythm of the night" develops an organic space. Another passage from *Satantango* describes organic space in a way reminiscent of how space appears in Tarr's long takes and of how long takes produce vertigo in general. This is how Estike experiences the organic space of her house:

> Her attention was almost exclusively restricted to the kitchen door, but she registered that with such keen sharpness it almost amounted to acute pain, every detail of the door impinging on her at once, the two dirty panes of glass above it, through which she glimpsed flashes of lace curtains fixed there with drawing pins, and below it, splashes of dried mud, and the line of the door handle as it bent toward the ground; in other words a terrifying network of shapes, colors, lines; not only that, but the precise condition of the door itself as it changed according to her curiously chopped-up sense of time, in which possible dangers presented themselves every moment. When any period of immobility came to a sudden end everything around her shifted with it: the walls of the house sped by her as did the crooked arc of the eaves, the window altered position, the pigsty and the neglected flowerbed drifted past her from left to right. (109)

The Long Take and Contemplation

In principle, long takes are organic because they convey the natural continuity of time. The tango-dancing scene in *Satantango* seemingly never ends because it was long in reality. A shot is not a sign or symbol for an event, for example, a mob riot. If there were a riot, it would have to be shown in its entire length. Cinematic time should be natural and not rationalized or calculated in terms of a logic established by editing. Clipping and editing are mathematical, Werckmeisterian activities. Editing will most probably work toward a climax, but, as Bordwell (2007) says, Tarr's "long takes don't present a beginning-middle-end-structure ... and there is no visual climax." Paradoxically, the feeling of circularity is mostly due to this contemplative kind of "naturalism." The circular structure is the eternal return of the same, which is no invention but "reality." Correspondingly, András Bálint Kovács finds that the long take's slowness is produced through a "circular structure, a structure producing the

Figure 12.1. Estike in *Satantango* (1994).

feeling that the return is inevitable" (2013: 118). In other words, when space is organic and uncentered, the feeling of circularity emerges.

The introduction made certain points about the cognitive condition of contemplation. It can now be concluded that contemplation, as opposed to mathematical analysis, locates an organic web of temporal and spatial relations in the form of an immanent, self-sufficient "natural logic." This logic is absent in the form of empirical facts or abstract rules. Therefore, the long take is by its nature related to contemplation. As mentioned, the philosophy of the organic has traditionally seen the organic order of nature as something that remains hidden for science but can be made visible by philosophers and artists. The contemplation of psychological realities, nature, music, or the stars is a purely "organic activity," as it looks for an organic order that is neither abstract nor concrete but "in between." All this means that the aesthetics of the long camera take depends on the premises formulated by the philosophy of the organic. This cinema makes use of long takes because it understands the logic of the organic precisely in the way laid down by philosophers of architecture. The most important point is that in slow cinema, time exists in the real world as time. While cutting and editing produce an artificial time dependent on the human ratio, slow cinema's long takes serve, just like an organic structure, as natural mechanisms able to produce time (in the same way the organic structure in architecture produces space). In other words, the camera merely "sees" or contemplates during the long take. The camera adopts its own viewpoint not to establish a geometrical perspective but to transcend the concept of perspective.

In organic cinema, the viewpoint is not subjective or produced by a camera angle. Tarr therefore most aptly says, "it's just a point of view, I show what happens, without any justification" (interview with Zeuxis, in Breteau-Skira 2010). The approach emphasizing the "just a point of view," which is detached from objectifying geometry, enables Tarr to "transmit life in a way that is autonomous with regard to the narrative" (Breton 2011: 100). Either the point of view is almost fixed—like in the case of the tavern dance scene that Tarr films in a pure documentary style, moving the camera only slightly, without close-ups, secondary elements (such as somebody entering the room), or dramatization—or the camera moves around objects or trails subjects by following them on their spider web trajectories. However, even in the latter case, the camera's point of view remains "fixed" in a metaphorical way because it does not change according to a narrative, creating an effect where, according to Peter Hames (2001), "the logic of events ... determines what we see," not the logic of the narrative. The point of view remains fixed like that of the doctor who eagerly notes everything he sees, filling notebook after notebook without editing anything. However, once the subjectivity of the narrator has been eliminated, the camera can autonomously establish its point of view. "Contemplation" describes precisely this nonsubjective way of seeing in which the point of view is neither geometrically fixed nor established by subjective editing.

The contemplating mind might also find something spiritual in the objects it contemplates, but such is the case not because some spiritual quantity has been invested "into" the viewed object by a calculating, subjective mind. Calculating, subjective minds usually depend on theories, ideologies, nationalisms, or religions. Contemplated spirituality, on the other hand, does not depend on such meta-narratives: it simply locates the organic web in the form of an immanent "natural logic." Krasznahorkai's sentence structures follow the same principle of the "long take" based on contemplation. It is not the author who decides to lengthen his sentences while editing his text; the sentence structure is no matter of editing at all. Rather, the sentences are long by nature. The writer does not attempt to impose another intonation on the sounds nature provides: he avoids applying a Werckmeisterian tuning to the natural harmony of sentences. Krasznahorkai supports this view when explaining in an interview, "When you want to convince somebody about something, that the world is such and such, then it's a natural process for the sentences to become always longer and longer because I needed less and less the dot, this artificial border between sentences" (Cardenas 2013). This is Krasznahorkai's way of explaining that nature cannot be rendered by grammar.

Werckmeisterian Realism

Krasznahorkai's aversion to what James Wood (2012) has called "grammatical antirealism" (or what I prefer to call antigrammatical realism) relates to Eszter's opposition to mathematical rules (see chapter 7). Reality cannot be grasped with the help of abstract grammar. The "realism argument" can also be applied to organic time and space. Both are "naturally real," though this is no simple realism—just like organic architecture is not simply realist. All of this points to an interesting relationship between reality and nature. In musical theory, one calls "natural harmony" what architecture calls the "organically created space." Drawing lines in architecture or editing a film in an Eisensteinian manner, however, represents a sort of Werckmeisterian tuning. Cutting and editing are the equivalent of the piano keyboard that cuts "natural sound" into twelve different tones despite the fact that tones "in nature" do not follow those mathematical laws. Lucie Wright and Emeric de Lastens are thus right when pointing out that Tarr's films contain a "naturalisme des profondeurs" (naturalism of depths, 2011: 88). This does not represent an attempt to invest aesthetics with an empirical notion of nature and to declare this notion of nature central for the aesthetics of cinema or architecture. Ecological philosophy usually undertakes such "centralizations," while in organic architecture, according to Sydney Robinson's formulation, "nature is a referent, not an origin" (1993: 9). Eisensteinian editing and Werckmeisterian tuning, on the other hand, distort nature. Geometrical architecture applies the same distortion to architectural space. According to Häring, space remained "natural" until humanity imposed the geometric order on space. Consequently, Häring opposes any technical concept of space controlled by coordinates.

An "Aristoxenusian" film, should it ever exist, will necessarily contain long takes and nothing else. Natural time is long, so the takes must be long, too. When Tarr says he favors the long take because its continuity matches that of real life, he does not mean he is copying reality, but rather he means the film's logic follows the "real" psychological processes of the protagonists. In other words, Tarr is not Werckmeister basing music on math but Eszter basing math on music. The impression of the organic as a phenomenon produced through a combination of both the static and self-contained motion ("dynamic paralysis") has been described by Kovács very well, who finds that in *Damnation*:

> the world is rather static; motions are repetitive, circular and have no direction. The camera moves about in this world of objects and almost frozen people sometimes in strange postures, revealing them one after the other, as if it were wandering around aimlessly in a dead landscape. In the long takes, camera movements and staging a feeling of both immersion and distanced self-consciousness are present. (2013: 59)

This is the Werckmeister-Aristoxenus controversy transposed to film theory. Music should not be submitted to the keyboard, but the keyboard should be submitted to "natural music." And the result will be "real music." Correspondingly, cinematic time should not be submitted to actions, but actions should be submitted to cinematic time. The action will only come to an end when the time permits and not the other way round. This is "real cinema" or organic cinema.

The same principle has existed in organic architecture for decades and has been spelled out as follows: space and form should not be submitted to architectural functions, but space should, according to Frank Lloyd Wright, be "determined form from within" (1941: 184). The reason is that organic space must be fluent. What all three—film, music, architecture—want to achieve by referring more or less explicitly to organic models of time and space is a sense of uncalculated, nonmathematical, and natural continuity as the highest achievement in their respective art. In this sense, the long take presents the world "as it is," meaning, the reality presented depends on nothing but its own organic structure.

In the end, a "real" tragedy narrated by a story from a subjective point of view is always absent in those contemplative films. When Tarr shows the enraged people ransacking the hospital, "this is it—and nothing else" (Bíró 2008: 168). There is neither drama nor narrative. In a similar vein, Rollet calls this approach a "radicalité phénoménologique" (2011: 101) because the phenomenon exposed is reduced to itself and stripped of psychological, religious, or artistic meta-reasons. Yvette Bíró therefore sees in Tarr's films "the existence of human beings deprived of action and events in their allotted time" (2008: 169). The same phenomenon can be observed in Krasznahorkai's text. In the popular revolt of *Werckmeister Harmonies,* "each thing moves at its own speed and tempo" and "the time of inner impulses is past explanation or measuring ... Everything lasts until full exhaustion [and] leads inevitably to self-degradation" (1998: 172). In the end, through these actions, organic time and organic space begin forming a whole. This holistic approach transcends formalist rationalism as well as the postmodern representation of reality and depicts reality in the form of random play.

The essential element holding all organic spaces together is not an abstract structure produced by editing but an organic "landscape" within which humans engage in self-contained actions. This is true for film as much as for architecture. Bíró uses an architectural metaphor when writing that Tarr's space "evokes the sense of the labyrinth, as there is no escape, everything moves in closed space and time" (2008: 170). Similarly, Fred Kelemen, Tarr's camera operator from *The Turin Horse,* points out that "in this world there is no other world than this one. There is no escape" (Koehler 2011). Similar to Krasznahorkai's sentences, Tarr creates in his films a claustrophobic labyrinth. If a dream-state appears in Tarr's films similar to the one we find in Tarkovsky, it's only because the organic-labyrinthine composition of the film makes us lose our point of view and invites us to dream.

No Form Follows Function

In architecture, the rationalist dictum that "form follows function" (coined by the organic-rationalist architect Louis Sullivan in his 1896 article "The Tall Office Building Artistically Considered") has been adopted by modernist architects like Le Corbusier. The dictum can be translated into cinema theory as follows: the length of a camera shot is defined by its function as a unit of narrative information. Like any artist striving to be "organic," Wright also rejected the "form follows function" concept. Instead, he wanted to create an organic expression in which "form and function are one" (1941: 181). This expression represented for him a "higher truth," higher than that of aesthetic laws or laws of comfort. In several respects, Wright's concept of the organic comes close to Goethe's morphology in which no distinction is made between form and function because function is believed to be "existence thought of as an activity" (Goethe 1833: 536). This is why Goethe's ur-type (original type) could represent a form that developed not out of a certain function but a being that aimed to express its existence directly through form.

Wright also does not want to obtain spaces that have been "edited" in terms of narrative architectural functions spelling out which form must follow which function. The highest architectural truth for Wright is the integration of form and function. Only this integration can create the spatial continuity characteristic of organic architecture, while all features that are "merely constructed" must be eliminated (1941: 182). Wright concludes that only when architecture stops seeing itself as a form following function can it become "architecture for the spirit of man … architecture spiritually (virtually) conceived as appropriate enclosure of interior space to be lived in" (189). The spirituality Wright mentions is here a sort of dynamic paralysis in which the "will to construct" has been restrained it is installed by applying the model of the organic: "Decoration should never be purposely constructed. True beauty results from that repose which the mind feels when the eye, the intellect, the affections, are satisfied from the absence of any want" (1987: 72). In the end, this is a true aesthetics of contemplation.

Finally, this phenomenon is similar to what happens in the performance of rituals. Makovecz does indeed understand the spatial structure his buildings evoke in such a ritualistic way: the "mythical time of primitive people where rituals re-enact events … seem to take place for them anew, despite being in the past of their collective unconscious" (Heathcote 1997: 21). Here, nature has neither been copied nor imitated, but reality, in its most cosmic sense, has been introduced into the organic whole that this architecture expresses. Accordingly, Makovecz believes his structures "create a connection between the sky and the earth, while, at the same time, interpreting and expressing the movement and place of human beings" (Gerle 2010: 20). Located between sky and earth is space (well demonstrated by Tarr through Valuska's staging of the astro-dance). This space provides authenticity because it attaches a cosmic structure to individual actions. For Makovecz, the illustration of this constellation is architecture's main task.

What space is for Makovecz is time for Tarr in this context. When Tarr avers that nothing happens in his movies, that "all that remains is time [and that] this is probably the only thing that's still genuine" (Ebert 2007), he is alluding to the authenticity of time in the same way organicists talk about the authenticity of nature. In this sense, Tarr's concept of time is similar to Makovecz's "mythical time": it is not an abstract structure, it cannot be measured, and it is not "something" to which we can point and say, "that's what time means."

Pure Time and Pure Space: Bergson

The organicism described in this book is not antimaterial but is almost synonymous with the "vital materialism" proclaimed by a philosophical line reaching from Henri Bergson to Gilles Deleuze. Tarr's long takes, as well as the "mythical time" announced by Makovecz, are produced in the organic mode of Bergson's *durée pure* (normally translated as "pure duration" or "lived duration"). Makovecz's "mythical time" can most successfully be defined in the sense of Bergson's *durée* as it evolves in its own way: its evolution is not necessarily successive. Like for the *durée*, the meaning of this time emerges in the form of an organic structure.

To use Bergson's *durée pure* to describe the functioning of the long take makes sense in several respects. For this most organic of all philosophers, *durée pure* accumulates and eternalizes within one and the same absolute present, a maximum of elements. In this sense, *durée pure* can also provide a perfect philosophical account of the long camera take. Bergson (1966) develops the idea of *durée pure* in the fifth lecture of *La Pensée et le mouvant* (*The Creative Mind*), where he opposes *durée pure* to mathematically constructed or "spatialized" time. Time as it is experienced is lived time in which the different steps of succession are not distinguished. Pure duration is always undivided. Lived time is experienced time that is fluent, organic, and intuitive. Whenever we experience the evolution of time, we do not divide it into steps. Those steps can only be imposed on time from an extra-temporal point of view (by clocks, for example). In other words, time is not a juxtaposition of moments but an organic whole.

Rollet sees an "absolute present" (2006: 101) in Tarr's films and concludes that in *Satantango*, there is a "present without borders, without past and without future, though suspended in an undefined expectation. For Karrer, the hero of *Damnation*, nothing can happen because everything has happened already: neither his wife's earlier suicide, nor the encounter with another woman, nor the separation of the lovers, and not even Karrer's final betrayal are able to represent for him an event" (2013: 2). The idea of Bergsonian time is also contained in *Werckmeister Harmonies*'s astronomical ruminations. Roger Ebert asks: "And what is time anyway but our agreement to divide one rotation of the earth around the sun into units? Could there be hours, minutes, seconds, on a planet without our year? Why would one earth second need to exist except as part of one earth year?" Ebert decides to link those reflections on time to the development of Tarr's long takes: "Perhaps such questions lead us into the extraordinary, funny, ingenious 11-minute shot at the start of the picture" (2009: 847).

The immersive power of long takes, just like the immersive power of the virtual, which shows many parallels with Bergson's *durée pure*,[1] has to do with the loss of the subjective and the objective, which is why Scott Foundas describes the logic of Tarr's long takes as autonomous developments: "You rarely ever feel in one of his films ... that the movement of the camera or the length of the shot is being dictated by anything other than the characters and the physical presences on the screen. The camera is moving with them, is dancing with them, not just when it's a dancing scene. He is really sort of immersing you in this world" (*Talking about Tarr* 2008: 11). This autonomous reality of the long take is also the "reality" of music as Eszter perceives it. Music has its own standards, which might be "illogical" from the point of view of a mathematically divided piano keyboard, but still this music is the only "real" music we have.

Tarr himself seems to allude to the two different ways of measuring time when making Irimiás in *Satantango* say, while waiting with his companion in the town hall of the village: "The two clocks show different times. Both wrong of course. This one here is too slow. The other one, instead of telling the time, seems to point at our hopeless condition. We cannot defend ourselves."[2] It is interesting to note that Hamvas has described this perception of time as typical for the melancholic subject because "in melancholy past, present and future are accumulated" (2008: 27–28). Hamvas believes, particularly in the melancholy of old age, all sections of a life are relived in real time. Moreover, curiously, some people have found that Hungarians "naturally" practice Bergson's accumulative concept of time. István Bori writes in the preface to *The Essential Guide to Being Hungarian:* "They pass the time mainly by 'looking forward into the past' says Jimmy Porter about his father-in-law's generation in John Osborn's play *Look Back in Anger*" (2012: i). Bori finds that this best characterizes the "Hungarian concept of time."

Another notion from Bergson associated with the essence of Tarr's organic cinema is the élan vital ("vital impetus"), which Bergson coined in 1907 in *L'Évolution créatrice* (*Creative Evolution*). The élan vital is an autonomous form of self-organization of life that advances in cultural works in an increasingly complex manner. Most importantly, the creative evolution is not submitted to static rules of a deterministic progress but evolves from within. We have seen that this is also how Wright wanted space to be developed in buildings: it should be "determined form from within" (1941: 184). And Makovecz shares a very Bergsonian view of time when writing: "time is not a series of successive events, but a flower which, as it grows, metamorphoses into a cluster of petals; all similar but never identical and unified" (Heathcote 1997: 8). There is an inner meaning of the *durée pure* of the long takes, just like "[t]here must be an inner meaning to every building, a kind of meaning which cannot be named, yet reveals itself during the planning process. I don't trust architects who claim the program must be learned as a function, the elements must be put together, and then we will arrive at a very clever and modern building. [The architect] discovers what kind of house he wants to build" (Gerle 2010: 33). This is an application of Bergson's "creative evolution" in building theory based on the *élan vital* as an inner development.

We also find this conception of space derived from the *élan vital* in Krasznahorkai's writings. Estike's experience of her house's organic space in *Satantango* has been analyzed above: "The walls of the house sped by her" and "the pigsty and the neglected flowerbed drifted past her from left to right" (2012a: 109). We might say Bergson's *élan vital* appears here in Deleuze's reconfigured form. According to Keith Ansell Pearson, the élan vital in Deleuze's hands becomes a substance in which the distinction between organic and inorganic matter is indiscernible, and the emergence of life undecidable. This is how the "difference of nature has itself become nature" and finally, "organic form decompos[es] into matter." Ansell Pearson believes that through this application to the organic, the élan vital remains an internal force but "loses its mystic appeal" (2012: 65). This is exactly what frequently happens in Krasznahorkai's texts, particularly in the above passage: organic matter becomes mystical in return.

The experience of "lived time" coincides with the aesthetics of the long camera take, as well as with the fluent and intuitive space of organic architecture (which is also suitably called "living architecture"). Space, which is always experienced in time, is not geometrically divided, but the juxtapositions of parts do form an organic whole within spatial experience. Therefore, organic cinema and architecture both propagate a sort of *espace pur* or "space-time continuum." In contemplative films, organic time is never the existential time where motivations, hopes, gains, or losses create behavioral structures that science can describe (and optimize) in terms of math, logic, and dramatic effects. In the *durée pure* of the hospital scene in *Werckmeister Harmonies*, for example, there is no past, present, or future, but things happen "just because." This would be an application of *espace pur*.

The problem of the long take is closely linked to Bergsonian duration. Janice Lee (2014) finds that "Tarr's long take tells as time itself would tell—as a time indifferent to the human experience of time." This depends, of course, on what we decide to call the "human experience of time." True, many humans would look at their watches when viewing the scene and conclude that it is simply too long. The problem is that statements about the length can only be made by dividing the time of the scene into mathematical units. In the *durée pure,* such segments do not exist because lived time is the original human experience of time. We are reminded of Saint Augustine's statement that he understands very well what time is when he does not reflect on it (*Confessions,* Book 10). Hans-Georg Gadamer, another main proponent of organic philosophy, particularly organic time, describes the "empty duration of time" as a "lingering, which—as lingering—is too long and therefore appears as agonizing boredom" (1970: 348–49). However, the lingering can be boring only as long as it appears "as time," which happens only in relationship with a generally defined time. If nothing happens in this time, then this time will indeed be found empty and boring.

The paradox persists in the fact that just because time is empty, this time will be experienced as something containing time. This means that mere separation from clock time does not help. On the contrary, this perception of time as "empty" is possible only *because* it is separated from the normal life time: "Only that which is separated from the cycle of life and isolated as something separate, 'has' time," writes Gadamer (348). In other words, we look at our watch in the cinema only because we still believe this experience is part of the general time system. However, the time feeling mentioned by Mary Ann Doane, which emerged in modernity "as a weight, as a source of anxiety, and as an acutely pressing problem of representation" (2002: 4), should not remain with us while we are watching the film, especially while we are watching an extremely long take. This is the secret of the long take and of slow cinema: though the long take has its own temporal dynamic, it is still part of a cycle of life and not as something isolated. Only then do we "know what time is" (in Augustine's sense), and only then does time become Bergson's "lived time." In isolation, time will still "have time" in the mathematical sense; paradoxically, just because this time has been isolated from the general flow of time, it will still be measured against this general flow of time. Tarkovsky describes the phenomenon of experiencing a long take through lived time without merely isolating the time experience from time itself: "If you extend the normal length of a shot, first you get bored; but if you extend it further still you become interested in it; and if you extend it even more a new quality, and new intensity of attention is born" (1999: 6). Slow cinema can have this liberating function only when time is—in the Augustinian sense—completely "forgotten."

Notes

1. Deleuze believes Bergson developed "the notion of the *virtual* to its highest degree" and that he based his entire philosophy on it (1988: 37). Deleuze identifies the virtual, considered a continuous multiplicity, with Bergson's *durée pure*.
2. The Bergsonian input is less clear in Krasznahorkai's text (here in Szirtes's translation): "The two clocks say different times, but it could be that neither of them is right. Our clock here is very late, while that one there measures not so much time as, well, the eternal reality of the exploited, and we to it are as the bough of a tree to the rain that falls upon it: in other words we are helpless" (2012a: 23).

Conclusion

This book has shown that the paradoxical nature of an "organic rhythm" manifests important overlaps with the principles of organic architecture. Rudolf Steiner explained, "whereas elsewhere the dynamic of geometry is merely presented in repetition so that like balances like, here one is concerned with the growth of one out of the other" (Pearson 2001: 29). Steiner also opposes formalism to organic thinking. Historically, it can be confirmed that just like organic theories of architecture strive to invert the theory of functionalism, organic theories of film strive to invert constructivist strategies. What organicist architects usually identify as "geometrical culture" has an equivalent in film in montage and editing. And in architecture, Andrei Tarkovsky's ideas about an organic cinema are very aptly paralleled by Hugo Häring's statement that "in nature form is the result of the organization of many individual entities in space in order that life can unfold and action take place, a fulfillment of both part and whole (whereas in the world of geometrical cultures form is derived from the laws of geometry)" (1925: 4). Tarkovsky would probably have willingly adopted Häring's idea that a creator should always work "from the essence of a task toward a yet unknown appearance" (Blundell Jones 1996: 9), a principle that could be a guideline for many directors of slow films. Furthermore, Béla Tarr's idea that one should follow not the logic of a story but the logic of life expresses a principle that Häring referred to as *Leistungsform* ("achievement form"), which is a predecessor of Häring's term "essential Gestalt" (*wesenhafte Gestalt*) that would become very important in later decades. For Häring, the *Leistungsform* is achieved by passing from an inner essence (of life) to a certain externally experienced appearance. Häring describes the *Leistungsform* as always elastic, maintaining an inner tension. This means it partly overlaps with Tarkovsky's (1986: 53) concept of "time pressure" (давление времени), that is, with the rhythm created through inherent movements within the original camera work.

The parallels between cinema and architecture have become manifest. Sergei Eisenstein is for Tarkovsky what Le Corbusier is for Häring.

For both Häring and Tarkovsky, the geometric-rationalist element is the enemy of the organic and, according to Häring, "geometrification" remains the "most effective way to suppress organ-like form" (Häring et al. 1964: 30). Le Corbusier, on the other hand, equipped with his quasi-Platonist belief in a universal order underlying nature, should be considered the Eisenstein of architecture. Even more, since Le Corbusier believed universal order is equivalent with geometry, he also represents natural theology in architecture. And when he declares that his modular proportioning system should be seen as both natural and universal, he looks like the Werckmeister of architectural theory.

The association of those two intellectualist artists, Le Corbusier and Eisenstein, is not far-fetched: both have been linked to organic thought, though in a special, restrictive way. The link with the organic is based on the idea that the technical and the mathematically constructed are not purely artificial but that they do follow the laws of nature. From this point of view, the mathematical can appear organic. This is the particularity of both le Corbusier and Eisenstein: though their works contradict elemental premises of organicism, they can also be seen as organic. Arnold Schoenberg and Anton Webern can be added to the same list of mathematically organic artists because, though their twelve-tone technique attempted to subordinate human subjectivity to mathematics, both have also been declared "organic" composers. One could say those artists entertained a sort of love–hate relationship with the organic or that they came close to the idea of the organic without being able to entirely assume it. The introduction showed that Gilles Deleuze believed Eisenstein to be organic because his representation "includes spatial and temporal caesuras" (1986: 152). Walter Curt Behrendt points out a similar particular love–hate relationship with the organic concerning Le Corbusier:

> The creations of modern technique, which excite Le Corbusier's highest admiration have not originated from mathematical calculations alone; the machine, the automobile, the airplane are typical creations of organic structure ... they really are products based on the evolutionary laws of organic nature. (1937: 163)

Louis Sullivan, who is often mentioned together with Frank Lloyd Wright as the founder of organic architecture, was working within a similarly contradictory framework. This organic architect coined the concept "form follows function," which Wright believed to contradict basic organic premises. The question is once again whether the organic can be resumed by math, which is precisely the problem of *Werckmeister*

Harmonies. Behrendt describes Le Corbusier as "the geometrical man" and thus as the antithesis of Wright because Le Corbusier's style follows the "universal law of Geometry" (1937: 163). Apart from Le Corbusier, one could also name the science-based quantitative functionalism of German modernists, especially Hannes Meyer of the Bauhaus School, as direct opponents of Häring and as proponents of Werckmeisterian tuning in architecture.

The presentation of organic structures has played an important role in Western culture, covering a historical lapse reaching from Renaissance humanism through Gothic architecture to Art Nouveau. The art of Béla Tarr, László Krasznahorkai, and Imre Makovecz appears at the end of this development. Those artists are particularly important in a world in which universalism is increasingly understood as a "centered" notion and where anti-universalisms tend to take refuge in simplistic relativisms. The cosmic art discussed in this book has a highly hermeneutic character because it believes in tensions; it is also pragmatic because it knows that no truth is simply universal in the sense of "one fitting for all." At the same time, organic thinking does not abandon the belief in truth but sticks to an idea of "cosmic" truth that transcends both the relative and the universal. Organic philosophy shows that the relationship between the universal and individual should be understood in terms not of oppositions but of paradoxes. Absolute truths cannot be established by religions, ideologies, or even science, but everything must be negotiated in a Werckmeisterian way. Furthermore, organicism sticks to the idea of modernity because organic expressions are not folkloristic, nor do they engage in a romanticization of the past. Organicism wants a different kind of modernity, and Hungary is a suitable ground for staging this experiment.

Bibliography

Adorno, Theodor W. (1925) 1981. "Über Bela Bartók" In *Béla Bartók*, ed. Heinz-Klaus Metzger and Rainer Riehn, 118–128. Munich: Text und Kritik.
Agamben, Giorgio. 2009. *Nudités*. Paris: Payot.
Alcmaeon of Croton. 1952. "Fragments." In *Die Fragmente der Vorsokratiker*, vol. 1, ed. Hermann Diels and Walther Kranz, 210–16. Dublin and Zürich: Weidmann.
Ando, Tadao. 1991. "Introduction." *Japan Architect* 1: 1–6.
Ando, Tadao. 1991b. "From the Periphery of Architecture" in *Japan Architect* 1, 12–20.
Andrew, Dudley. 2005. Foreword to *What Is Cinema?* vol. 2, André Bazin, xi–xxvi. Berkeley: University of California Press.
Ansell Pearson, Keith. 2012. *Germinal Life: The Difference and Repetition of Deleuze*. New York: Routledge.
Aristoxenus. 1868. *Aristoxenoy Armonika Stoicheia: The Harmonics of Aristoxenus*, ed. Henry Stewart Macran. Oxford: Clarendon Press.
Arnason, Johann P. 2005. "Alternating Modernities: The Case of Czechoslovakia." *European Journal of Social Theory* 8(4) 435–51.
Auerbach, David. 2010. "The Mythology of László Krasznahorkai." *The Quarterly Conversation*, June 7. Accessed 5 May 2016. http://quarterlyconversation.com/the-mythology-of-lszl-krasznahorkai.
———. 2013. "The Pythagorean Comma and the Howl of the Wolf." Special issue on László Krasznahorkai, Béla Tarr, and Max Neumann, *Music and Literature* 2: 145–61.
Bakhtin, Mikhail. 1981. "Forms of Time and Chronotope in the Novel." In *The Dialogic Imagination: Four Essays*, 84–258. Austin: University of Texas Press.
Barber, Benjamin R. 1995. *Jihad vs. McWorld: How Globalism and Tribalism Are Reshaping the World*. New York: Times Books.
Barthes, Roland. 1987. *Mythologies*. New York: Hill and Wang.
Bauman, Zygmunt. 2007. *Liquid Times: Living in an Age of Uncertainty*. Cambridge: Polity.
Bazin, André. 1961. *Qu'est-ce que le cinéma?* 4 vols. Paris: Cerf.
———. 2005. *What Is Cinema?* 2 vols. Berkeley: University of California Press.
Behrendt, Walter Curt. 1937. *Modern Building: Its Nature, Problems, and Forms*. New York: Harcourt Brace.

Beke, László. 1987. "Versuch einer Zusammenfassung der Architektur von Imre Makovecz." In *Urform und Baugestalt: Architektur von Imre Makovecz*, 25–33. Budapest: Fellbach.
Benjamin, Walter. 1978. *Briefe II*, ed. Gershom Scholem and Theodor W. Adorno. Frankfurt: Suhrkamp.
———. 1999. "Paris, the Capital of the Nineteenth Century (Exposé of 1935)." In *The Arcades Project*. Cambridge, MA: Belknap Press of Harvard University Press.
Beplate, Justin. 2013. "The Universal Labyrinth." Special issue on László Krasznahorkai, Béla Tarr, and Max Neumann, *Music and Literature* 2: 162–65.
Berger, Peter L. and Thomas Luckmann. 1966. *The Social Construction of Reality: A Treatise in the Sociology of Knowledge*. Harmondsworth: Penguin.
Bergson, Henri. (1907) 1991. *L'Evolution créatrice*. Paris: Alcan. Published in English as *Creative Evolution*, trans. A. Mitchell (New York: The Modern Library, 1944).
———. (1934) 1966. *La Pensée et le mouvant*. Paris: Presses Universitaires de France. Published in English as *The Creative Mind: An Introduction to Metaphysics*, trans. Mabelle L. Andison (New York: Kensington Publishing Corp, 1946).
Berque, Augustin. 2015a. "La Cosmisation d'un territoire: Haïku et milieu Nippon." Paper presented at the University of Corsica in Corte, March 26.
———. 2011. "Mesologics and Mesology (as opposed to Ecology)." *ODIP: The Online Dictionary of Intercultural Philosophy*, ed. Thorsten Botz-Bornstein. Accessed 5 May 2016. http://media.wix.com/ugd/c49976_698ce79e28914a 2d940d133936e7193b.pdf.
Bíró, Yvette. 2008. *Turbulence and Flow in Film: The Rhythmic Design*. Bloomington: Indiana University Press.
Black, Monica. 2010. *Death in Berlin: From Weimar to Divided Germany*. Cambridge: Cambridge University Press.
Blokker, Paul. 2013. "The Ruins of a Myth or a Myth in Ruins? Freedom and Cohabitation in Central Europe." In *The Inhabited Ruins of Central Europe Re-imagining Space, History, and Memory*, ed. Derek Sayer and Dariusz Gafijczuk, 40–54. New York: Palgrave.
Blumenberg, Hans. 1983. *The Legitimacy of the Modern Age*. Cambridge, MA: MIT Press.
———. 1987. *The Genesis of the Copernican World*. Cambridge, MA: MIT Press.
Bloom, Allan. 1987. *The Closing of the American Mind: How Higher Education Has Failed Democracy and Impoverished the Souls of Today's Students*. New York: Simon and Schuster.
Bloom, Harold, and Lionel Trilling, ed. 1973. *The Oxford Anthology of English Literature: Romantic Poetry and Prose*. Oxford: Oxford University Press.
Blundell Jones, Peter. 1996. Preface to *Seeking Structure from Nature*, Jeffrey Cook, 6–8. Basel: Birkhäuser.
Blundell Jones, Peter. 1999. *Hugo Häring: The Organic versus the Geometric*. Stuttgart: Axel Menges.

Bognar, Botond. 1982. "Vivre Dans L'Austérité et dépouillement." In *Tadao Ando: Minimalismes,* ed. François Chaslin, 26–29. Paris: Electa Moniteur.
Bordwell, David. 2007. "The Sarcastic Lament of Béla Tarr." *David Bordwell's Website on Cinema,* 19 September. Accessed 5 May 2016. http://www.davidbordwell.net/blog/2007/09/19/the-sarcastic-laments-of-bela-tarr.
Bori, István. 2012. Preface to *The Essential Guide to Being Hungarian,* ed. István Bori, 1–3. North Adams, MA: New Europe Books.
Boromisza-Habashi, David. 2012. *Speaking Hatefully: Culture, Communication, and Political Action in Hungary.* University Park, PA: Penn State University Press.
Botz-Bornstein, Thorsten. 2007a. *Films and Dreams: Tarkovsky, Bergman, Sokurov, Kubrick, and Wong Kar-wai.* Lanham, MD: Lexington Books.
——. 2007b. "Empathy vs. Abstraction: Twentieth Century Interactions of German and Russian Aesthetics or Attempts to Retrieve the World." *CLCWeb: Comparative Literature and Culture* 9(2): 1–9.
——. 2015. *Transcultural Architecture: The Limits and Opportunities of Critical Regionalism.* Farnham: Ashgate.
Botz-Bornstein, Thorsten, and Giannis Stamatellos, eds. 2017. *Plotinus and the Moving Image: Neoplatonism and Film Studies.* Leiden: Brill.
Boyer, M. Christine. 1996. *CyberCities: Visual Perception in the Age of Electronic Communication.* New York: Princeton Architectural Press.
Boyers, Robert. 2005. "Stiflings: László Krasznahorkai." In *Dictator's Dictation: The Politics of Novels and Novelists,* 169–78. New York: Columbia University Press.
Bradatan, Costica. 2010. "Editorial Introduction." *Angelaki: Journal of the Theoretical Humanities* 15(3): 1–8.
——. 2014. "The Two Abysses of the Soul." *Los Angeles Review of Books,* 31 July.
Braidotti, Rosi. 2013. *The Posthuman.* Cambridge: Polity.
Brandow-Faller, Megan. 2011. "Art Nouveau and Hungarian Cultural Nationalism." In Tötösy de Zepetnek and Vasvári 2011, 182–93.
Breteau-Skira, Gisèle. 2010. *Les Entretiens de Zeuxis: Les cinéastes de la mélancolie.* Paris: Séguier.
Breton, Émile. 2011. "Quelques Jalons dans une œuvre vouée au noir." *Vertigo* 41: 96–101.
Buslowska, Elzbieta. 2009. "Cinema as Art and Philosophy in Béla Tarr's Creative Exploration of Reality." *Acta Universitatis Sapientiae, Film and Media Studies* 1: 107–16.
Cairns, Graham. 2014. *The Architecture of the Screen: Essays in Cinematographic Space.* Bristol: Intellect.
Cardenas, Mauro Javier. 2013. "Conversations with László Krasznahorkai." *Music and Literature,* 12 December. Accessed 5 May 2016. http://www.musicandliterature.org/features/2013/12/11/a-conversation-with-lszl-krasznahorkai.
Cassirer, Ernst. 1946. *Language and Myth.* New York and London: Harper.
Coleridge, Samuel Taylor. 1965. *Theory of Life: Biographia Literaria.* London: Cass.

———. 1987. *Lectures 1808–1819 on Literature,* vol. 2, ed. by Reginald A. Foakes. The Collected Works of Samuel Taylor Coleridge. Princeton, NJ: Princeton University Press.

Comte, Auguste. 1875–1877. *System of Positive Polity,* 4 vols. London: Longmans, Green & Co. Originally published as *Système de politique positive, ou traité de sociologie instituant la religion de l'Humanité* (Paris: Carilian-Goeury, 1851–1854).

Cook, Jeffrey. 1996. *Seeking Structure from Nature: The Organic Architecture of Hungary.* Basel, Switzerland: Birkhäuser.

———. 1997. "Hungarian Folk Traditions that Displaced Modernism: Farmhouse Roofs, Chair Backs, and Grave Markers as 'Pure Sources.'" *Traditional Dwellings and Settlements Review* 9(1): 7–19.

Dabernig, Josef. 2011. "Béla Tarr, Satantango." Text for exhibition in the Galerie Andreas Huber as part of the Vienna Art Fair series "Art and Film."

Dányi, Endre. 2013. "Democracy in Ruins: The Case of the Hungarian Parliament." In *The Inhabited Ruins of Central Europe: Re-imagining Space, History, and Memory,* ed. Derek Sayer and Dariusz Gafijczuk, 55–77. New York: Palgrave.

Darwin, Charles. (1871) 2004. *The Descent of Man.* London: Penguin.

de Certeau, Michel. 1984. *The Practice of Everyday Life.* Berkeley: University of California Press.

Deleuze, Gilles. 1988. *Bergonism,* trans. Hugh Tomlinson and Barbara Habberjam. New York: Zone Books. Originally published as *Le Bergsonisme* (Paris: Presses Universitaires de France, 1966).

———. 1986. *Cinema 1: The Movement-Image,* trans. Hugh Tomlinson and Barbara Habberjam. Minneapolis: University of Minnesota Press.

———. 1989. *Cinema 2: The Time-Image,* trans. Hugh Tomlinson and Robert Galeta. Minneapolis: University of Minnesota Press.

Deleuze, Gilles, and Felix Guattari. 1987. *A Thousand Plateaus: Capitalism and Schizophrenia.* Minneapolis: University of Minnesota Press, trans. Brian Massumi. Originally published as *Mille plateaux: Capitalisme et schizophrénie* (Paris: Minuit, 1980).

Derham, William. 1714. *Astro-theology: Or, a Demonstration of the Being and Attributes of God, from the Survey of the Heavens.* London: W. and J. Innys.

Derrida, Jacques. (1962) 1978. *Edmund Husserl's Origin of Geometry: An Introduction,* trans. John P. Leavey. Omaha: University of Nebraska Press.

———. 1967. *De la Grammatologie.* Paris: Minuit.

———. (1972) 1981. *Positions,* trans. Alan Bass. Chicago: University of Chicago Press.

———. 1976. *Of Grammatology,* trans. Gayatri Chakravorty Spivak. Baltimore: John Hopkins University Press.

———. 1978. *Writing and Difference,* trans. Alan Bass. Chicago: Chicago University Press. Originally published as *L'Ecriture et la différence* (Paris: Seuil, 1967).

de Man, Paul. 1971. *Blindness and Insight: Essays in the Rhetoric of Contemporary Criticism.* Minneapolis: University of Minnesota Press.
Doane, Mary Ann. 2002. *The Emergence of Cinematic Time: Modernity, Contingency, the Archive.* Cambridge, MA: Harvard University Press.
Drexler, Eric. 1992. *Nanosystems: Molecular Machinery, Manufacturing, and Computation.* New York: John Wiley.
Dunaújvárosi Hírlap [Dunaujvaros newspaper]. 1962. "Góliáth Dunaújvárosban," 13 February. Retrieved 5 May 2016 from http://ujvaros.tumblr.com/post/44448260083/goliath-dunaujvarosban-vilagjaro-utja-soran.
Ebert, Roger. 2007. "Werckmeister Harmonies," 8 September. Accessed 5 May 2016. http://www.rogerebert.com/reviews/werckmeister-harmonies-2000.
———. 2009. *Roger Ebert's Four-Star Reviews 1967–2007.* Kansas City, MO: Andrews McMeel.
Eisenstein, Sergei. 1988. *Selected Works, Vol. 1: Writings 1922–1934*, trans. Richard Taylor. Bloomington: Indiana University Press.
Eletkert Pavilon facebook page. Accessed 26 December 2016. https://www.facebook.com/%C3%89letkert-Pavilon-509113619188460/
Esposito, Scott. 2013. "Interview with Ottilie Mulzet." Special issue on László Krasznahorkai, Béla Tarr, and Max Neumann, *Music and Literature* 2: 108–26.
Esslin, Martin. 2001. *The Theater of the Absurd.* New York: Vintage.
Fabbri, Roberto. 2016. *Max Bill: Espaces.* Zurich: Infolio.
Fehérváry, Krisztina. 2012. "From Socialist Modern to Super-Natural Organicism: Cosmological Transformations." *Cultural Anthropology* 27(4): 615–40.
Felbick, Lutz. 2012. *Lorenz Christoph Mizler de Kolof: Schüler Bachs und pythagoreischer "Apostel der Wolffischen Philosophie."* Hochschule für Musik und Theater "Felix Mendelssohn Bartholdy" Leipzig-Schriften, Bd. 5. Hildesheim: Georg Olms Verlag.
Ferkai, András. 1998. "Hungarian Architecture in the Postwar Years." In *The Architecture of Historic Hungary*, ed. Dora Wiebenson and József Sisa, 277–97. Cambridge, MA: MIT Press.
Fink, Eugen. 1960. *Spiel als Weltsymbol.* Stuttgart: Kohlhammer.
Foucault, Michel. 1973. *The Order of Things.* London: Vintage.
Frampton, Daniel. 2006. *Filmosophy.* London: Wallflower Press.
Freud, Sigmund. (1917) 1957. "Mourning and Melancholia," trans. by Joan Riviere. In *Standard Edition*, vol. 14, 239–60. London: Hogarth Press.
Frigyesi, Judit. 2000. *Béla Bartók and Turn-of-the-Century Budapest.* Berkeley: University of California Press.
Funzine Media. 2012. "Urban Legends: The Whale of the CIA." Accessed 5 May 2016. http://www.funzine.hu/2012-03-urban-legends-the-whale-of-the-cia.
Gadamer, Hans-Georg. 1970. "Concerning Empty and Ful-Filled Time." *Southern Journal of Philosophy* 8(4): 341–53. Originally published as "Über leere und erfüllte Zeit." In *Gesammelte Werke*, vol. 4 (Neuere Philosophie II), 137–53 (Tübingen: Mohr, 1969).

———. 1971. "Replik." In *Hermeneutik und Ideologiekritik*, ed. Karl-Otto Apel, 314–17. Frankfurt: Suhrkamp, 314–17.
———. 1976. "The Scope and Function of Hermeneutical Reflection." In *Philosophical Hermeneutics*, ed. and trans. David E. Linge, 18–43. Berkeley: University of California Press.
———. 1989. *Truth and Method*, trans. Joel Weinsheimer and Donald G. Marshall. New York: Continuum.
Gans, Deborah. 2003. Introduction to *The Organic Approach to Architecture*, ed. Deborah Gans and Zehra Kuz, v–xx. Chichester: Wiley.
Garton Ash, Timothy. 1985. "The Hungarian Lesson." *New York Review of Books*, 5 December, 5–9.
Gebser, Jean. 1985. *The Ever-Present Origin*. Athens: University of Ohio Press.
Gerle, János. 1985. "Organische Architektur in Ungarn" in *Bauwelt* 39, 1560–1578.
———. 1998. "Hungarian Architecture from 1900 to 1918." In *The Architecture of Historic Hungary*, ed. Dora Wiebenson and József Sisa, 223–44. Cambridge, MA: MIT Press.
———, ed. 2010. *Architecture as Philosophy: The Work of Imre Makovecz*. Stuttgart: Edition Axel Menges.
Goethe, Johann Wolfgang. 1772. "Von deutscher Baukunst." Gesammelte Werke, Berliner Ausgabe, Bd. 19, 7–12. Berlin: Aufbau Verlag.
———. 1817. "Morphologie." In *Naturwissenschaftliche Schriften* (Gesammelte Werke, Hamburger Ausgabe), Bd. 13, 55–56. Hamburg: Wegener.
———. 1833. *Maximen und Reflexionen*. München: Deutscher Taschenbuch Verlag.
Goodwin, James. 1993. *Eisenstein, Cinema, and History*. Urbana-Champaign: University of Illinois Press.
Górski, Eugeniusz. 2002. "From 'Socialist' to Postmodern Pluralism in Poland." *Eastern European Politics and Societies* 16: 249–77.
Gray, Hugh. 2005. Introduction to *What Is Cinema?* vol. 2, ed. André Bazin, 1–15. Berkeley: University of California Press.
Green, Peter. 1987. "Apocalypse and Sacrifice." *Sight and Sound* 56(2): 111–18.
Groys, Boris. 1992. *The Total Art of Stalinism: Avant-Garde, Aesthetic Dictatorship, and Beyond*. Princeton, NJ: Princeton University Press.
Gyáni, Gábor. (1998) 2002. *Parlor and Kitchen: Housing and Domestic Culture in Budapest, 1870–1940*. Budapest: Central European University Press.
Haeckel, Ernst. 1899–1904. *Kunstformen der Natur*. 10 vols. Leipzig: Verlag des Bibliographischen Instituts.
———. 1900. *The Riddle of the Universe*. Amherst, NY: Prometheus Books.
———. 1900. *The Riddle of the Universe*. Amherst, NY: Prometheus Books. Halligan, Benjamin. 2000. "The Long Take That Kills: Tarkovsky's Rejection of Montage." *Central Europe Review* 2(39). http://www.ce-review.org/00/39/kinoeye39_halligan.html.
Hames, Peter. 2001. "The Melancholy of Resistance: The Films of Béla Tarr." *Ki-*

noeye: New Perspectives on European Film 1(1). http://www.kinoeye.org/01/01/hames01.php.
Hamvas, Béla. 2007. "The Seventh Symphony and the Metaphysics of Music," trans. Dániel Antall and Sam Poole. http://www.hamvasbela.org/2011/12/bela-hamvas-seventh-symphony-and.html. Accessed 27 December 2016.
———. 2008. *Die Melancholie der Spätwerke*. Berlin: Matthes & Seitz. Häring, Hugo. 1925. "Wege zur Form." *Die Form* 1: 3–5.
———. 1968. *Die Ausbildung des Geistes zur Arbeit und der Gestalt: Fragmente*. Berlin: Mann.
Häring, Hugo, Heinrich Lauterbach, and Jürgen Joedicke. 1964. *Hugo Häring: Schriften, Entwürfe, Bauten*. Stuttgart: Karl Krämer Verlag.
Hauser, Arnold. 1911. "Beethoven's 9th Symphony." *Temesvári Hírlap* [The Temeswar chronicle], 6 April, 1–2.
Heathcote, Edwin. 1997. *Imre Makovecz: The Wings of the Soul*. Architectural Monographs 47. Chichester: Academy Editions.
———. 2006. "Hungary: The Organic and the Rational Traditions." *Architectural Design* 76(3): 34–39.
Heidegger, Martin. 1969. *Zur Sache des Denkens*. Tübingen: Max Niemayer.
Heller, Agnes. 1982. *A Theory of History*. Oxford: Blackwell.
Hodgkins, John. 2009. "Not Fade Away: Adapting History and Trauma in László Krasznahorkai's *The Melancholy of Resistance* and Béla Tarr's *Werckmeister Harmonies*." *Adaptation* 2(1): 49–64.
Hoppál, Mihály. 1984. *Shamanism in Eurasia*, 2 vols. Göttingen: Herodot.
———. 2007. *Shamans and Traditions*. Budapest: Akadémiai Kiadó.
Isenschmid, Andreas. 2015. "Artists, Eccentrics, Solitaries, and Saints: On László Krasznahorkai's *Seiobo There Below*." *Music and Literature*, 20 May. Accessed 13 November 2016. http://www.musicandliterature.org/reviews/2015/5/15/artists-eccentrics-solitaries-and-saints-on-lszl-krasznahorkais-seiobo-there-below.
Jaffe, Ira. 2014. *Slow Movies: Countering the Cinema of Action*. New York: Wallflower Press.
James, Beverly A. 2005. *Imagining Postcommunism: Visual Narratives of Hungary's 1956 Revolution*. College Station: Texas A&M University Press.
James, William. 2008. *A Pluralistic Universe*. Rockville, MD: Arc Manor.
Janaszek-Ivaničková, Halina. 1997. "Postmodernism in Poland." In *International Postmodernism: Theory and Literary Practice*, ed. Hans Bertens and Douwe Fokkema, 423–28. Amsterdam: John Benjamins.
Jencks, Charles. 2002. *The New Paradigm in Architecture: The Language of Postmodernism*. New Haven: Yale University Press.
Jobbit, Steven. 2011. "Memory and Modernity in Fodor's Work on Hungary." In Tötösy de Zepetnek and Vasvári 2011, 59–71.
Joullié, Jean-Etienne. 2013. *Will to Power: Nietzsche's Last Idol*. London: Palgrave.
Kadare, Ismail. 2013. *Chronicle in Stone*. New York: Skyhorse.

Kant, Immanuel. 1781. *Kritik der reinen Vernunft*, Werkausgabe, vol. 3. Frankfurt: Suhrkamp.
———. 1929. *Critique of Pure Reason*, trans. N. Kemp Smith. Basingstoke: Palgrave Macmillian.
Kerman, Joseph. 1983. "A Few Canonic Variations." *Critical Inquiry* 10: 107–25.
Khan, Abraham. 1985. "Melancholy, Irony, and Kierkegaard." *International Journal for Philosophy of Religion* 17(1–2): 67–85.
Koehler, Robert. 2011. "Interview—The Thinking Image: Fred Kelemen on Béla Tarr and *The Turin Horse*." *Cinema Scope* 46. http://cinema-scope.com/cinema-scope-magazine/interview-the-thinking-image-fred-kelemen-on-bela-tarr-and-the-turin-horse.
Koffka, Kurt. 1936. *Principles of Gestalt Psychology*. New York: Routledge.
Kohn, Hans. 1953. *Pan-Slavism: Its History and Ideology*. Notre Dame, IN: University of Notre Dame Press.
Konrád, György. 1995. *Melancholy of Rebirth: Essays from Post-Communist Central Europe, 1989–1994*. New York: Harcourt Brace.
Koyré, Alexandre. 1962. *Du Monde clos à l'univers infini* [From the closed world to the infinite universe]. Paris: Presses Universitaires de Paris.
Kovács, András Bálint. 2004. "Sátántangó." In *The Cinema of Central Europe*, ed. Peter Hames, 237–45. London: Wallflower.
———. 2008. "The World According to Béla Tarr." *KinoKultura*. Accessed 5 May 2016. http://www.kinokultura.com/specials/7/kovacs.shtml.
———. 2013. *The Cinema of Béla Tarr: The Circle Closes*. London: Wallflower.
Kracauer, Siegfried. 1973. *Theorie des Films*. Frankfurt: Suhrkamp.
Krasznahorkai, László. 1998. *The Melancholy of Resistance*, trans. George Szirtes. New York: New Directions. Originally published as *Az ellenállás melankóliája* (Budapest: Magvető, 1989).
———. 2001. *Le Thésée universel* [The universal theseus], trans. Joëlle Dufeuilly. Paris: Vagabonde. Originally published as *A Théseus-általános* (Budapest: Széphalom Kvműhely, 1993).
———. 2005. *Im Norden ein Berg, im Süden ein See, im Westen Wege, im Osten ein Fluß* [From the north by hill, from the south by lake, from the west by roads], trans. Christina Viragh. Zurich: Ammann. Originally published as Északról hegy, Délről tó, Nyugatról utak, Keletről folyó (Budapest: Magvető, 2003).
———. 2006. *War and War*, trans. George Szirtes. New York: New Directions. Originally published as *Háború és háború* (Budapest: Magvető, 1999).
———. 2009. "El último Lobo," trans. George Szirtes. *Words without Borders*, August. Accessed 5 May 2016. http://wordswithoutborders.org/article/el-ultimo-lobo.
———. 2012a. *Satantango*, trans. George Szirtes. London: Atlantic Books. Originally published as *Sátántangó* (Budapest: Magvető, 1985).
———. 2012b. "The Disciplined Madness." Interview. *Guernica: A Magazine of Art and Politics*, 26 April. Accessed 5 May 2016. https://www.guernicamag.com/daily/laszlo-krasznahorkai-the-disciplined-madness.

———. 2013a. "About a Photographer." Special issue on László Krasznahorkai, Béla Tarr, and Max Neumann, *Music and Literature* 2: 11–14.
———. 2013b. *The Bill: For Palma Vecchio, at Venice*. London: Sylph.
———. 2013c. *Seiobo There Below*, trans. Ottilie Mulzet. New York: New Directions. Originally published as *Seiobo járt odalent* (Budapest: Magvető, 2008).
———. 2014. *Animalinside*, trans. Ottilie Mulzet. London: Sylph. Originally published as Állatvanbent (Budapest: Magvető, 2010).
———. 2015a. *Der Gefangene von Urga* [The prisoner of Urga], trans. Hans Skirecky. Originally published as *Az urgai fogoly* (Budapest: Szephalom Konyzmuhely, 1992).
———. 2015b. *Die Welt voran* [Going to the world], trans. Heike Flemming. Frankfurt: Fischer. Originally published as *Megy a világ* (Budapest: Magvető, 2013).
———. 2015c. *Sous le coup de la grâce* [Under the conditions of grace], trans. Marc Martin. Paris: Vagabonde, Originally published as *Kegyelmi viszonyok* (Budapest: Magvető, 1986).
Kraus, Karl. 1914 . "In dieser großen Zeit." *Die Fackel* 16(404): 1–20. Reprinted as "In These Great Times" in *In These Great Times: A Karl Kraus Reader*, ed. Harry Zohn, 64–83 (Manchester: Carcanet, 1984).
Kuhn, Thomas S. 1957. *The Copernican Revolution: Planetary Astronomy in the Development of Western Thought*. Cambridge, MA: Harvard University Press.
Kuma, Kengo. 2009. *Studies in Organic*. Tokyo: TOTO Shuppan.
Kundera, Milan. 1984. "The Tragedy of Central Europe." *New York Review of Books*, 26 April.
Kurg, Andres. 2009. "Architects of the Tallinn School and the Critique of Soviet Modernism in Estonia." *The Journal of Architecture* 14(1): 85–108.
Lacoue-Labarthe, Philippe. 1987. *La fiction du politique*. Paris: Christian Bourgeois.
Lee, Janice. 2014. "Apocalypse Withheld: On Slowness and the Long Take in Béla Tarr's Satantango." *Entropymag*, 15 May. Accessed 5 May 2016. http://entropymag.org/apocalypse-withheld-on-slowness-the-long-take-in-bela-tarrs-satantango.
Ligeti, György. 2001. *The Ligeti Project II*. Audio CD. Teldec Classics.
Lim, Song Hwee. 2014. *Tsai Ming-Liang and a Cinema of Slowness*. Honolulu: University of Hawai'i Press.
Lodder, Christina, and Benjamin Benus. 2012. "Constructivism." *Grove Art Online/Oxford Art Online*. Oxford University Press. Accessed 5 May 2016. http://www.oxfordartonline.com/subscriber/article/grove/art/T019194.
Lossky, Nicolas. 1928. *The World as an Organic Whole*. Oxford: Oxford University Press.
Lukács, Georg. (1920) 1971. *The Theory of the Novel: A Historico-Philosophical Essay on the Forms of Great Epic Literature*, trans. Anna Bostock. London: Merlin Press.
Lyotard, Jean-François. 1991. *The Inhuman*. Stanford: Stanford University Press.
Macheray, Pierre. 1970. *A Theory of Literary Production*. London: Routledge and Kegan Paul.

Mackay, Robin, ed. 2015. *When Site Lost the Plot*. Falmouth, UK: Urbanomic.
Magyar, Zoltan. 1991. "Der ungarische Architekt Imre Makovecz und seine Sakralbauten." *Das Münster* 1: 17–23.
Makovecz, Imre. 1993. "Anthropomorphic Architecture: The Borderline between Heaven and Earth." *Architectural Design* 63(6): 15–20.
——. 2014. *Makovecz Imre*. Budapest: Magyar Muveszeti Akademia.
Márai, Sándor. 2008. *Esther's Inheritance*, trans. George Szirtes. New York: Knopf Doubleday. Originally published as *Eszter hagyatéka* (Budapest: Révai, 1939).
Marchand, Steven. 2009. "Nothing Counts: Shot and Event in *Werckmeister Harmonies*." *New Cinemas: Journal of Contemporary Film* 7(2): 137–54.
Marcus, Judith, and Zoltán Tarr. 1989. *Georg Lukács: Theory, Culture, and Politics*. New Jersey: Transaction.
McKibbin, Tony. 2005. "Cinema of Damnation: Negative Capabilities in Contemporary Central and Eastern European Film." *Senses of Cinema* 34. http://sensesofcinema.com/2005/feature-articles/cinema_of_damnation/.
McLaren, Rose. 2012. "The Prosaic Sublime of Béla Tarr." *The White Rose Review* 6. http://www.thewhitereview.org/features/the-prosaic-sublime-of-bela-tarr.
McLuhan, Marshall. 1964. *Understanding Media: The Extensions of Man*. New York: McGraw Hill.
Mizler, Lorenz Christoph. 1736 "Werckmeisters General Baß. Wobey dessen Unterricht—wie man ein Clavier wohl stimmen soll—angehänget." *Musikalische Bibliothek* 1(5): 67–71. Retrieved 5 May 2016 from http://reader.digitale-sammlungen.de/de/fs1/object/goToPage/bsb10599089.html?pageNo=423.
Molnár, Virág. 2005. "Cultural Politics and Modernist Architecture: The Tulip Debate in Postwar Hungary." *American Sociological Review* 70(1): 111–35.
Müller, Max. 1855. *The Languages of the Seat of War in the East—With a Survey of the Three Families of Language: Semitic, Arian, and Turanian*. London: Williams and Norgate.
Neubauer, John. 2009. "Organicism and Music Theory." In *New Paths: Aspects of Music Theory and Aesthetics in the Age of Romanticism*, ed. Darla Crispin, 11–35. Leuven: Leuven University Press.
Nietzsche, Friedrich. (1883–1891) 1978. *Thus Spake Zarathustra*. Harmondsworth: Penguin.
——. 1998. *Beyond Good and Evil*, trans. Marion Faber. Oxford: Oxford University Press.
Norris, Christopher. 2005. "Music Theory, Analysis and Deconstruction: How They Might (Just) Get Along Together." *International Review of the Aesthetics and Sociology of Music* 36(1): 37–82.
Ohio State University, School of Music. N.d. "Some Notes Regarding Tuning and Temperament." Accessed 13 November 2016. http://www.music-cog.ohiostate.edu/Music829B/tuning.html.
Parti Nagy, Lajos. 2006. "Giuseppe undo Pusztay." In *A Fagyott Kutya Lába* [A frozen dog's leg]. 25–33. Budapest: Magvető.

Pearson, David. 2001. *New Organic Architecture: The Breaking Wave.* Berkeley: University of California Press.
Perkins, V. F., Ian Cameron, Paul Mayersberg, and Mark Shivas. 1963. "Movie Differences: A Discussion." *Movie* 8: 28–34.
Petric, Vlada. 1989. "Tarkovsky's Dream Imagery." *Film Quarterly* 43(2): 28–34.
Petrova, Evgenia. 2003. *Kazimir Malevich: Suprematism.* Exhibition catalog. New York: Guggenheim Museum.
Prince, Bart. 2001. "Inside Out." In *New Organic Architecture: The Breaking Wave,* ed. David Pearson, 86–93. Berkeley: University of California Press.
Proust, Marcel. 1922. *Swann's Way,* trans. C. K. Scott-Moncrieff. New York: Holt.
Rancière, Jacques. 2002. Preface to *L'Eternité par les astres* [Eternity by the stars], Auguste Blanqui, 5–26. Paris: Les Impressions Nouvelles.
———. 2013. *Béla Tarr, the Time After,* trans. Erik Beranek. Minneapolis: Univocal. Originally published as *Béla Tarr, le Temps Après* (Nantes: Capricci, 2011).
Rattenbury, Kester. 1994. "Echo and Narcissus." *Architectural Design* 64(6): 34–37.
Ráz, Péter. 2012 "Fate." In *The Essential Guide to Being Hungarian,* ed. István Bori, 4–7. North Adams, MA: New Europe Books.
Ritzer, George. 2001. *Explorations in the Sociology of Consumption: Fast Food, Credit Cards and Casinos.* London: Sage.
Robinson, Sydney K. 1993. "Building as if in Eden." *Architectural Design* 63(6): 9–14.
Rockwell, John. 1992. "The Talk of Seville: In Expo Architecture, Mishmash Means Eclectic" *New York Times,* 7 May.
Rodych, Victor. 2008. "Mathematical Sense: Wittgenstein's Syntactical Structuralism." In *Wittgenstein and the Philosophy of Information: Proceedings of the 30th Wittgenstein Symposium in Kirchberg,* ed. Alois Pichler and Herbert Hrachovec, 81–104. Berlin: De Gruyter.
Rollet, Sylvie. 2006. "Béla Tarr ou le temps inhabitable." *Positif* 542: 101–3.
———. 2011. "Une phénoménologie du chaos." *Vertigo* 41: 102–6.
———. 2013. "Filmer la figure humaine 'au milieu' des choses: Le cinéma selon Béla Tarr." *Appareil* 12: 1–8.
Rorty, Richard. 1989. *Contingency, Irony, and Solidarity.* Cambridge, MA: Cambridge University Press.
Rousseau, Jean-Jacques. 1998. *Essay on the Origin of Languages and Writings Related to Music,* trans. and ed. John T. Scott. Hanover, NH: University Press of New England. Originally printed as *Essai sur l'origine des langues où il est parlé de la mélodie et de l'imitation musicale* (Paris: Aubier Montaigne, 1781).
Roy, Nilanjana S. 2015. "Slow Reading." *Business Standard,* 25 May. Accessed 5 May 2016. http://www.business-standard.com/article/opinion/nilanjana-s-roy-slow-reading-115052501366_1.html.
Said, Edward W. 2006. *On Late Style: Music and Literature Against the Grain.* New York: Pantheon Books.
Samocki, Jean-Marie. 2011. "Tant de Nuits." *Vertigo* 41: 118–21.

Saussure, Ferdinand. (1916) 1995. *Cours de linguistique générale*. Paris: Payot.
Schelling, Friedrich Wilhelm Joseph. (1798) 1967. "Ideen zu einer Philosophie der Natur als Einleitung in das Studium dieser Wissenschaften." In *Schriften von 1794–1798*. Darmstadt: Wissenschaftliche Buchgesellschaft. Engl. trans. by Errol E. Harris and Peter Heath, *Ideas for a Philosophy of Nature* (Cambridge: Cambridge University Press, 1988).
Schlegel, August Wilhelm. (1845) 1963. *Kritische Schriften und Briefe XVII*, Bd. 2. Stuttgart: Lohner.
———. 1833. *A Course of Lectures on Dramatic Art and Literature*, trans. John Black. Philadelphia: Hogan and Thompson.
Schleicher, Hans J. 1987. *Architektur als Welterfahrung: Rudolf Steiners organischer Baustil und die Architektur der Waldorfschulen*. Frankfurt: Fischer.
Schneider, David E. 2006. *Bartók, Hungary, and the Renewal of Tradition*. Berkeley: University of California Press.
Schoenberg, Arnold. (1946) 1975. "New Music, Outmoded Music, Style, and Idea." In *Style and Idea: Selected Writings of Arnold Schoenberg*, ed. Leonard Stein, 113–24. Berkeley: University of California Press.
Schrader, Paul. 1972. *Transcendental Style in Film: Ozu, Bresson, Dreyer*. New York: Da Capo.
Sebald, W. G. 2000. Blurb to László Krasznahorkai's *The Melancholy of Resistance*. New York: New Directions.
Shusterman, Richard. 1989. "Organic Unity: Analysis and Deconstruction." In *Redrawing the Lines: Analytic Philosophy, Deconstruction, and Literary Theory*, ed. Reed Way Dasenbrock, 92–115. Minneapolis: University of Minnesota Press.
Stauffer, George. 2005. "Review of *Bach and the Meanings of Counterpoint*, by David Yearsley." *Journal of the American Musicological Society* 58(3): 710–17.
Steiner, Peter. 1979. *From Formalism to Structuralism: A Comparative Study of Russian Formalism and Prague Structuralism*. Ann Arbor, MI: University Microfilms International.
Steiner, Rudolf. 1883. *Einleitungen zu Goethes Naturwissenschaftliche Schriften*. Dornach: Steiner Verlag.
Sullivan, Louis H. 1896. "The Tall Office Building Artistically Considered." *Lippincott's Magazine* (March): 403–9.
Sushytska, Julia. 2010. "What Is Eastern Europe?" *Angelaki: Journal of the Theoretical Humanities* 15(3): 53–65.
Szakolczai, Arpad. 2005. "Moving Beyond the Sophists: Intellectuals in East Central Europe and the Return of Transcendence." *European Journal of Social Theory* 8(4): 417–33.
Szakolczai, Arpad, and Harald Wydra. 2006. "Contemporary East Central European Social Theory." In *Handbook of Contemporary European Social Theory*, ed. Gerard Delanty, 138–52. London: Routledge.
Talking about Tarr: A Symposium at Facets. 2008. Booklet accompanying the CD of the Facets edition of *Satantango*. Chicago: Facets Multi-Media.

Tamás, Gáspár Miklós. 2007. "Elátkozott magyar ünnepek" [Cursed Hungarian celebrations]. *Népszava Online*, 18 August.
———. 2013. "Words from Budapest—Interview." *New Left Review* 80: 5–27.
Tarkovsky, Andrei. 1986. *Sculpting in Time: Reflections on the Cinema*, trans. Kitty Hunter-Blair. London: The Bodley Head.
———. 1999. *Collected Screenplays*, trans. William Powell and Natasha Synessios. London: Faber and Faber.
Tarr, Béla. 2000. "Interview with Béla Tarr: About *Werckmeister Harmonies* (Canne 2000, Director's Fortnight)." By Eric Schlosser. *Bright Lights*, 30 October. Accessed 5 May 2016. http://www.brightlightsfilm.com/30/belatarr1.php#.VEylLvmUd8E.
———. 2001. "Waiting for the Prince: An Interview with Béla Tarr." By Fergus Daly and Maximilian Le Chain. *Senses of Cinema* 12. http://sensesofcinema.com/2001/feature-articles/tarr-2 (accessed 19 November 2016).
———. 2004. "In Search of Truth: Béla Tarr Interviewed." By Phil Ballard. *Kinoeye: New Perspectives on European Film* 4(2). http://www.kinoeye.org/04/02/ballard02.php.
———. 2008. "Radio Interview by Laure Adler on France Culture." Transcript available at *Unspoken Cinema*. Accessed 5 May 2016. http://unspokencinema.blogspot.com/2009/01/bla-tarr-2008-interview-on-french-radio.html.
———. 2014. "My Master's Voice: Béla Tarr Interviewed by J R Robinson." *The Quietus*, 5 November. Accessed 5 May 2016. http://thequietus.com/articles/16564-bela-tarr-interview-wrekmeister-harmonies.
Todd, Emmanuel. 1976 (1979). *La chute finale: Essai sur la décomposition de la sphère soviétique*. Paris: Laffont. Reprinted as *The Final Fall: An Essay on the Decomposition of the Soviet Sphere*, trans. John Waggoner (New York: Karz Publishers).
Töke, Lilla. 2011. "The Absurd as a Form of Realism in Hungarian Literature." In Tötösy de Zepetnek and Vasvári 2011, 102–12.
Töttössy, Beatrice. 1995. "Hungarian Postmodernity and Post-Coloniality: The Epistemology of a Literature." In "Postcolonial Literatures: Theory and Practice," ed. Steven Tötösy de Zepetnek and Sneja Gunew. Special issue, *Canadian Review of Comparative Literature* 22(3–4): 881–91.
Toy, Maggie. 1993. "Organic Architecture: Subtlety and Power." *Architectural Design* 63(6): 1–7.
Tuttle, Harry. 2007. "Yvette Bíró on Béla Tarr." *Unspoken Cinema*, 5 October. Accessed 5 May 2016. http://unspokencinema.blogspot.com/2007/10/yvette-biro-on-bela-tarr.html.
Ungváry, Krisztián. 2012. "Turanism: The 'New' Ideology of the Far Right." *Budapest Times*, 5 February. Accessed 5 May 2016. http://budapesttimes.hu/2012/02/05/turanism-the-new-ideology-of-the-far-right.
"Milan 2015 Expo." "Hungary's Pavilion Draws Life From the Purest Source." Acessed 26 December 2016. http://www.expo2015.org/archive/en/news/all-news/il-padiglione-ungherese-prende-vita-dalla-fonte-piu-pura.html

Vági, Zoltán, László Csősz, and Gábor Kádár. 2013. *The Holocaust in Hungary: Evolution of a Genocide.* Lanham, MD: AltaMira Press.
van de Velde, Henry. 1901. *Die Renaissance im modernen Kunstgewerbe.* Berlin: Cassirer.
Vásáry, István. 2005. *Cumans and Tatars: Oriental military in the pre-Ottoman Balkans, 1185-1365.* Cambridge University Press.
Venturi, Robert, Denise Scott Brown, and Steven Izenour. 1972. *Learning from Las Vegas: The Forgotten Symbolisms of Architectural Form.* Cambridge, MA: MIT Press.
Virilio, Paul. 1977. *Vitesse et politique: Essai de dromologie.* Paris: Galilée. Reprinted as *Speed and Politics,* trans. Mark Polizziotti (Cambridge, MA: MIT Press, 2006).
———. 2002. *Desert Screen: War at the Speed of Light,* trans. Michael Degener. London: Athlone Press.
Vitruvius. *De architectura (Ten Books on Architecture).* Retrieved 5 May 2016 from http://penelope.uchicago.edu/Thayer/E/Roman/Texts/Vitruvius/home.html.
Volkov, Solomon. 2004. *Shostakovich and Stalin: The Extraordinary Relationship between the Great Composer and the Brutal Dictator.* New York: Knopf.
Wallace, Robert M. 1987. Preface to *The Genesis of the Copernican World,* Hans Blumenberg, xi–xlvi. Cambridge, MA: MIT Press.
Webern, Anton. 1963. *The Path to the New Music* (1932–33), ed. Willi Reich. Bryn Mawr: Theodore Press.
Wellek, René. 1982. *The Attack on Literature and Other Essays.* Chapel Hill: University of North Carolina Press.
Werckmeister, Andreas. (1707) 2007. *Musikalische Paradoxal-Discourse* (Quendlinburg Edition). Laaber: Laaber Verlag. Retrieved 5 May 2016 from http://reader.digitale-sammlungen.de/de/fs1/object/display/bsb10527832_00014.html.
Winder, Simon. 2013. *Danubia: A Personal History of Habsburg Europe.* London: Picador.
Wesselényi-Garay, Andor. 2008. "Utopian Traditions: From the Architectural Model to a Possible Alternative." *Epiteszforum,* 15 August. Accessed 5 May 2016. http://epiteszforum.hu/utopian-traditions-from-the-architectural-model-to-a-possible-alternative.
Wittgenstein, Ludwig. (1921) 1990. *Tractatus Logico-Philosophicus.* Leipzig: Reclam.
Wood, James. 2011. "Madness and Civilization: The Very Strange Fictions of László Krasznahorkai." *New Yorker,* 4 July. http://www.newyorker.com/magazine/2011/07/04/madness-and-civilization
———. 2012. "Reality Examined to the Point of Madness: László Krasznahorkai." In *The Fun Stuff and Other Essays,* 279–91. New York: Farrar, Strauss and Giroux.

Wright, Frank Lloyd. 1941. "Organic Architecture." In *Frank Lloyd Wright on Architecture*, ed. Frederick Gutheim, 177–91. New York: Macmillan. First published in *The Architects' Journal*, 6 August 1936.

———. 1975. *In the Cause of Architecture: Essays by Frank Lloyd Wright for the Architectural Record, 1908–1952*, ed. Frederick Gutheim. New York: McGraw-Hill.

———. 1979. *Organic Architecture: The Architecture of Democracy*. London: Lund Humphries.

———. 1987. *Truth Against the World: Frank Lloyd Wright Speak for an Organic Architecture*, ed. Patrick Meehan. New York: Wiley.

———. 2003. "The Art and Craft of the Machine." In *The Industrial Design Reader*, ed. Carma Gorman, 55–64. New York: Skyhorse.

Wright, Lucie, and Emeric de Lastens. 2011. "*Ecce Homines*: La pesanteur et la grâce selon Béla Tarr." *Vertigo* 41: 88–95.

Zavaliy, Andrei. 2012. "Cosmism." In *ODIP: The Online Dictionary of Intercultural Philosophy*, ed. Thorsten Botz-Bornstein. Accessed 5 May 2016. http://media.wix.com/ugd/c49976_e6458b678efa4ae2a178197d53531443.pdf.

Zevi, Bruno. 1950. *Toward an Organic Architecture*. London: Faber and Faber.

Filmography

Films by Béla Tarr

1981. *The Outsider* [*Szabadgyalog*].
1982. *The Prefab People* [*Panelkapcsolat*].
1985. *Almanac of Fall* [*Őszi almanach*].
1988. *Damnation* [*Kárhozat*].
1994. *Satantango* [*Sátántangó*].
1995. *Journey on the Plain* [*Utazás az alföldön*].
1997. *Family Nest* [*Családi tűzfészek*].
2000. *Werckmeister Harmonies* [*Werckmeister harmóniák*].
2004. *Visions of Europe*.
2007. *The Man from London* [*A londoni férfi*].
2011. *The Turin Horse* [*A torinói ló*].

Other films

4 Months, 3 Weeks and 2 Days [*4 luni, 3 saptamâni si 2 zile*]. Dir. Cristian Mungiu. Mobra Films, 2007.

Andrei Tarkovsky: A Poet of the Cinema. Dir. Donatella Baglivo [*Un poeta nel Cinema: Andreij Tarkovskij*] (documentary supplemental to the DVD of Andrei Rublev), 1984.

Bálint Fábián Meets God [*Fábián Bálint* találkozása Istenne]. Dir. Zoltán Fabri. Dialóg Filmstúdió, 1980.
Elephant. Dir. Gus Van Sant. HBO Films, 2003.
Hungarians [*Magyarok*]. Dir. Zoltán Fabri. Hungarofilm / Mafilm, 1978.
Liverpool. Dir. Lisandro Alonso. 4L, 2008.
Nostalghia. Dir. Andrei Tarkovsky. Mosfilm/Gaumont, 1983.
Ossos. Dir. Pedro Costa. Madragoa Fims, 1997.
Solaris. Dir. Andrei Tarkovsky. Mosfilm, 1972.
Stalker. Dir. Andrei Tarkovsky. Mosfilm, 1970.
Still Life [*Sanxia haoren*]. Dir. Jia Zhangke. Xstream Pictures, 2006.
Stranger Than Paradise. Dir. Jim Jarmusch. Cinesthesia Productions, 1984.
The Death of Mr. Lazarescu [*Moartea domnului Lazarescu*]. Dir. Cristi Puiu. Mandragora, 2005.
The Sacrifice [*Offret*]. Dir. Andrei Tarkovsky. Katinka Farago, 1986.

Index

A
Aalto, Alvar, 29
Abduh, Muhammad, 50
absurdity, 81, 84, 154, 157
Adorno, Theodor, 19
Agamben Giorgio, 162
al-Afghani, Jamal ad-Din, 50
Alcmaeon of Croton, 68
All-Unity, 53, 99, 122
Almanac of Fall, 3
anamnesis, 13–14
Ando, Tadao, 6, 9
Andrew, Dudley, 7
Angelopoulos, Theo, 2
Animalinside, 94–95
Antonioni, Michelangolo, 5, 24, 34
Aquinas, Thomas, 103
Aristotle, 11, 51, 124, 159
Aristoxenus, 90, 110
Art Nouveau, 19, 44, 81–82, 91–92, 131, 151, 201
Association of New Architects (ASNOVA), 139
Astronomy, 158–61
Astro-theology, 160

B
Bakhtin, Mikhail, 54
Balázs, Béla, 175
Barthes, Roland, 20, 124
Bartók, Béla, 29, 32, 45, 101
Bauhaus, 92, 201
Bauman, Zygmunt, 63
Bazin, André, 20–21, 35–37, 55, 107–8, 138, 180
Beckett, Samuel, 32
Benjamin, Walter, 96, 169
Berdyaev, Nicolai, 53
Bergman, Ingmar, 119
Bergson, Henri, 53, 171, 193–97
Berque, Augustin, 21, 165
Bill, Max, 92
biology, 35, 50, 52–55
Bíró, Yvette, 15, 132, 172, 190–91
Blanqui, Louis Auguste, 159
Bloom, Allan, 49, 133
Blumenberg, Hans, 13, 120, 160
Bordwell, David, 96, 179
Braidotti, Rosi, 164–65
Bresson, Robert, 133
Budapest, 19, 41
Byzantium, 118, 185

C
Cantor, Georg, 93–94
Capra, Fritjof, 166
Cassirer, Ernst, 163, 166–67
Celts, 166
Central Asia, 145
Central Europe. *See* Eastern Europe
chôra, 51, 126
circularity, 29–30, 186–87
Coleridge, Samuel Taylor, 4, 52, 56n2, 134
communism, 42, 147–48
Comte, Auguste, 159
constructivism, 15
contemplation, 11–12, 182, 186–88 ; contemplation vs. analysis, 11, contemplative cinema, 1–2, 7, 8, 30, 37
Copernicus, 13, 117, 158
cosmology, 3, 55, 81, 96–98, 159–61, 165; acosmic, 21
Csete, György, 43, 148

D

da Vinci, Leonardo, 117
Damnation (synopsis), 2
Darwin, Charles, 5, 86–87
de Man, Paul, 124–25
decay (decomposition), 41, 86, 153
deconstruction, 15–16, 20, 86, 120–24
Deleuze, Gilles, 5–6, 122, 193
democracy, 113
Derham, William, 160
Derrida, Jacques, 64n2, 123–129, 163
Descartes, René, 35
determinism, 86
Dewey, John, 115n6, 124
différance, 64, 125, 182
digital, 83, 122
Dilthey, Wilhelm, 46
diversity, 87
Dostoevsky, Fyodor, 143
dream, 178
durée pure, 53, 193–97
dynamics, 29–30, 49, 117, 169–70, 182

E

Eastern Europe, 3, 22n4, 39–42, 87, 132, 143–44, 151
Einfühlung, 53, 122, 166, 181
Eisenstein, Sergei, 4–5, 181, 199
empathy. See *Einfühlung*
Enlightenment, 117–19, 125, 159
Erdem, Reha, 2
Esterházy, Peter, 87
Eurasianism, 20
existentialism, 12
Expo, 2015, 145

F

Fabri, Zoltan, 3
face, 174–78
Family Nest, 24
Farkasrét Mortuary Chapel, 26, 151
Fedorov, Nicolai, 99
feeling, 7, 53, 196
Fellini, Federico, 24
Fink, Eugen, 98
Fodor, Ferenc, 46
folklore, 144–45
formalism, 54, 181, 183

Foucault, 163
Foucault, Michel, 64, 124
Fourier, Charles, 159
Frampton, Daniel, 4
Freud, Sigmund, 12–13, 59–60
functionalism, 151
fundamentalism, 65–66

G

Gadamer, Hans-Georg, 50, 65, 196
Gaudí, Antonio, 43, 151
Gebser, Jean, 185
genes, 62
geography, 67
geometry, 100, 183, 199–200
Gestalt, 2, 61, 99–100, 167, 199
globalization, 49
God, 60–61, 66, 103, 108, 133
Godard, Jean-Luc, 5
Goethe, Johann Wolfgang, 4, 52–53, 67, 100, 191–92
Goff, Bruce, 77
gothic, 30–34, 52, 167
Groys, Boris, 20, 157
Guattari, Felix, 126
Gyáni, Gábor, 41

H

Habsburg, 44
Haeckel, Ernst, 83, 131
Hamvas, Béla, 9, 57–59, 182, 194
Häring, Hugo, 2, 29, 61, 81, 86, 97–98, 118, 170, 185, 199
harmony, 42–43, 46, 113, 117, 127–29, 141, 171, 180–81
Hauser, Arnold, 101
Hegel, Georg Wilhelm Friedrich, 51, 126
Heidegger, Martin, 168
Heller, Agnes, 117
hermeneutics, 12, 17, 50
Human Genome Project, 55
Humanism, 117–19
Hungariannes, 44
Hungary, 7, 40–41, 45–46, 144; Hungarian history, 67, 74; Hungarian geography, 46; Hungarian music, 46
Husserl, Edmund, 101

I

identity, 146
irony, 59
Islam, 2, 50

J

Jaffe, Ira, 9, 22n1, 30–34, 37, 174
Japan, 93
Jencks, Charles, 77
Journey on the Plain, 24

K

Kadare, Ismail, 142
Kamerarealität, 36
Kant, Immanuel, 108–9
Kaurismäki, Aki, 2
kenosis, 183
Kepler, Johannes, 159
Kierkegaard, Soren, 59
kitsch, 70–75, 138, 149
Kodály, Zoltán, 46, 144
Koffka, Kurt, 99
Konrád, György, 41, 85
Kós, Károly, 43
Kotsis, Iván, 80
Kovács, András Bálint, 57, 68, 87, 133–34, 153, 157, 178, 186–87, 190
Koyré, Alexandre, 158
Kracauer, Siegfried, 35–36
Krasznahorkai, Laszlo, 16–17, 24
Kraus, Karl. 122
Kuhn, Thomas S., 13, 117
Kundera, Milan, 42

L

Lacoue-Labarthe, Philippe, 66
Lajta, Béla, 44
Lamarck, Jean-Baptiste, 51
landscapes, 176–78
Laplace, Pierre-Simon, 159
Le Corbusier, 191, 200
Lechner, Ödön, 43–45
Leclerc, Georges-Louis, 35
Leviathan, 26
Ligeti, György, 136
Lossky, Nicolas, 54
Lukács, Georg, 14, 42, 58–60, 64n1, 101, 159

M

Macheray, Pierre, 152n1
Makovecz, Imre, 18–19, 23
Malevich, Kazimir, 105
Man from London, 24–25, 168–69
Márai, Sándor, 142
Marchand, Steven, 5
materiality, 7
mathematics, 11, 30, 54–55, 89–90, 93–94, 100–102, 109
McLuhan, Marshall, 32
Medvigy, Gábor, 17
Melancholy of Resistance (synopsis), 8
melancholy, 13, 57–60, 85
melody, 127
metaphor, 8
metaphysics, 65
metonymy, 8, 180
Mies van der Rohe, Ludwig, 62
minimalism, 31–32, 70
Mitteleuropa, 41
Mizler, Lorenz Christof, 104, 160
montage, 5–6, 29, 35–36, 179
Morris, William, 52
Müller, Max, 145
music, 52, 60, 73, 89–90, 94–95, 103–6, 114, 137, 141
musical theology, 104
mysticism, 51, 123, 150
myths, 81, 162–63, 192–93

N

nano science, 62
nationalism, 49, 145
nature, 54–55, 59, 60–61, 63, 129, 140, 162
Nazis, 66, 79, 146
Newton, Isaac, 103
Nietzsche, Friedrich, 86–87, 114, 129–133
nihilism, 139–40
Nishida, Kitaro, 53
Nostalgia, 157
Nouveau Roman, 31
Nouvel, Jean, 6
Nouvelle Vague, 5, 31

O

Old Testament, 26
Orbán, Viktor, 38, 146

organic (definition), 51
Orthodox Church, 20

P
Paks Church, 164–65, 184
Palladio, Andrea, 52
Pan-Slavism, 44
Pécs Group, 43, 77, 83, 98, 144–45
perfection, 91
perspective, 184–85
Pethő, Sandor, 46
Plato, 11, 12, 67, 93
Plotinus, 51
postmodernism, 15, 76–83
Pragmatism, 112–14
Prefab People, 24
Proust, Marcel, 96, 180
Pudovkin, Vsevolod, 34
Pythagoras, 110

R
Rameau, Jean-Philippe, 128
Rancière, Jacques, 84, 96, 159, 179
Ranke, Leopold, 46
rationalism, 45–46
realism, 36, 106–8, 121, 122, 137–38, 157, 189–91
reality, 62, 84–86, 100
relativism, 49, 97, 112–14
religion, 131–32, 154
Renaissance, 117–19, 184–85
repetition, 40
rhizome, 73, 126
rhythm, 2, 180–86
Romanticism, 108–9
Rorty, Richard, 65, 114, 124
Rousseau, Jean-Jacques, 127–29
Russian philosophy, 53–54

S
Sacifice, The, 156–58
Said, Edward, 58
Saint Augustin, 196
Satantango (synopsis), 2
Saussure, Ferdinand, 125
Schelling, F.W.J., 54, 109
Schlegel, August Wilhelm, 4, 51–52, 56n2
Schleicher, Hans, 166

Schoenberg, Arnold, 29, 32, 75
Sebald, W.G., 98
Seiobo There Below, 40
Seville Pavilion, 26, 76, 147, 149
Shostakovich, Dmitri, 139
Shusterman, Richard, 124–26
silence, 9–10
Siófok Church, 26, 175
Slavophiles, 53
Slow Cinema. *See* Contemplative Cinema
Slow Food, 8
slow motion, 34
slowness, 184
sobornost, 53
socialism, 45, 98, 137–39, 149
Socrates, 67
Solaris, 177
Soloviov, Vladimir, 53
space, 94–95, 166–70, 183–85, 193–97
Spinoza, 51
spiritual, 153–55
Stalin, Joseph, 120, 133, 136–39, 143–44
Stalker, 113, 155, 156, 176–77
Steiner, Rudolf, 53, 199
step printing, 34
Stoicism, 133
Strohheim, Erich von, 35
style, 75, 161
Sullivan, Louis, 191, 200
symbolism, 81
Szekfű, Gyula, 46
Szigetvár Cultural Center, 82

T
Tamás, Gáspár Miklós, 40, 119, 144, 157
Tarkovsky, Andrei, 2, 4, 7, 8, 34, 36, 113, 131–32, 134, 153–58, 176–77, 181–82, 200
Tarr, Béla, 23–24
time, 6, 9, 182, 195–96
Todd, Emmanuel, 17
totalitarianism, 49–50, 123, 142
transculturalism, 50
Transylvania, 163
Tsai Ming-Liang, 9
Turanism, 145
Turin Expo (1911), 150

Turin Horse, The, 168, 170, 174, 191
Twelve-Tone Technique, 92

U
Universal Theseus, 18, 26
universalism, 2, 49–51, 96, 123
Urbanomic, 6
utopia, 65, 114

V
van de Velde, Henri, 92, 131
Venturi, Robert, 74–75
Verfremdung, 75, 181
Vig, Mihály, 29–30, 73, 153
Viragh, Pál, 80
Virilio, Paul, 8
virtual, 5
Visions of Europe, 176
Vitruvius, 52, 117–18

W
Wagner, Otto, 45
walls, 25
War and War, 63, 68
Webern, Anton, 29, 32, 92
Wellek, René, 86, 131
Werckmeister Harmonies, 2, 3–4, 89–92, 104–5, 160, 184
whales, 26–28, 37n1, 37n2, 70, 151–52, 176
Wittgenstein, Ludwig, 10, 100–101
Wolff, Christian, 104
Wong, Kar-wai, 34
Worringer, Wilhelm, 53
Wright, Frank Lloyd, 4, 25, 28–29, 51, 62, 75, 86, 168, 184, 191

Z
Zevi, Bruno, 47
Zhdanov decree, 139